BLACK
ECUMENISM

BLACK
ECUMENISM

Implementing
the Demands
of Justice

MARY R. SAWYER

TRINITY PRESS INTERNATIONAL
Valley Forge, Pennsylvania

Trinity Press International, P.O. Box 851, Valley Forge, PA 19482–0851

Library of Congress Cataloging-in-Publication Data

Sawyer, Mary R.
    Black ecumenism : Implementing the demands of justice / Mary R. Sawyer.
        p.   cm.
    Includes bibliographical references and index.
    ISBN 1-56338-092-7
    1. Afro-American churches. 2. Afro-Americans—Religion.
3. Christian union. 4. Church and social problems—United States.
5. United States—Church history.   I. Title.
    BR563.N4S38   1994
    277.3'082'08996073—dc20   94-4922
                                                          CIP

Printed in the United States of America

94   95   96   97   98   99   10   9   8   7   6   5   4   3   2   1

Power, properly understood, is the ability to achieve purpose. It is the strength required to bring about social, political or economic changes. In this sense power is not only desirable but necessary in order to implement the demands of love and justice. One of the greatest problems of history is that the concepts of love and power are usually contrasted as polar opposites. Love is identified with a resignation of power and power with a denial of love. . . . What is needed is a realization that power without love is reckless and abusive and that love without power is sentimental and anemic. Power at its best is love implementing the demands of justice. Justice at its best is love correcting everything that stands against love.

—Martin Luther King, Jr.
Where Do We Go from Here:
Chaos or Community?

For all my teachers,
both in the academy
and in the street

CONTENTS

TABLES

PREFACE

Contemporary black ecumenical movements are in large part a product of the black consciousness movement of the 1960s. Their agenda is empowerment and liberation. Their goal is participation as equals among equals in an ethnically pluralistic American society *and* in a universal Christian Church comprised of culturally defined particularities. Their strategy is cooperative, interdenominational action involving the historic black denominations and black enclaves within predominantly white denominations, both Protestant and Catholic.

Ecumenists are often among the more progressive, visionary leaders of the Church. As the most established component of the Church, local congregations tend to be the conservators of tradition. Ecumenical organizations, in contrast, are typically open to new ideas, to new relationships — to change. Thus, the black ecumenical movements that were the products of social change have, in turn, characteristically been proponents and agents of social change. It would be mistaken, however, to think of black ecumenical movements as strictly political entities. Like the Black Church from which they issue, they are religious organizations, concerned for the soul as well as the body, for the spiritual as well as the material. If black ecumenism is action oriented, the action is preceded by theological reflection, and theological reflection by the experienced authenticity of the faith. At the core of black ecumenism is the abiding conviction that the wholeness and the holiness of God's children are of a piece. As an organizational study, this book features prominently the structural aspects of the various movements, but the intent is never to silence or deny the spiritual realities that give life and meaning to the structures.

Three interrelated objectives governed this exploration of that aspect of the African American religious experience that we name black ecumenism. The work was first an extension of my longstanding interest in the relationship of the Black Church to issues of social justice. Second, in the effort to gauge the social change potential of these movements, I was challenged to explore the meaning of black ecumenism on the one hand, and the ways in which black ecumenism differs from other ecumenical expressions on the other. Third was an increasingly apparent need to collect descriptive and historical information about the various ecumenical endeavors and in so doing to fill a gap in documented Black Church history. In conducting this inquiry, I attempted, insofar as possible, to let the voices of the movements speak for themselves, to approach the organizations and their spokespersons from an empathetic, yet critical, stance. Inevitably, the project itself entered into the ecumenical dialogue, so that what is presented here is both product and ongoing process.

In one sense, this work began as my doctoral dissertation, and even before then, as my master's thesis while in seminary. But in another sense, it began some thirty years ago when, as a beginning college student fresh from rural Nebraska, I first encountered the insidiousness of racism. Stunned by the flagrant discrepancy between the tenets of Christianity as I had learned them as a child and the realities of race relations in adult society, I was propelled into civil rights activism. The University of Northern Colorado was unceremonious in rejecting my efforts to help it eliminate its discriminatory practices, instead ejecting me from the privileged arena of academe. So began an education that far surpassed the offerings of any institution of higher learning, as I followed the inclinings of my heart.

Two persons extended their support as dismissal from school led to eviction from my university-approved apartment and to termination from my job: first, Professor Edward Tomich, faculty sponsor of our campus CORE chapter, and, second, the resident campus minister, whose name has long since been lost from my memory, but whose actions effectively countered those of the hometown minister whose letters inveighed dire consequences in the afterlife did I not cease my "sinful associations with the descendants of Ham."

The professor and the preacher became my guides as I embarked on a journey that ultimately took me to south central Los Angeles; east Oakland; Washington, D.C.; the projects of Kansas City; the southernness of North Carolina — from human relations work to urban administration to black electoral politics, all in the interests of ameliorating the ravages of racism. And all along the way I gathered teachers: from storefront churches, tenant associations, Model Cities programs, black militant organizations, the corner grocery, my next door neighbors — adults and children alike. They were street-wise, often weary, but always willing teachers, ever so gentle with my naivete and inexperience. The gifts of civil rights teachers were equally bountiful — from the impassioned oratory of Dr. Martin Luther King, Jr., to the organizing lessons of Colorado State Senator and Denver Urban League director George Brown, to the theological instruction of the Rev. Phillip Lawson; all bid me keep the faith, the racism of the white church notwithstanding.

Then came more formal teachers: Dean Lawrence Jones and all the faculty of Howard University Divinity School in Washington, D.C., including Professor James Cone, whose commutes from Union Theological Seminary in New York City made his seminars accessible to me; Professors C. Eric Lincoln, Charles Long, and William Chafe at Duke University — all of whom affirmed me in my insistence on merging the experiential and the theoretical. Dr. Benjamin E. Mays, Bishop Reverdy C. Ransom, and Bishop William J. Walls were among the ecumenical teachers who spoke to me from the past. They were joined by contemporary ecumenists: the Rev. John H. Satterwhite, Bishop John Hurst Adams, the Rev. Marshall Lorenzo Shepard. None was more instructive than the Rev. Gayraud Wilmore, whose contributions to ecumenism in this day are inestimable and whose vision and faithfulness inspired and sustained me throughout the preparation of this book.

I am blessed in the teachers I have had.

My indebtedness extends to many others as well, and to none more than those individuals who generously granted me interviews and made available their contacts and files. The research and writing of this work was supported by two grants from the Lilly Endowment, Inc. The Working Group on African American Religion and Politics at Harvard University's W. E. B. Du Bois Institute for Afro-American Research provided a congenial cohort of colleagues and critics. Supportive friends and colleagues in the Iowa State University and Ames community are too numerous to name; they will know who they are. Margaret Langloss graciously assumed the tedious task of manuscript preparation. Graduate assistants Cynthia Bragg and Margaret Hanson proved both able researchers and compassionate friends. My Howard classmate William Key fortuitously introduced me to my publisher, Harold Rast, and to managing editor Laura Barrett. Their collective enthusiasm gave me the motivation I needed. The Sisters of St. Francis in Dubuque, Iowa, provided quiet space for reflection and writing. I am especially grateful to Carole Freking, OSF, for her encouragement at critical moments.

My sisters, Kathy Tegtman and Polly Richter, and their families are a source of much joy in my life. Through all the years of my journey, with all of its perplexing turns, my mother, Polly Kentfield Sawyer, has stood by me, modeling unconditional love. I thank her from the bottom of my heart. As my very first teacher, she is preeminently included in the dedication.

As collective a project as this book may be, I alone am responsible for whatever the shortcomings of its contents. Inasmuch as this is a work in process, my hope is that others will join in the conversation and particularly that the voices of women ecumenists will become more audible. May our words lead to deeds as the models of ecumenical activity presented here are revisioned and adapted to respond to the needs of our sisters and brothers who hunger and thirst after justice, freedom, and righteousness, but who are not yet filled.

ACRONYMS

AME	African Methodist Episcopal Church
AMEZ	African Methodist Episcopal Zion Church
BTP	Black Theology Project
CME	Christian Methodist Episcopal Church
CNBC	The Congress of National Black Churches
COCU	Consultation on Church Union
COGIC	Church of God in Christ
CORLE	Commission on Regional and Local Ecumenism
ITC	Interdenominational Theological Center
NAES	National Association of Ecumenical Staff
NBCA	National Baptist Convention of America, Inc.
NBC, USA, Inc.	National Baptist Convention, U.S.A., Inc.
NBEA	National Black Evangelical Association
NBPC	National Black Pastors Conference
NCBC	National Conference of Black Christians
NCC	National Council of Churches of Christ in the United States of America
NMBCA	National Missionary Baptist Convention of America
PIE	Partners in Ecumenism
PNBC	Progressive National Baptist Convention, Inc.

Chronology of
Predominantly White Ecumenical Movements

1908   Federal Council of Churches of Christ in America (FCC)

1910   World Missionary Conference, Edinburgh, Scotland

1921   International Missionary Council

1925   Universal Christian Conference on Life and Work

1927   First World Conference on Faith and Order

1942   National Association of Evangelicals (NAE)

1948   World Council of Churches (WCC)

1950   National Council of Churches of Christ in the United States of America (NCC)

1962   Consultation on Church Union (COCU)

Chronology of
Black Ecumenical Movements

1930

Fraternal Council of
Negro Churches
1935   (1934–64)

1940

1945

1950

        Southern Christian
1955   Leadership Conference
        (SCLC) (1957–)

1960

                        National Negro
                        Evangelical Association
                        (NNEA) (1963–73)   National Committee of
1965   Negro Churchmen
                            | (NCNC) (1967–68)
                            | National Committee of
                            | Black Churchmen
                            | (NCBC) (1968–73)
1970 |
                        National Black |
                        Evangelical Association National Conference of
        Black Theology Project (NBEA) (1973–) Black Churchmen
1975   (1975/77–)   (NCBC) (1973–83)
        Partners in Ecumenism |
        (PIE) (1978–89) |
        National Black Pastors Congress of National |
        Conference (NBPC)   Black Churches (CNBC) |
1980   (1979–81)   (1978–) |
                                                        |
                                                 National Conference of
                                                 Black Christians
1985   (NCBC) (1983–84)

        Black Ecumenical
        Advocacy Ministries
        (BEAM) (1989–)
1990

INTRODUCTION

The Black Church is both one and many. It is one in that all believers participate in the black experience in America, sharing in the religious ambiance which that experience creates. But it is many in the variety of structural components through which black religion is expressed. Were this not the case, there would be no occasion for ecumenical activity within the fold of African American Christians.[1]

The Black Church, of course, is itself a fragment of the universal Christian Church. Accordingly, African Americans have long been represented in the Protestant ecumenical movement, which counts among its progeny the Federal Council of Churches (FCC), the World Council of Churches (WCC), the National Council of Churches (NCC), and the Consultation on Church Union (COCU).[2]

These two levels of ecumenical engagement point to three categories of African American participation. The first category involves African Americans who participate in the wider religious world — WCC, NCC, COCU — on an individual basis, though perhaps as representatives of their respective denominations. Typically, these persons, who may or may not also be committed to unity of the Black Church, operate within the framework of integration, risking assimilation and absorption into the ethos and modality of white Christendom. The relationship is that of minority to majority, powerless to empowered, part to whole.

In the second category are those persons concerned preeminently with the black particularity, whose activities, through a consciousness raising process, serve to solidify the black cosmos — that is, the world as experienced by African Americans. Contact with the larger world is marginal; their relationship with the larger Church — so far as deliberate overtures are concerned — is one of nonrelationship, of

1

studied indifference. In this instance, the doctrine of One Church remains tacit in deference to pragmatically grounded cooperative efforts within the boundaries of the black Christian experience. The legitimacy of the transcending doctrine is not denied; it is simply not compelling.

The third category, then, consists of those who negotiate the terrain of the universal Church from the base of a black ecumenical group, who cultivate relationships in the larger world based on a model of pluralism. The relationship is more that of Church to Church, of particularity to particularity, each having equal status, each unit having equal claims to legitimacy and authority. For such persons, the doctrine of One Church may be the overtly articulated premise on which the appeal is based for white churches to join in cooperative efforts to address the needs and concerns of African Americans.

These second and third categories of ecumenical activity constitute two poles between which there is constant, dynamic motion. The two types of involvement — the first, to solidify the black cosmos, the second, to establish pluralism in the universal Church — must be viewed in creative tension. It is the degree of intactness of the cosmos that enables participation in the universal Church — without being controlled, manipulated, exploited, or ignored. It is the integrity of pluralistic relationships that brings resources of the Church to bear in such a way as to enhance the particularity. In short, it is the function of black ecumenical activity both to make the divided cosmos whole and to make the One Church plural.

Perhaps no one exemplified this inextricable relation of the particular and the universal so well as Howard Thurman. "My roots are deep in the throbbing reality of the Negro idiom," he wrote,

> and from it I draw a full measure of inspiration and vitality. I know that a man must be at home somewhere before he can feel at home anywhere. . . . Nevertheless, a strange necessity has been laid upon me to devote my life to the central concern that transcends the walls that divide and would achieve in literal fact what is experienced as literal truth: Human life is one and all men are members one of another. And this insight is spiritual and it is the hard core of religious experience.[3]

Existing in tandem with this transcendent vision in the black religious ethos, however, is a pragmatic and historically grounded skepticism toward the white institutional church. Mirroring the secular involvement of the Western world in slavery and colonialism, the early European and North American missionary movements were steeped in racism and cultural imperialism. This mind-set carried over into the early missionary conferences,[4] as well as the early period of the World Council of Churches, which was characterized by a marked coolness toward African American participation.

The impact on the Black Church of the "whiteness" of the Euro-American dominated movement was twofold. First, in keeping with the prophetic tradition of the Black Church, African American ecumenists began adopting an evangelical stance toward white ecumenists. Permeating the black ecumenical perspective is a persistent intimation that the white churches of Europe and the United States may be devoid of authentic Christianity and that the Black Church, as the preserver of the faith, is likewise the source of ecumenical possibility.[5] "Inclusiveness," from this perspective, is not a matter of blacks and other disinherited peoples clamoring to be admitted to the white church, but of whites being invited by blacks and others of the Two-Thirds World to return to the fold. Accordingly, the aspiration of black ecumenists who engage in common efforts with white church representatives reaches beyond integration into, or reconciliation with, structures-as-they-exist and extends to transformation of those structures such that African Americans may participate in the universal Church as free persons — liberated from white domination, insensitivity, and indifference.

The second and more far-reaching impact of white exclusivity in the ecumenical movement was the impetus given to self-conscious black ecumenism. Indeed, a case can be made for the inevitability of a movement toward black ecumenism, given the demeanor not only of the international movement, but of the ecumenical players within the United States.

The Federal Council of Churches of Christ in America (FCC) had come into being in 1908 as a voice of the social gospel movement of the late nineteenth and early twentieth centuries. Both the social gospel movement and ecumenism were responses to industrialization and attendant labor issues. Race and racism and their socioeconomic — or moral — ramifications were not pressing considerations in the establishment of ecumenical bodies. As the American working classes unionized to challenge industrial management, many Protestant churches redefined their constituency accordingly. But since African Americans were largely excluded from the working classes by virtue of their caste status, the churches' new definitions of constituency included blacks no more than had the old.

Black denominations were invited to participate in the FCC and were represented by such notable personages as Benjamin Mays, Reverdy Ransom, William Jernagin, Mary McLeod Bethune, and George Edmund Haynes, who for twenty-five years headed the FCC's Commission on Race Relations. Notwithstanding the positive work of this Commission, the truculence of the FCC is apparent in the fact that it was not until 1946 — thirty-eight years after the founding of the FCC and twenty-five years after the creation of the Commission on Race Relations — that the Council passed a resolution officially and publicly opposing segregation. By then, the discrepancy within the FCC between black expectations and white intentions had long since prompted the formation of a black ecumenical body, which was known as the Fraternal Council of Negro Churches (see chapter 1).

In 1941 the FCC, along with seven other interdenominational agencies, formed a Committee on Closer Relationships of General Interdenominational Agencies. The result, after nearly a decade of work, was the National Council of the Churches of Christ in the United States of America (NCC), in which six black denominations became formal members. African Americans have been represented on NCC's many commissions and committees and have held key appointive and elective administrative posts, including the presidency of the Council on three separate occasions.

Numerous offices have been created within the Council's elaborate structure to address on an ongoing basis matters of concern to African Americans, as well as to other ethnic minority groups. Though consistently in the liberal mode, the involvements and positions of the NCC mirror the changing social climate, so that the apex of attention to racial matters occurred during the civil rights movement of the 1960s. On the positive side, involvement in key campaigns of the movement brought the Council into a working relationship with a major black ecumenical body, the Southern Christian Leadership Conference (see chapter 2). The black power movement of the later 1960s proved a greater challenge than the Council was up to, however, and in its stumbling the Council inadvertently helped foster a climate that brought into being two new black ecumenical groups, the National Conference of Black Christians and Partners in Ecumenism (see chapters 3 and 6).

The black Methodist churches gave white ecumenism yet another trial through their participation in the Consultation on Church Union (COCU), organized in 1962. African Americans have been a strong presence in COCU, holding office as associate general secretary and president. But when, in 1970, a plan for organic union was put forth, the black denominations found themselves in the forefront of the opposition for two reasons: first, because the black membership would be proportionately so small as to cause them to lose their identity; second, because the failure of the white churches to come to terms with their racism could only mean oppression for blacks who attempted to function within the proposed structure.

After a decade of groping and regrouping, COCU shifted its focus from organic union to theological consensus, producing a new proposal for a "covenant" arrangement in which ministerial orders, baptism, and communion would be shared and recognized mutually by all of the participating churches — including the black denominations who have given interim endorsement to the plan. If, at some future time, organic union once more becomes a priority goal, the posture of participating African Americans may well shift again. But as one observer noted, "For these denominations even to participate in COCU is a display of grace and forgiveness that commands respect."[6]

That the same might be said of black participation in white ecumenism generally is attested by recent experiences with the World Council of Churches. In the mid-1980s a group of U.S. black theologians presented to WCC's Faith and Order Commission a report entitled, "Toward a Common Expression of Faith: A Black North American Perspective," which pointedly expressed the perspective of black ecumenism as it sought to be understood in the larger context of worldwide ecumenism:

> We have...a profound hermeneutical suspicion about any movement for unity that is dominated by North Atlantic attitudes and assumptions. We have observed that when our white brothers and sisters speak of unity they often mean being together on terms that carefully maintain their political, economic and cultural hegemony. Unity is frequently confused with "Anglo-conformity" — strict adherence to premises and perspectives based upon the world view and ethos of the North Atlantic community with its history of racial oppression....

Blackness is one of God's gifts for the realization of the unity
of the Church and humankind at this critical stage of history.
... The meaning of unity is related to the meaning of Blackness
for the Afro-American Church and points to its vocation as a
church of the poor and oppressed who claim liberation in the
Black Messiah of God and want to share the humanizing experience of suffering and joy in struggle with others who want to
work for a world of justice and equality for all. Unity is possible
only when there is acceptance of suffering under Christ's work
of liberation and when there is commitment to his mission.[7]

The report was received by the membership of the WCC Commission
with disinterested silence.[8]

From the beginning faith has called African Americans to participate in white ecumenical movements, and when they are betrayed,
either passively or overtly, faith calls them to work apart. The major
thrust of black ecumenical activity thus turns to the interior life and
role of the Black Church.

Ecumenism within the black religious community plays out in two
distinct ways. First is the quest for structural merger. Since 1864, the
African Methodist Episcopal (AME) Church and the African Methodist Episcopal Zion (AMEZ) Church have put forth intermittent
proposals for merger. Throughout the 1980s and early 1990s such
conversations were ongoing between the AMEZ and Christian Methodist Episcopal (CME) Churches. Significantly, explorations of organic
union generally are restricted to one orientation; that is, the conversations do not extend across the boundaries of denominational
"families." Discussions are held among the Methodists, or among the
Baptists — and mostly the former. Such efforts at times have succeeded, a case in point being the creation in 1895 of the National
Baptist Convention out of three predecessor bodies. In another instance, the AME Zion Church, which split into two factions in 1852,
was reunited in 1860. But the continued existence of separate denominations is its own evidence that the initiatives to overcome structural
fragmentation have enjoyed less than total success.[9]

The second model of ecumenism is that of cooperative, interdenominational activity undertaken in the pursuit of goals and objectives transcendent of church organization. Informal interdenominational activities seeking to foster a larger sense of fellowship, such
as pulpit exchanges and joint musical programs, are a longstand-

ing tradition among black churches. Of recent vintage, however, is a form of endeavor far more intentional and ambitious than the Black Church had previously known. The story of this more potent form of black ecumenism is told in the movements and organizations that emerged from the black religious community in the half-century from the 1930s to the 1980s and that have in common a liberating agenda of empowerment. It is the recounting of this story that constitutes the task of this work.[10]

For some, the idea of ecumenical movements within the Black Church may seem a contradiction in terms; for others, the very phrase "Black Church" is a point of confusion. In part, the confusion stems from the absence of a consistent definition of the Black Church among scholars and church practitioners. The Black Church for many is simply the sum of local, individual congregations. For others, however, it is a gestalt — that whole which is greater than the sum of its parts. Those persons subscribing to the former perspective utilize a strictly institutional definition, and since there is no one institutional entity that can be called "the Black Church," many of these individuals eschew the use of the phrase.

Others who utilize an institutional definition, among them AME Bishop John Hurst Adams, stress the factor of control over resources and the decision making process as the primary criterion of what is included in the Black Church. For Bishop Adams, the Black Church properly defined excludes blacks in the white denominations and, conversely, is limited to the historic black denominations and sects.[11] Sharply departing from this perspective is C. Eric Lincoln, whose definition is functional rather than structural. For him the Black Church consists of those who share in the black experience in America and thereby have common needs; the Black Church encompasses all those who participate in black ethnicity, which transcends doctrine, dogma, and structural demarcations.[12]

Gayraud Wilmore's understanding is similar to Lincoln's, encompassing in the Black Church those persons who share a certain cultural affinity formed by "a blend of diasporic African culture with a culture of poverty" and by a common history of suffering and struggle.[13] Peter Paris, from yet another perspective, predicates his definition on unified opposition to racism, so that the oneness of the Black Church hinges on the shared ethical principle of racial liberation, which in turn derives from the principle of the parenthood of God and the kinship of all people.[14]

On balance, the case for speaking of a "Black Church" is more compelling than the argument against. The structural divisions that obscure unity are mostly denominational and relatively few; the eight largest denominations, seven of which are either Methodist or Baptist, account for over 80 percent of all formal church members. The relative insignificance of even these divisions is attested by the fluidity among them. Churchgoers commonly alternate membership in Baptist and Methodist churches and — continuing a routine established in rural church life — often make a practice of regularly attending three or four different churches. It is neither unusual nor a source of dissension for members of a given household to hold membership in different churches.

Boundaries are introduced at the level of denominational hierarchies, where separate budgets, organizations, meetings, communication systems — as well as "tradition," personal ambition and ego, and territorial imperative — come into play. Denominational lines here become undeniable realities, as may passions for respective, corresponding doctrines — infant baptism, for example, or sanctification. Nevertheless, not only philosophically but in practice, ethnicity generally does transcend both church structure and doctrine.

What, then, is the task of ecumenism in relationship to this "both one and many" entity? The objective of black ecumenism, unlike that of white ecumenical movements, is neither structural unity nor doctrinal consensus; rather, it is the bringing together of the manifold resources of the Black Church to address the circumstances of African Americans as an oppressed people. It is mission-oriented, emphasizing black development and liberation; it is directed toward securing a position of strength and self-sufficiency.

If white exclusivity gave impetus to black ecumenism, it was further fueled by the black consciousness movement of the 1960s, which caused black America to undergo a veritable metamorphosis. Newfound ethnic awareness and pride; the themes of unity, solidarity, cultural heritage, beauty in blackness; the process of defining new self-identities and structuring new relationships — all of these resulted in new meanings being imputed to old symbols, not excepting the symbols of the Black Church. For the Church, black consciousness meant a number of things. First was a reappropriation and renewed appreciation of the rich political and social activist heritage of the Black Church.[15] Second was a profound analytical shift in the understanding of the nature of the dilemma facing black America, and therefore of the nature of the solution as well: from an individualistic, one-on-one, integrationist model that relied on evangelical proclamation, to a systemic, corporate, structural model calling for organized strategies and actions.[16] Third was the articulation of a systematic black liberation theology positing economic and political liberation and empowerment as the gospel mandate.

Collectively, these developments called into being new vehicles for pursuing justice, vehicles that transcended denominational divisions, that enabled relationships with secular activists, and that gave concreteness to the black consciousness vision of political liberation. These new vehicles took the form of ecumenical organizations.[17]

If the Fraternal Council of Negro Churches represented the first stage of black ecumenism and the Southern Christian Leadership Conference constituted a second stage, the black theology movement — given impetus by the black power movement and by the National Council of Churches' reaction to it — provided a framework for the third stage of ecumenical activity, which extended from the 1960s into the 1970s. In addition to the earlier mentioned National Conference of Black Christians, the National Black Evangelical Association and the Black Theology Project were a part of this stage (see chapter 5), as were numerous local ecumenical bodies such as the Black Ecumenical Commission of Massachusetts and the Philadelphia Council of Black Clergy (see chapter 4).

As the 1980s approached, a fourth stage of ecumenism was inaugurated with the emergence of Partners in Ecumenism (see chapter 6), housed within the National Council of Churches, and the independent Congress of National Black Churches (see chapter 7). On balance, these groups were less overtly activist than their predecessors and more oriented toward social service delivery and the long-term project of institution building. The agenda remained constant: empowerment within the framework of liberation theology. But a shift in strategies and tactics was mandated by a radically altered social climate in the nation at large that had far-reaching consequences for the Black Nation.

Even before the 1960s came to a close, the election of Richard Nixon signaled the beginning of a new era, which was bracketed on the other end by the eight-year reign of Ronald Reagan in the 1980s, and by the administration of his successor, George Bush. White backlash, benign neglect, and officially sanctioned dismantling of the gains of the civil rights era combined to produce a starkly different mood and reality. Optimism and celebration succumbed in many quarters to disillusionment and despair, as ethnic solidarity yielded to a class fissure that appeared irreparable. On the one hand, the liberal agenda of economic growth conjoined with the Reagan ideology of elitism to give marginal accommodation to an upwardly mobile segment of the African American population. In the central cities, on the other hand, poverty not only worsened but was compounded by the devastation of crack cocaine, gang violence, AIDS, and teenage parenthood. Staggering unemployment, deteriorating housing, homelessness, inadequate medical care, and declining literacy rates all attested that if equity had been attained by some, it was but a cruel fantasy for others. For those trapped in such circumstances, the task of sheer survival rendered mute, to a large degree, the integration-nationalism debate that so preoccupied the 1960s and 1970s.

The new configuration of economic polarization in the black community in no way negated the importance of race. Rather, it brought into sharp relief the historic reality that in the United States those who are assailed by racism are also assaulted by an economic system whose end is monetary profit and whose means is exploitation of human labor — including the discarding of "obsolete" labor. That 33 percent of blacks in America are in poverty, as compared to 10 percent of whites; that the median income of black families is $17,000 as compared to $30,000 for white families — that is a function not only of this society's cultural ideology of white superiority, but of corporate America's vested economic interests, which that ideology is designed to protect. Thus, the challenge of black ecumenism in this day is to confront not just racial discrimination or economic discrimination, but the convergence and interaction of these two dehumanizing social forces.[18]

That is not to say that the Black Church is compelled or inclined to endorse overtly a particular counterideology. More important than the ideological label may be the characteristics of the strategies employed. As one writer put it, "A justice which is integrally relational, creative, liberating, and vindicating of the poor cuts against some of the bias and self-interests of nearly all political movements and ideologies to be found on the political scene."[19] In fact, many black religious leaders, as well as religiously based political leaders, have traditionally eschewed endorsing particular ideologies, invoking instead a transcendent, biblically grounded ethic of justice. But that stance has often failed to bring the issue of economic stratification to the forefront of the agenda of either black denominations or local congregations, the economic analyses of the Hebrew prophets notwithstanding.

Racial liberation was the dominant paradigm for social action from the beginning of the black religious experience in America. The efforts of such modern-day prophets as Martin Luther King, Jr., to shift the dialogue and the movement to a more adequate level of analysis that acknowledged the complex interrelations of racism, militarism, and economic exploitation met with modest success at best. The Black Church was led to become more attentive to the matter of poverty, and in the 1990s some awareness has been developed of the gender factor in economic stratification. Nevertheless, the category of racial oppression remains the primary focus.[20] Where there are exceptions, they are most often found in an ecumenical context. As the progressive edge of the Black Church, ecumenical organizations, in varying degrees, have attempted to address poverty not merely as a racial matter, but as a class issue as well, finding ideological formulations not necessarily incompatible with a biblical ethic.

The merit of reviewing the case studies contained in this volume may reside not so much in honoring what has been done as in assessing what to do. In the larger context of our sociopolitical world, the movements described here appear as minor actors with modest impact. Yet they may well delineate a means of harnessing the power that is latent in the Black Church and of bringing to bear on the life conditions of millions of men, women, and children the resources of the institution that is most central in African American culture.

The degree of success in such a formidable undertaking will hinge in large measure on the internal characteristics of these organizations — characteristics such as cultural ideology, economic philosophy, model of governance, sources of funding, degree of inclusiveness of women and laity and of the various components of the African American Christian family, and political/spiritual balance. Indeed, these characteristics are among the more critical criteria for conducting the ongoing critique of African American religio-political movements that is essential in any social change effort. Accordingly, attention is given in this work to the prominent features of each organization relative to this set of characteristics, an exercise that yields a constellation of continuums that are corollary to the dialectical model of the Black Church suggested by C. Eric Lincoln and

Lawrence H. Mamiya in *The Black Church in the African American Experience.*[21]

Lincoln and Mamiya pose a set of polarities held in dialectical tension that provide a holistic picture of black churches. These include: priestly and prophetic functions, other-worldly and this-worldly stances, universalism and particularism, communal and privatistic emphases, charismatic and bureaucratic leadership, resistance and accommodation. Locating black ecumenical movements in this model, they clearly move toward the prophetic, this-worldly, particularism, communal, resistance ends of the continuums, with some variation with regard to the charismatic and bureaucratic polarities. A second set of characteristics may be posited, then, that present a holistic picture of black ecumenical organizations, although in some instances the categories deviate from the conventional pairings. None of the organizations, for example, is socialist in any doctrinaire sense, but some envision a form of mixed economy or economic democracy. None is nationalist in the extreme of advocating separatism; the framework of pluralism, however, contains elements of nationalism — e.g., Pan-Africanism and self-determination — along with a transformative agenda for society as a whole. In contrast is the goal of integration into the "system" as it exists. Thus, the continuums of characteristics of black ecumenical organizations include the following:

- from pluralist philosophy to integrationist philosophy
- from mixed economy to capitalist economy
- from democratic governance to autocratic governance
- from fiscal independence to dependence on white funding sources
- from inclusiveness to exclusiveness — of women, laity, and the various components of the Black Church
- from political/spiritual balance to political/spiritual imbalance[22]

Regardless of internal characteristics, there should be no illusion that church-identified movements alone can solve the problems confronting black America. Indeed, the elective ecumenical strategy may be to join with other justice-minded organizations and movements in a multicultural coalition approach. Or it may be to link hands and resources across denominational lines — and class and gender lines — to organize the local neighborhood for institution building and political action.

Whatever path is chosen, it is difficult to conceive that a black religious presence would not be in the forefront, for while it is true that the fundamental purpose of the church is spiritual, it is also tradition that in the black community "the secular is mediated by the sacred."[23] Furthermore, the crisis of black urban America at its core is a normative crisis, a crisis of meaning and purpose and values. The same may be said, of course, of suburban America, both white and black, and it may well be that in its ecumenical program of inclusive caring and restoration of unity, the Black Church will be a healing balm for the nation as a whole.

Chapter One

TO UPLIFT THE RACE
The Fraternal Council of Negro Churches

Context

Prominent among the features of black life in the 1930s were Jim Crow segregation, economic depression, spiritual and physical lynchings. For many blacks, sheer survival constituted the overriding challenge. The prevailing image of the Black Church in that day — indeed, of the black populace as a whole — is one of political passivity, of a turning inward and heavenward. Yet the decade and those preceding were also a time of nascent nationalism, and black church leaders were not immune to its pull. The appeal of nationalism was especially strong for AME Bishop Reverdy C. Ransom, whose vision of black church unity found concreteness in the Fraternal Council of Negro Churches, which he founded in 1934.

The Fraternal Council represented a response to the prevailing climate both within the church and in the society at large. With regard to the church, on the positive side, it was an era of ecumenism; black clergy had had experience with ecumenism and knew the language of ecumenism. On the negative side was the failure of the white church to fully include blacks not only in the conciliar movement, but in the denominational mergers taking place in that period. The proposal of the white Methodists for creating a racially segregated Central Jurisdiction, for example, surely gave incentive to self-elected separatism.

Portions of this chapter appeared previously in *Church History* 59, no. 1 (March 1990), copyright 1990, The American Society of Church History.

As early as 1917, the editor of the *Christian Recorder* posited a need for an "ecumenical council of dark skinned Christians" to address issues attendant to black migration.[1] In March 1927 an organization called the National Inter-denominational Ministerial Alliance was formed and met at least one other time, in 1930, under the leadership of CME minister C. L. Russell. A proposal for a second such organization was put forth in 1929 by the Rev. Lacey Kirk Williams, president of the National Baptist Convention, U.S.A., Inc., and a member of the Federal Council of Churches (FCC). Black clergy members of the FCC held one planning session at Howard University, but a subsequent meeting scheduled at Hampton Institute failed to materialize.[2]

Impetus for creating such organizations was provided by the discrepancy within the FCC between black expectations and white intentions. White FCC members, for example, declined to support anti-lynching legislation or to condemn the Ku Klux Klan. Disillusioned by such insensitivity to compelling black concerns, Bishop Ransom came to place his hope for relief of racial oppression in the structural merger of black church bodies.[3] When merger efforts faltered, he initiated the third effort at organizing a federal council of *black* churches.

The formation of separate ecumenical organizations was never a betrayal of commitment to the ultimate unity of the whole Church, and at no time did the existence of black church organizations preclude simultaneous participation by blacks in the larger ecumenical movement. What the Fraternal Council did signify was a recognition that black solidarity was a condition of freedom and that freedom was a condition of reconciliation. "Freedom" in the 1920s and 1930s was defined in large part as a matter of both *de jure* and *de facto* desegregation. Freedom was knowing the protection of the law rather than its brutality. Freedom meant access to restaurants and hotels, theaters and trains, hospitals and educational institutions. It meant the opportunity to vote, to elect public representatives, to serve on juries — in short, exercise of the fundamental rights of citizenship.

If the Fraternal Council was ahead of the times in its quest for civil rights, so were other secular and quasi-religious movements of the day that pursued a political agenda. Most prominent among these movements was the Garvey-led Universal Negro Improvement Association (UNIA), which flourished from 1919 to 1927. The UNIA itself had a strong religious dimension and claimed among its participants some 250 black clergy.[4] While not officially a member, Bishop

Ransom on more than one occasion in the early 1920s editorialized favorably on behalf of the UNIA in the *AME Church Review*.[5] He was also likely exposed to the philosophy of church unity espoused by such church leaders as A. A. Maloney, a black Episcopal priest whose views were published in the *Negro World*, the official organ of the UNIA.[6]

The need for black unification was also recognized in the formation of the Joint Committee on National Recovery, a coalition of some twenty black organizations formed in the early 1930s to protect the rights of blacks in the implementation of New Deal programs. This Joint Committee joined with the Division of Social Science at Howard University to found the National Negro Congress, the goals of which were economic and social justice for blacks.[7] The Congress convened for the first time in 1936 under the presidency of labor leader A. Philip Randolph; the preceding year, the Fraternal Council of Negro Churches officially endorsed the effort to create the new organization.[8] Further, the person who was to become president of the Fraternal Council after 1938, William Jernagin, was elected vice president of the Second and Third National Negro Congresses. In 1940 Randolph, disillusioned by Communist infiltration of the National Negro Congress, was commending the Fraternal Council as an alternative body committed to black development and liberation.[9] Such reciprocity in program endorsements points to a mutuality of agendas, as well as to an extant network of like-minded leaders, both religious and secular. As a representative of the Black Church establishment who had been an active participant in the Niagara movement, Ransom resonated more to nationalist than integrationist activity.[10] Thus, if the Fraternal Council was a departure from the interracialist approach of the FCC's Commission on Race Relations, it was of a piece with other black change-oriented movements and organizations of its time. At the very least, the Council provided an alternative forum for church leaders who rejected the extremes of "back to Africa" advocates, but who felt the prophetic mandate to critique and to protest America's shortcomings.

Founding

The call for denominational representatives to assemble to discuss a basis for united action was issued by Bishop Ransom in 1933.

"Impelled," as Bishop Ransom later recorded, "by a deep sense of the need of our racial group for an authoritative voice to speak for us on social, economic, industrial and political questions, and believing that a united Negro church could best supply this need," interested clergy convened in Washington, D.C., on January 5, 1934, and "bound themselves together in what they designated as a 'Voluntary Committee on the Federation of Negro Religious Denominations in the United States of America.' "[11]

Participants in the Washington meeting, held at Mount Carmel Baptist Church, consisted for the most part of individuals who represented the three black Methodist churches and the National Baptists in the FCC. This initial session was followed by a second meeting on June 27 in Cincinnati. This planning meeting in turn resulted in the convening of a national conference of black church representatives at Bethesda Baptist Church in Chicago on August 22 and 23 of the same year. At this time, the assembly of 152 delegates formally organized the Fraternal Council of Negro Churches of America, adopting a constitution and electing officers. Represented were six black denominations — the National Baptist Convention, U.S.A., Inc.; National Baptist Convention of America; AME Church; AME Zion Church; CME Church; and Union American Methodist Episcopal Church — along with delegates from the Methodist Episcopal, Congregational, and Community Center Churches.[12] The proceedings of this first conference culminated in the issuance of a public statement of self-identity and intentions:

> While not acting under the authority of our different communions, we as officials and leaders feel that the present plight of our race in this country calls for the united strength, wisdom and influence of its religious leadership. We start with the distinct understanding that in this proposal for the Federation of Negro Churches, the question of religious doctrine, creed, polity or any interference with denominational independence, authority or control is not to enter into our deliberation. We propose that the Negro religious denominations shall cooperate on all questions touching the spiritual, moral, social, political, economic and industrial welfare of our people. It is agreed that Negroes in other communions such as Methodist Episcopals, Presbyterians, Congregationalists and Episcopalians may come and cooperate on an equal footing.[13]

The Fraternal Council thus early established that its interests were neither doctrinal consensus nor structural merger — though it periodically served as a forum for advocacy of the latter.[14] Further indications of the Council's motives are apparent in the invitations extended to a wide range of smaller black denominations and sects to participate in the organization. Included were Holiness and Pentecostal bodies that had not previously enlisted in any ecumenical endeavors.[15] Church unity clearly was an objective of the founder, as it was of other participants, but the unity was to come through cooperative action — not the cooperative action of conventional mission work or evangelism, but social action directed toward the achievement of racial justice.

That the official organizing meeting of the Council was convened in Chicago and attended predominantly by northern ministers pastoring urban churches was no coincidence.[16] Ransom had been editorializing in the *AME Review* since 1917 for interdenominational cooperation and coordination of services to blacks in northern urban ghettos who had migrated from the South during the War and Depression years.[17] The Fraternal Council, as Ransom envisioned it, was thus in no small part a response to the problems of this particular population. However, positions taken by the Council in subsequent meetings demonstrate concern not only for the problems engendered by urban life, but for the "plight of the sharecropper in the cotton regions of the south."[18] At the same time, their deliberations point to a keen awareness of the larger world dynamics that entered into the twin scourges of racism and economic discrimination.

The Fraternal Council met a second time in Cleveland, Ohio, at Saint Paul AME Zion Church on August 21, 22, and 23, 1935. The nearly two hundred delegates who attended this session, "upon the earnest request of a number of Negro Churchmen affiliated with white denominations," changed the name of the Council to " 'The Negro Fraternal Council of Churches of America,' so that the Negroes of all churches might be accepted as members."[19] This name change seems to have never taken hold; the organization was subsequently referred to as the "National Fraternal Council of Negro Churches, U.S.A.," and was so incorporated on May 27, 1947.

The more substantive action taken at the 1935 Cleveland meeting was the issuance of "A Message to the Churches and to the Public" which, as a statement of the ecumenical and theological orientation of the Council, merits quoting at length:

For more than three hundred years Americans of African descent have embraced every creed and form of religious belief that would admit them to membership in their churches. They had nothing to do with the bitter religious controversies and divisions that gave birth to the numerous communions and sects that divide American Protestant Christianity. They have produced no Martin Luthers, John Calvins, or John Wesleys. They have never been called upon to suffer persecution for conscience sake because of religious belief. They have simply divided and followed the many divergent paths where their white fellow Christians had paved the way. But these religious divisions have left us weak and almost helpless of power to protest and defend ourselves in the social, industrial, economic and political framework of American society....

In the United States we have about four million Jews who always stand together when the interests of Jewry are at stake. We have here, five million Negroes organized into many different churches, each acting separately and apart, so far as the interests of the race as a whole are concerned. Neither the Baptists nor the Methodists, however numerous, however strong they each may be within themselves, are powerful enough to face the pitiable plight that confronts our people without the reinforcement and cooperation of the others....

The hour is at hand when the Negro church should unite to fearlessly challenge the faithless stewardship of American Christianity by submitting it to the test of political, social, and economic justice, a justice that accepts no peace on the basis of submission, compromise, or surrender.

Shall the American Negro, whose broadest boast is the patriotic devotion and loyalty with which he has defended our flag in all wars, be less devoted and loyal to the cross of Christ when all that it stands for in human relations is either openly denied or menaced, in social, economic and political denial with which it is flouted or assailed?

Those who have joined the Fraternal Council have found joy in the larger freedom and fellowship. We call upon ministers and lay members in all the churches to cross the boundary lines of their denominationalism to join in the common task of working in the present to secure the future peace and justice not only of our race, but of all underprivileged and oppressed.[20]

In addition to its cogent appeal for black cross-denominational unity, this statement is noteworthy for its explicit critique of white churches. Theologically, that critique is predicated on justice for the "underprivileged and oppressed" — language that anticipated by over thirty years the National Conference of Black Christians (NCBC) and the black theology movement to which NCBC gave birth. The securing of justice is clearly posited as the appropriate measure of faithfulness not only of the white church, but of the Black Church as well.

The statement was attended by a series of resolutions addressing a wide range of pragmatic issues, among them exclusion of farm laborers and domestic workers — "more than half the Negro population" — from the new Social Security Act; the "condition of virtual serfdom" of black sharecroppers; the exclusion of blacks from labor organizations; and discrimination in the administration of government relief programs. Regarding Italy's threatened assault on Ethiopia, one resolution read: "While by sympathy, principle, and ideals we are Americans to the core, we cannot be deaf to the cry that comes from a menaced nation in the land of our fathers' fathers." And on the subject of evangelism: "We urge our ministers to study their Bibles with particular reference to the . . . teachings of Jesus regarding social justice and brotherhood. . . . We also urge that our people be encouraged to organize whenever they can."[21]

In an "Address to the Country" issued the following year, in 1936, the Fraternal Council spoke to many of the same issues but included appeals for blacks themselves to utilize their potential political and economic power. The Council also added this word of clarification, which in important respects anticipated the philosophy of cultural pluralism that emerged from the black consciousness movement of the 1960s and early 1970s:

> We would not . . . have it understood that by urging organization along racial lines we are urging antagonism to the white people of our country. Far be it from that. We are offering the only method of cooperating with white people. The Negroes cannot hope to cooperate individually, but only collectively. We are of very little power today because we act as individuals. We must act as a body in order to cooperate with other bodies working in the same field.[22]

Beyond issuing such statements, little evidence is to be found of program activity in the first eight years of the Council's life. The

Fraternal Council's original constitution stated its purpose as simply
the uniting of "various denominational Church Organizations for the
purpose of making more practical the principles of Christian Religion
in their application to the Civic, Economic and Social condition of
the Negro in America and the World." The 1950 revised constitution
elaborated somewhat:

> The purpose of the organization shall be: (1) To develop co-
> operative relations among all member denominations, and to
> take appropriate collective measures to strengthen this bond of
> Christian Unity, so that they may work together as one United
> Church to bring about racial and economic justice, progressive
> measures of nonpartisan political legislation and social reform.
> (2) To afford a center for coordinating the actions of the de-
> nominations in the achievement of their common goals. (3) To
> cooperate with other programs of like nature in seeking to foster
> the worldwide program of Christ.

Active participation in the Council is also difficult to ascertain.
Through the 1930s attendance at the annual assemblies was generally
something less than two hundred, which compared favorably with
the average total attendance of four hundred to five hundred at the
FCC annual meetings.[23] Most "individual" members of the Fraternal
Council were persons from the local host city who attended the annual session on a one-time basis; this was also the primary source of
lay participation as local ministers took church members to the Council's meetings.[24] The coffers of the organization likewise provide no
clue of the level of support, except that it did not come in the form
of financial contributions. The reports of the officers and staff contain
endless pleas for more adequate funding. The *Negro Journal of Religion*,
which according to its masthead was "officially authorized to publish
for the Fraternal Council of Negro Churches," was even moved to
editorialize on the matter:

> [The Fraternal Council's] chief problem is that of financial sup-
> port. To make surveys, keep in touch with the denominations
> of the country, and push forward a sane program of publicity it
> must have funds. In the absence of big gifts from financiers it
> must struggle along on the dues of the members, who pay one
> dollar annually, when pressed to do so.

Some of the larger denominations have failed to make a single contribution as a group. Yet they declare and set forth just what the Council should do. Well, how shall they do it? Shall they make brick and straw too? There will be a meeting of the Council soon. Have you paid your dues?[25]

Financial constraints notwithstanding, the Council maintained an organizational structure throughout the Depression years — an accomplishment of no small magnitude, particularly in light of the fact that it was entirely dependent on dues and offerings, accepting no funds from white churches or foundations. The Council as a whole met annually from 1934 through 1950, with the exception of 1941, and erratically thereafter (Table 1.1). Committee meetings were convened at the annual sessions, while the executive committee ostensibly met twice a year. Significantly, members of the executive committee were not required to be ministers, which enabled the appointment of women. In fact, two members of the original thirty-nine-member executive committee were women — Belle Hendon from Chicago, representing the National Baptist Convention of America (NBCA), and Ida Mae Myller, of Gary, Indiana, from the Community Center Church. Whereas the original constitution had provided for some fifteen standing committees, in 1950 these were reduced to seven: Evangelism and Worship, Education, Human Relations, Public Relations, Washington Bureau, Social Welfare, and African Affairs. The Washington Bureau Committee, alone among these, developed a sustained program. Indeed, the establishment of the Washington Bureau in the nation's capital in 1943 marks the second major stage in the life of the Fraternal Council. (See Appendix II for additional information on organizational structure.)

Stage Two: The Washington Bureau

First located at 1934 Eleventh Street, N.W., in 1949 the Fraternal Council purchased a building at 318 Third Street, S.W., to serve as the national headquarters of the Council and as the office of the executive secretary, as well as the office of the Washington Bureau. Described as "a ten room house, in first class condition, with four rooms furnished, and a piano and a frigidaire included," the property was purchased for $16,000 cash, nearly half of which was raised by participating

Table 1.1. Chronology, Fraternal Council of Negro Churches

Year	President	Exec. Comm. Chair	Executive Secretary	Bureau Director	Annual Meeting
1934	R.C. Ransom	—	L.W. Kyles	—	Chicago
1935	"	—	"	—	Cleveland
1936	"	—	"	—	Nashville
1937	"	—	"	—	?
1938	W.H. Jernagin	—	"	—	Washington
1939	"	—	L.C. Ridley	—	Charlotte
1940	L.W. Kyles	W.H. Jernagin	"	—	Charlotte
1941	"	"	"	—	None
1942	J.A. Bray	"	R.R. Wright	—	Cleveland
1943	"	"	"	W.H. Jernagin	Memphis
1944	L.E. King/ A.P. Shaw	"	"	"	St. Louis
1945	A.P. Shaw	"	"	"	Washington
1946	J.H. Clayborn	J.L. Horace	"	"	Little Rock
1947	"	W.J. Walls	C.K. Stalnaker	"	Baltimore
1948	J.M. Bracy	J.H. Clayborn	"	C.T. Murray	St. Louis
1949	J.M. Bracy (Special Session)	"	"	L.M. Suitt	Richmond Washington
1950	W.J. Walls	J.M. Bracy	G.W. Lucas	B.L. Derrick	Buffalo
1951	"	"	"	A. Fowler	?
1952	A.W. Womack	W.H. Jernagin	"	"	Atlanta
1953	"	"	"	"	?
1954*	E.A. Love	"	"	"	St. Louis
1955	"	"	"	"	?
1956	?	"	"	"	?
1957	S.L. Greene	"	J.T. McMillan	"	?
1958	W.H. Borders	S.L. Greene	"	"	Miami
1959	"	"	"	"	Washington
1960†	H.T. Medford	"	"	"	?

*After 1954, the records of the Council's meetings and elections become erratic.

†Rev. Medford served at least through 1964. Correspondence of the late 1960s refers to E.P. Murchison as the president. Exactly how and when he became president is not clear. George W. Lucas served as acting chair of the executive committee through the early 1970s for purposes of representing the Council in business transactions. The last...and unsuccessfully...attempted meeting of the Council was in 1971 in Washington, D.C.

denominations, while the balance was secured through loans.[26] It was perhaps the sole moment of opulence in the life of the Council. The Rev. Andrew Fowler, who was appointed director of the Washington Bureau in 1951 and who continued to utilize the title into the early 1990s, was hired on terms of $50 per month salary. As of the early 1990s—some forty years later—he had yet to receive the first $50.[27]

The presidency of the Council passed from Bishop Ransom to Rev. William H. Jernagin in 1938. In addition to pastoring Mount Carmel Baptist Church in Washington, D.C., where the initial organizing meeting of the Fraternal Council was held, Rev. Jernagin served for over thirty years as president of the National Sunday School and Baptist Training Union of the National Baptist Convention, U.S.A., Inc. For more than ten years he sat on the executive board of the Baptist World Alliance, and he was a representative to the Federal Council of Churches before the Fraternal Council came into existence. No less creditable than his denominational and ecumenical credentials were his credentials as an activist. His opposition to the enactment of Jim Crow laws when Oklahoma became a state in 1907 led ultimately to the 1915 Supreme Court decision outlawing the "grandfather clause," which had so effectively disenfranchised blacks following Reconstruction.[28] Years later, in the 1950s, a test case brought by Jernagin and Mary Church Terrell led to the Supreme Court decision outlawing segregation in public accommodations in Washington, D.C.[29] In 1954 Jernagin succeeded Terrell as chair of the Coordinating Committee for the Enforcement of the D.C. Anti-Discrimination Laws.[30]

Jernagin's political prominence is further attested by the fact that the FBI maintained a "main" file on him, as well as a "cross-referenced" file on the Council, from the early 1940s into the 1950s. The FBI's interest in Jernagin was based on his affiliation with various organizations "known as fronts for Communist Party Activity," most of which were cited by the Congressional Committee on Un-American Activities. According to the FBI files, Jernagin testified before the Committee in March 1950.[31] The files also indicate that a woman employed by the Council in 1943 or 1944 as Jernagin's administrative assistant was an FBI informant.[32] As a civil rights activist, Jernagin could not have been unaffected by the Communist activity of the 1940s and 1950s: the aggressive proselytization of blacks, the recruiting of blacks into "front organizations," and the special attention paid to black ministers. Nor could he escape completely the frenzied witchhunts of the day, although he apparently was himself never so much a target of McCarthyism as were a handful of other black ministers. Indeed, one FBI memo states: "Although he [Jernagin] has been associated with a number of organizations known to have been controlled and dominated by the Communist Party, he is not believed to be a member of the Communist Party, although he will cooperate with it in regard to its campaign on racial equality." Jernagin was forthright, however, in his defense of fellow ministers who were so targeted.[33]

Jernagin's role with the Fraternal Council was also consonant with his political involvement within the National Baptist Convention; he was an active participant, for example, in the "Progressive" faction that first surfaced in 1931 in opposition to then president Lacey Kirk Williams.[34]

In 1940 Jernagin became chair of the Fraternal Council's executive committee, holding that office for six years. While serving in that capacity, Jernagin proposed and established the Washington Bureau. He then served as the first director of the Bureau. As a result of conflicts with the executive secretary, who was the appointed administrator of the Council, Jernagin moved to sever the Bureau from his administrative oversight. Thereafter, the Bureau reported directly to the executive committee — which Jernagin chaired. The autonomy of the Bureau was thus assured. Jernagin officially resigned in 1947 on complaint that he himself had had to raise the funds to support the Bureau's work and that his request to the executive committee for staff support had been ignored.[35] He maintained his relationship to the Bureau in the capacity of adviser and consultant, however, and for all practical purposes continued to direct its program. In 1952 Jernagin again became chair of the executive committee, retaining that position until his death in 1958, at age 89. With both the Washington Bureau and the executive committee under his command, Jernagin in effect *was* the Fraternal Council. Nor did his influence terminate with his death. The official director of the Washington Bureau during those years, Andrew Fowler, was a protégé of Jernagin. Even in the 1990s Fowler has continued to regard the Council as a trust bequeathed to him by Jernagin.[36]

Jernagin's conflict with the executive secretary, who was a Methodist bishop, was symptomatic of denominational conflict that persisted at least throughout the 1940s. In 1944 the Associated Negro Press reported that the executive secretary, Bishop R. R. Wright, Jr., had been censored for "engaging in political activities" contrary to the interests of the Council. In reply, allegations were leveled that the meeting at which this action was taken was in fact an illegal meeting that "had been packed with Baptist ministers serving as proxies for elected board members." The Council's treasurer, Rev. V. M. Townsend, charged that "certain forces had sought constantly to inject denominationalism into the organization, an effort which its officers had fought."[37]

Efforts to have Bishop Wright replaced apparently persisted, and in 1947 the Baptists succeeded in installing the Rev. J. Stalnaker as executive secretary, an action which the Methodists initially contested. This controversy prompted the chair of the executive committee at that time, the Rev. J. L. Horace, to issue a statement decrying the fact that personalities and self-importance were being permitted to interfere with "the cause." "I am afraid," said Horace, "we are not ready yet to work together across denominational lines. I am considering resigning in the near future from the executive committee rather than waste time in friction with so-called high churchmen bent on having their own end or wrecking the program."[38]

Rev. Stalnaker was succeeded as executive secretary after three years by another Baptist, the Rev. George W. Lucas, who served in that capacity for seven years. Although the presidency of the Council rotated, the Methodists did not again take command fully until 1958. AME Bishop S. L. Greene became president in 1957 and marked the occasion by noting that coincident with his installation "the AME Church was able to get in her man for Executive Secretary, the Rev. J. T. McMillan."[39] The following year, upon the death of Rev. Jernagin, Bishop Greene became chair of the executive committee.

If the Council, in the transition from Ransom's leadership to Jernagin's, underwent a shift from a conciliar model to a more autocratic model, it also moved from merely issuing public pronouncements — though it continued to do that — to pragmatic activism. As a result of Jernagin's leadership, the Washington Bureau was for twenty years the voice of the Black Church on executive and legislative matters pertaining to the struggle of black Americans to secure their civil rights. From 1943 to 1964, the Bureau's staff met and corresponded with Presidents Roosevelt to Johnson; testified before House and Senate Committees on such issues as the Fair Employment Practices Commission, anti-lynching and anti–poll-tax bills, desegregation of interstate travel, housing and education aid, civil rights for the District of Columbia, and the 1957 and 1964 Civil Rights Acts; protested incidents of discrimination in the armed services; published the monthly *Capitol Letter* as a means of informing local church constituencies; cooperated with A. Philip Randolph on labor issues and with Clarence Mitchell on the NAACP's legislative program; and organized civil rights conferences, prayer vigils, and pilgrimages.

Significantly, the Council never restricted itself to domestic issues, but was concerned with international affairs as well. The report of the Committee on the State of the Country issued at the 1950 annual session, for example, had this to say:

The hope of everyone, the dream, the deep and abiding desire of all is for Peace. Yet it would appear that our method of arriving at such is altogether foreign to our deepest yearnings. The church, aware of the armament race of the nations of the world, a race in which this our nation seems to be outstripping all others, would point out that peace, World Peace, is not to be attained by the production of more and better weapons of war, but by rising to great stature, great moral and spiritual stature in world and domestic character. We cannot but deplore the decision of the government to proceed with [humankind's] most devastating and utterly destructive... experiment in self-annihilation.[40]

In 1943 the Bureau was instrumental in arranging for black churchmen to visit soldiers in overseas war zones. In 1944 it sponsored the "National Conference of Christians for Religion, Democracy, and Building a Community of World Brotherhood." The conference issued a "Manifesto" for action to the nation and the government noting that "we are in the process of defeating master racism abroad, but master racism is in the process of defeating us at home."[41] The Bureau sponsored three church observers at the organizing meeting of the United Nations. In 1948 the Fraternal Council organized a National Prayer March in Washington attended by nearly two hundred ministers from seventeen states. The "Statement on Negro Citizens and Human Rights, Addressed to the Country," issued by the delegation on that occasion, read in part as follows:

We believe in the necessity of a strong Navy, a well equipped Army and ships and planes to protect our national borders and the peace of the world against international violators of human rights; but we also believe these things to be most important in the absence of the Good Neighbor principles. We therefore urge that our national leaders shall look wisely to the spending of more millions for education, good homes and other vehicles of goodwill, and that they do more in legislation and in practice to conquer the prejudices against sections, races and groups, and thereby establish a sense of security among all our citizens.[42]

One of the most ambitious projects of the Council and Bureau was the organizing of Committees of One Hundred in major cities, consisting of ministers who could be called on to lobby for the passage of legislation. In fact, such calls were issued and ministers did travel to Washington to lobby their representatives.[43] This model was later to be adopted by Partners in Ecumenism, which for several years devoted a portion of its annual meetings to active legislative lobbying. A Committee of One Hundred was also organized in Washington, D.C., and apparently functioned as an adjunct of the Bureau. Rev. Jernagin himself was officially registered as a lobbyist for the Fraternal Council following passage of the Legislative Reorganization Act of 1946. The dynamism of the Council and its concrete contributions in the 1940s were given eloquent testimony by a 1945 article in the *Pittsburgh Courier*, which described the Council and its Washington Bureau as "mobilized Christian theology in action" and as "one of the most revolutionary developments of our time . . . with its dramatic technique of organizing Negro preachers." The Negro preacher, the article went on to say, "the all-time leader of a patient flock of believers, is gradually realizing that the 'keys to the kingdom' can be found in militant social action. . . . A growing number of ministers think that the church cannot be reborn unless it is through a movement of the disinherited and dispossessed."[44]

This theologically grounded activism continued into the 1950s. On September 22, 1954, the Fraternal Council sponsored a Lincoln Thanksgiving Pilgrimage at the Lincoln Memorial in celebration of the Supreme Court decision setting aside the "separate but equal" doctrine in pubic education. The Council also presented a citation to Thurgood Marshall and voted to contribute $20,000 to the Freedom Rally Fund of the NAACP. In 1956 Jernagin led a movement that culminated in a National Prayer Day for "victims of Montgomery, Alabama's Bus Protest." That event, observed on March 28, resulted in several thousands of dollars being raised to help with the "Montgomery problem." The Council participated in the 1957 Civil Rights Conference, resolutions from which called for establishment of a U.S. Civil Rights Commission and aid to dislocated persons in Hungary and the Middle East. The Conference also commended and expressed support for Martin Luther King, Jr., and other participants in the emerging civil rights movement of the South. In 1963 the Council co-sponsored a citywide mass meeting in observance of the centennial anniversary of the signing of the Emancipation Proclamation.[45]

One of the Council's last major acts was its decision to support and participate in the 1963 March on Washington.[46] That it would do so was consonant with the precedent for nonviolent protest established in 1948 and continued throughout the 1950s. By 1963, however, activities of the Washington Bureau were being directed primarily to issues indigenous to the District of Columbia.[47] With the advent of the civil rights movement, the Fraternal Council was eclipsed, its work functionally concluded and its potential supporters drawn to other organizations. Thereafter it existed in name and in the faithfulness of Rev. Fowler and a few long-time members.

Somewhat surprisingly, there is more evidence of involvement by women in the years under Jernagin's administration than under Ransom's. Jernagin maintained a close working relation with Nannie Helen Burroughs, who headed NBC's National Training and Professional School for Women and Girls in Washington, D.C. Burroughs served on at least one committee of the Council[48] and spoke at the 1949 meeting of the Council in Richmond, Virginia. Significantly, her address was given during the "women's hour." At that same meeting the Council voted to "authorize the establishment of women's auxiliaries in various states."[49] Except for a group in St. Louis, no evidence exists that such appendages ever became active. In 1950, however, a women's auxiliary was organized at the national level and was for several years headed by Mrs. Jernagin. In keeping with this typical Baptist model, the participation of women outside the auxiliary was limited, although the same year the auxiliary was formed, a woman, Berta L. Derrick, did serve as associate director of the Council.[50] Several women were involved in the planning of the Prayer Pilgrimage held in Washington, D.C., under the sponsorship of the Fraternal Council following the 1954 Supreme Court decision in *Brown v. Topeka Board of Education*. Burma Whitted, Dorothy Ferebee, and Jane Spaulding were all co-chairs of major committees.[51]

Demise

Long before the 1960s — indeed, in the very inception of the organization — the Council was laden with structural features that seriously impaired its performance. Its constitutional framework failed to bind member denominations to its policies, and at no time were the denominations obliged to pay the assessed dues. So serious were the consequences of these omissions that the Council faltered in the early 1940s, necessitating the formulation of a plan for reorganization in 1942.[52] Later in the decade, as previously noted, the Council was beset with sectarian feuding. One may speculate that other issues affected the well-being of the Council as well: residual feelings from the 1915 schism of the National Baptists; expectations concerning authority attendant to disparate polities; and perhaps a divided mind on the part of Methodists, at least, as to whether merger or cooperation should take precedence. A further impediment to graceful cooperation was the failure to organize local or state branches of the Council, although the constitution as revised in 1950 did provide for the formation of such units.

At no time did the Council even begin to fulfill the original vision of Bishop Ransom of a mass movement by a united Black Church. Although the potential for mass action was hinted in the prayer vigils and organized lobbying, the Council's preeminent strategy was to position itself within the system and to agitate for change through resolutions, legislation, and lobbying of persons in positions of power. In this manner, it did at least provide an instrument through which the black churches could speak as a collective voice. In time, however, the Council fell victim to its own increasing tendencies toward moderation and to its faulty memory of blacks' experience with the Federal Council of Churches.

The reasons for the Fraternal Council's ultimate demise are multiple, not least of which was the death of Rev. Jernagin and, indeed, the aging of all its initial organizers. Put another way, the Council suffered from the long-term domination of one personality — made possible by the aforementioned structural deficiencies — and, conversely, from the lack of broad-based support, either in personnel or funding. Younger participants were attracted to more activist movements and the Southern Christian Leadership Conference, as another church-based organization, was among the more appealing. In fact, before SCLC was even organized, the Fraternal Council approached Martin Luther King, Jr., inviting him to become executive secretary of the Council.[53] King declined, but the very act of asking signified the Council's endorsement not only of King's philosophy of nonviolent protest, but of the philosophy of integration.

The impact of the new passion for integration on the Council first became evident in 1949 when the Council voted to change its name to the National Fraternal Council of Churches U.S.A., Inc., dropping the word "Negro" altogether. In so doing, the Council "bowed to the pressure of those who denounced the Council as a 'segregated organization' ";[54] a number of black ministers, especially some in white denominations, refused on that basis to affiliate with the Council.[55]

This sentiment was enhanced by the organizing of the National Council of Churches, which led some of the representatives of the black denominations to feel that a separate black ecumenical organization was no longer needed.[56] Their confidence in the validity of that view was further bolstered by the 1954 Supreme Court decision. The formation of NCC was also a factor in terms of financial support for the Fraternal Council, since the dues that denominations joining NCC were required to pay exceeded the dues of the Fraternal Council. Some denominations felt they could not afford both — even if they were so inclined — and opted for NCC.[57]

The Fraternal Council, at a special meeting called in 1954, even considered merging with NCC. Recalled one of those present, George Lucas:

> Although all of us present realized that this was a desperate attempt to keep the work alive, most of us were not ready for the Council to lose its identity by merging with the National Council of Churches. We were faced with the reality of whether the National Council was the best organization to represent our goals.[58]

A faithful participant of the Council in its last years, Lucas attributed the decline of the Fraternal Council to the fact that so many of its members "bought into the integration agenda," trusting the National Council of Churches to fully include blacks and fully incorporate their concerns in its program.[59] The trust proved to be ill-founded, and when the National Committee of Negro Churchmen came into being as a witness to that fact, Rev. Lucas wrote the fledgling organization:

> I, along with a few others, share a feeling of nostalgia about the National Fraternal Council, which was inaugurated in 1933 [sic] for the same purpose to which you subscribe. It was my privilege to serve as Executive Secretary from 1950 to 1957. The years of my service were somewhat paralyzed because so many of our Negro leaders thought that the National Council of Churches had subsumed our role.
>
> Things change. Now that a growing number are taking pride in our identity and contribution, I should like for us to give some consideration to dialogue between these two movements.

Lucas then quoted a letter from the president of the Fraternal Council, saying, "In my opinion, it might be more effective if the two organizations would merge into a third organization which would be different from either one as they presently exist."[60]

Nothing substantive came of these overtures, although Lucas himself went on to become the first president of Partners in Ecumenism and a member of the original executive committee of the Congress of National Black Churches. In reality, except for the property it owned in Washington, D.C., the Fraternal Council had little to offer another organization — save a legacy of being twice disappointed by the white ecumenical movement in the United States. Both in its origins and in its demise, this earliest black ecumenical organization was inextricably tied to the larger and predominantly white movement, a circumstance that would partially foretell the fate of subsequent black ecumenical movements as well.

Summary

On the continuums of characteristics suggested in the Introduction, the Fraternal Council may be depicted as follows:[61]

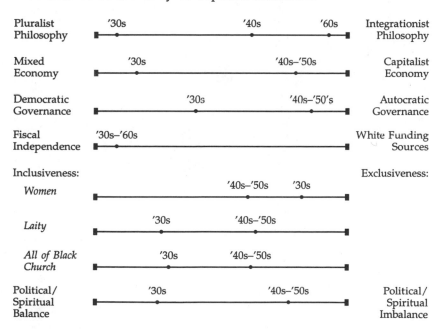

More so than later organizations, in large part on account of its longer tenure, the Fraternal Council presents two contrasting profiles, one reflective of the influence of Bishop Ransom, the other of Rev. Jernagin. In its final days, Rev. Lucas sought valiantly to bring the Council full circle to the earlier vision of Bishop Ransom. That effort proved too little, too late. Nevertheless, overall the Council merits an honored place in the history of Black Church organizations. External impediments and internal shortcomings notwithstanding, the Fraternal Council of Negro Churches represents an important effort on the part of the Black Church to overcome denominational divisions in order to improve the social, economic, and political status of the black populace. Further, its existence provides a partial corrective to the image of the Black Church in this era as accommodationist, pointing to an enduring impulse of activism and cultural revitalization in the black religious tradition. The Council can hardly be faulted for having been overtaken by new times; contrarily, not a few seeds of its planting surely came to fruition in successor religio-political organizations of the 1960s.

Chapter Two

TO SAVE THE SOUL OF AMERICA
The Southern Christian
Leadership Conference

Context

One of the great paradoxes of the twentieth century is that its most reactionary decade was also the decade that spawned the contemporary
freedom movement. In the United States of the 1950s, "communism"
was the code word for "enemy." But "enemy" included far more than
the Eastern bloc. To a power structure threatened by the modest economic reforms of the New Deal and by the embryonic realignment of
the races brought by World War II, "enemy" meant any type of labor,
civil rights, or populist movement. Accordingly, prominent among the
features of the late 1940s and the 1950s were vicious name-calling,
witch hunts, silencing — immobilization — of would-be seekers after
justice. Yet, in the midst of pervasive death, there was resurrection.

Perhaps no development in the recent history of the United States
attests more persuasively to the interaction of religion and society
than that of the contemporary civil rights movement. In the years
from 1954 to 1968 — from *Brown v. Topeka Board of Education* to the
assassination of Martin Luther King, Jr. — black churches and their
pastors and members helped stage a drama that challenged the nation and captivated the world. The flagship organization in this
compelling production was the Southern Christian Leadership Conference (SCLC). SCLC was bracketed, however, by older organizations
that laid the foundation for its work and by younger organizations

that extended its accomplishments. And few of these fellow actors were without religious connections.

The oldest civil rights organization, the NAACP, was created out of the spiritual-political vision of progressive black clergy such as Bishop Reverdy Ransom and the Rev. Francis Grimké, the intellectual prowess of W. E. B. Du Bois, and the social consciousness of a handful of whites — all of them seeking a vehicle for altering the structure of American society. Preeminently, the northern-based NAACP mandated legal action as the prescribed mode for seeking change. In the South, however, local NAACP representatives were drawn into roles that were more directly responsive to the circumstances at hand. Many of these representatives were black clergy whose local churches became the centers for community meetings, membership recruitment, and fund raising. From 1918, when an NAACP presence was established in the South, through the 1940s, these clergy advocates were deemed harmless enough and left in relative peace. In the 1950s, however, the NAACP's campaign to desegregate southern public schools greatly heightened the visibility of both black churches and local NAACP units. The result was a coordinated attack on the NAACP that lasted the decade, with local units being outlawed in five southern states, a circumstance that made this cadre of activist ministers both amenable to and available to a newly emergent protest organization, SCLC.[1]

As the NAACP was compelled to recede in the South, another northern-based civil rights organization — the Congress of Racial Equality (CORE) — gained ascendancy. Although organized in 1942, CORE's first black executive director, James Farmer, was appointed in 1961. Farmer had been one of the principal founders of CORE, which received its initial support from the Fellowship of Reconciliation, a pacifist organization that played a central role in early civil rights campaigns by training key participants in the tactic of nonviolent resistance. Although CORE itself was not founded as a religious organization, Farmer was trained as a minister, having graduated from Howard University Divinity School. It was under his leadership that CORE initiated the famous "Freedom Rides" that were so instrumental in desegregating southern transportation systems.

The Student Nonviolent Coordinating Committee (SNCC) was the youth arm of the civil rights movement, originating in the student sit-ins in Greensboro, North Carolina, and Nashville, Tennessee, in 1960. While the tone of SNCC changed drastically quite early in its tenure, it was initially rooted in a religious ethos, in no small part because of its ties to SCLC. James Lawson, a committed pacifist and theology student at Vanderbilt University, trained the Nashville students in nonviolence prior to the sit-ins and subsequently wrote SNCC's original statement of purpose. Lawson was later ordained a United Methodist minister and became a key aide to Martin Luther King, Jr. Dr. King encouraged the students' activism, and Ella Baker, a key personality in SCLC, was instrumental in assisting them to form their own separate organization. Further, it was the Rev. Kelly Miller Smith, head of the Nashville Christian Leadership Council, an SCLC affiliate, who provided the primary support to the students throughout the Nashville sit-ins. One of these students, John Lewis, became a Baptist minister and served as the chair of SNCC from 1963 to 1966. In addition to the sit-ins, which desegregated public accommodations in towns and cities across the South, SNCC played a leading role in voter registration campaigns through the mid-1960s.

But if SCLC found at least marginal spiritual kinship with these sister organizations, it far surpassed them in the depth and breadth of its connections to the Church. Though not usually characterized as an ecumenical organization, SCLC was in fact the first of this new genre of black religious movements to appear in the second half of the century. As the vehicle for the nonviolent social change movement led by Martin Luther King, Jr., SCLC was dominated in its early years by the charismatic personality of this Baptist preacher, while its board of directors consisted almost entirely of black ministers. That it was a self-consciously religious organization was evidenced by its very name. Moreover, in campaign after campaign in rural communities across the South, the lifeblood of SCLC was the Baptist and Methodist and Pentecostal ministers and church members who crossed denominational lines to confront terror and danger in order to "be the church" — to affirm the parenthood of God and the kinship of all people. In the process, they desegregated America.

SCLC Origins

In the mid-1950s a half-dozen boycotts of segregated bus systems took place in southern cities. The first, in Baton Rouge, Louisiana, in 1953, was led by the Rev. T. J. Jemison, then national secretary of the largest black denomination, the National Baptist Convention, U.S.A.,

Inc. (NBC). This fortuitous connection subsequently resulted in the NBC's becoming a conduit for dissemination of the Baton Rouge model to other activist clergy. Among those who consulted with Jemison were fellow members of the Convention, the Rev. Dr. Martin Luther King, Jr., and the Rev. Ralph David Abernathy in Montgomery, Alabama.[2]

The Montgomery bus boycott, sparked by the actions of Rosa Parks, had been initiated in December 1955 by an attorney, Fred Gray; a railroad porter, E. D. Nixon; and a college teacher, Jo Ann Robinson. All three were heads of political clubs. Robinson's Women's Political Council, especially, was instrumental in getting the boycott underway, whereupon it was taken over by a group of Montgomery ministers who formed the Montgomery Improvement Association (MIA).[3] The Rev. L. Roy Bennett, head of the local Interdenominational Ministerial Alliance, became the chair of the MIA, while the young Dr. King was chosen as president.

The year-long Montgomery protest acted as a powerful catalyst, stirring protest activity across the South and generating what Aldon Morris describes as "movement centers." In Tallahassee, Florida, the bus boycott organized by the Inter Civic Council (ICC) was led by the Rev. C. K. Steele, president of the local NAACP, and Dr. James Hudson, president of the Interdenominational Ministerial Alliance. In Birmingham, the Alabama Christian Movement for Human Rights (ACMHR) was headed by the Rev. Fred Shuttlesworth. The Rev. Josephs Lowery president of the Interdenominational Ministerial Alliance in Mobile, Alabama, gave leadership to protest activity through the Mobile Civic Association (MCA).[4] In these centers and others, it was clergy involvement that lent a moral framework and religious enthusiasm to the unprecedented demands for social change. It was lay church members who responded, with as many as 98 percent of the members of the local movement centers being church members.[5]

After Montgomery, the leaders of the major movement centers — Steele, Shuttlesworth, Jemison, and Lowery — regularly consulted with King and Abernathy and with one another. Out of their continuing dialogue came recognition of a need to somehow coordinate the local protests that were steadily multiplying. The idea of creating a new organization to assist and coordinate the burgeoning protests was given concreteness at a meeting in New York City in December 1956 of a group called "In Friendship." In Friendship had been organized early in 1956 by Ella Baker, Stanley Levison, and Bayard

Rustin. A. Philip Randolph was subsequently recruited as the chair of the organization. Each of these individuals had close ties to the northern political left, or what Adam Fairclough describes as "the socialist-liberal-labor forces." Each was to play a crucial role in the development of SCLC, with repercussions for King both positive and negative.[6]

In Friendship itself was formed to provide financial support to the southern protest movement and to help bring to the nation's awareness the scope of racial injustice. The Montgomery boycott was one of the beneficiaries of their efforts, and as the members of In Friendship reflected on the significance of that movement, a plan began to take shape for a larger, more activist organization. Recognizing that the initiative for a southern coordinating body needed to be indigenous, Rev. C. K. Steele was approached to issue a call to southern activists to attend a regional conference. Such an invitation was extended by King, Shuttlesworth, and Steele on January 1, 1957. In response, some sixty persons from twenty-nine communities in ten states convened at Ebenezer Baptist Church in Atlanta on January 10 and 11. Most of the persons attending were ministers, although the gathering also included three businessmen, two labor leaders, two college professors, and one farmer.[7] The outcome of the meeting was an organization called the "Southern Negro Leaders' Conference on Transportation and Nonviolent Integration."

The agenda of that initial meeting consisted in part of discussion of seven working papers, written by Bayard Rustin, that set forth a philosophical and programmatic framework for regionwide facilitation of a mass protest movement. The first position paper stated emphatically that "the campaign is based on the most stable institution in Negro culture — the church," and noted the contributions of the church in providing economic assistance and "community spirit" to the local movements already underway.[8] Thus, from the beginning the foundation of the new organization was understood to be the Black Church. Both the philosophy and method of change were understood to be nonviolence, as was emphasized in "A Statement to the South and Nation," prepared by conference participants.[9]

A second organizing meeting was convened the following month, on February 14, at New Zion Baptist Church in New Orleans. Nearly a hundred delegates from thirty-four cities were present to designate officers and a board of directors — including the naming of King as president — and to change the name of the organization to the Southern Leadership Conference.[10] This time several lawyers were also present, but the composition remained overwhelmingly ministerial.

A third meeting, held at Holt Street Church in Montgomery on August 8 and 9 and attended by over a hundred individuals, is regarded as the first convention of the new organization, the name of which was changed yet again to Southern Christian Leadership Conference.[11] David Garrow reports it was King who suggested inclusion of the name "Christian" in the name, to emphasize the organization's church base.[12] Other accounts credit a minister from Little Rock who argued, "Since they were doing Christ-like work, why not include the name Christian."[13] Either way, the recommendation no doubt reflected the preference of other participating ministers. It also did not pass unnoted that an overt Christian identity might protect the new organization from the charge of being a Communist front. As if to accent the moral thrust of the new endeavor, participants at the first convention adopted as SCLC's motto, "To Save the Soul of America."[14]

It was also at the first convention that King proposed SCLC's first programmatic venture. The "Crusade for Citizenship" was to be a voter education and registration project carried out in selected southern cities. Ella Baker was deployed to Atlanta to implement the program, but the effort met with only marginal success. Baker returned to New York briefly, only to return to Atlanta in early 1958 to begin the process of establishing permanent headquarters for the fledgling organization.

A second convention was held in November 1957 at Mt. Olive CME Cathedral in Memphis. Two more meetings were convened in 1958, a May meeting in Clarksdale, Mississippi, and an October meeting in Norfolk, Virginia (Table 2.1). SCLC was officially incorporated in 1958, with the articles of incorporation specifying the arena of operation as sixteen southern states, although the bylaws stipulated that resources and support would be received nationwide.[15] While the initial board of directors, organized at SCLC's first convention, consisted of twenty-five members — twenty-one clergy and four lay — the adopted constitution specified thirty-three board members. Officers totaled nine, including president, three vice presidents, secretary, corresponding secretary, treasurer, chaplain, and historian. Of the first board to serve under the new guidelines, all members were black, one was a woman, some two-thirds were ministers. Lay members

Table 2.1. SCLC Meetings

Organizing Meetings

| 1. January 10–11, 1957 | Atlanta |
| 2. February 14, 1957 | New Orleans |

Conventions

1. August 7–8 or 8–9, 1957	Montgomery
2. November 5, 1957	Memphis
3. May 29, 1958	Clarksdale, Miss.
4. October 1–2, 1958	Norfolk, Va.
5. May 1959	Tallahassee
6. September 1959	Columbia, S.C.
1960	—
7. September 1961	Nashville
8. September 1962	Birmingham
9. September 1963	Richmond, Va.
10. September 1964	Savannah
11. August 1965	Birmingham
12. September (?) 1966	Jackson
13. September (?) 1967	Atlanta

Source: David J. Garrow, *Bearing the Cross: Martin Luther King, Jr., and the Southern Christian Leadership Conference* (New York: Wm. Morrow, 1986).

included a dentist, a pharmacist, a history professor, several business-men, and one union official. Of the clergy members, approximately 80 percent were Baptist and 20 percent Methodist.[16] A thirteen-member administrative committee was also composed overwhelmingly of clergy. Other committees were established as particular programs and campaigns were initiated over the years.

Even as SCLC was being born, King himself, capitalizing on the visibility gained from the Montgomery campaign, found himself engaged in national diplomacy and leadership. Frustrated that over-tures to President Eisenhower from other civil rights leaders were being spurned, King proposed at the February 1957 meeting of SCLC that a Prayer Pilgrimage to Washington, D.C., be organized. With the cooperation and support of Roy Wilkins, head of the NAACP, and of A. Philip Randolph, the pilgrimage took place at the Lincoln Memorial on the historic date of May 17, the third anniversary of the 1954 Supreme Court decision. The highlight of the event was King's dramatic "Give Us the Ballot" speech. The next month, King was granted an audience with Vice President Richard Nixon. A year later, a renewed request for a conference with President Eisenhower was granted. SCLC's president, at least, had been established as a force to be reckoned with.

Over the course of its early years SCLC evolved a statement of purpose and philosophy that was published as a brochure called "This Is SCLC." That statement made clear the initial intent of SCLC: "achieving full citizenship rights, equality, and the integration of the Negro in all aspects of American life." The "ultimate aim" was to "foster and create the 'beloved community' in America where brotherhood [sic] is a reality." The "ultimate goal" was "genuine intergroup and interpersonal living — *integration.*"[17]

Integration was unequivocally SCLC's vision for America. Indeed, the "beloved community" became Dr. King's rhetorical trademark. In pursuit of that vision, SCLC's "focal points" were twofold: "the use of nonviolent philosophy as a means of creative protest; and securing the right of the ballot for every citizen." Specifically, SCLC members anchored their agenda in "Christian nonviolence," at the center of which was understood to be "redemptive love." "Creatively used," they asserted, the philosophy of nonviolence could "restore the broken community in America," for "nonviolence is the most potent force available to an oppressed people in their struggle for freedom and dignity."[18]

Further, civil disobedience was understood to be "a natural consequence of nonviolence when the resister is confronted by unjust and immoral laws" — an unjust law being "one that is out of harmony with the moral law of the universe, or, as the religionist would say, out of harmony with the Law of God. More concretely, an unjust law is one in which the minority is compelled to observe a code which is not binding on the majority." It is a law "which people are required to obey" although they had "no part in [its] making because they were denied the right to vote."[19]

In conjunction with defying unjust laws, securing the right to vote became the pragmatic path to fulfillment of SCLC's vision. The "beloved community" might represent a biblical ideal, but the organization was committed to realizing that ideal in the here and now through true participatory democracy. That the electoral political process could be an instrument for securing freedom was a fundamental tenet in SCLC's faith.

If exercise of the ballot was a necessary condition for securing freedom, however, it was not a sufficient condition. Overcoming segregation was a parallel requirement and "overcoming" had two compelling components: First was the dismantling of the system of codes and customs that constituted segregation; second was attendance to "the demoralization caused by the legacy of slavery and segregation — inferior schools, slums, and second-class citizenship.... There *must*," read the organization's manifesto, "be a balance between attacking the causes and healing the effects of segregation."[20] The former was to prove far more susceptible to SCLC forays than the latter.

The Movement Years, 1960–65

Membership in SCLC consisted of local affiliate organizations rather than individuals.[21] Consequently, SCLC functioned in two tiers: first, as an umbrella organization providing support to local groups; second, as the initiator and administrator of its own programs.

In part, the affiliate structure was built from local church-based protests initiated before SCLC came into being. The "movement centers" in Montgomery, Baton Rouge, Mobile, Tallahassee, and Birmingham, for example, that were instrumental in SCLC's creation, subsequent to that creation became official affiliates. Many of the ministers who participated in the first meetings of SCLC either affiliated their home church or affiliated new direct action groups organized by them in their respective communities. Many local Interdenominational Ministerial Alliances affiliated, as did local Baptist Conferences. Nor were all affiliates church-based, but ranged from civic leagues to lodges to labor organizations to voter registration projects. Any such group could become a member of SCLC by paying a $25 fee and signing a charter that committed them to organize their community to carry out direct action protests.[22]

In organizing local movements, affiliates were charged with responding to community grievances. Thus, local protests frequently had as their focus bus boycotts, voting rights, or school integration.[23] The broader scope of activity is suggested in the following breakdown of actions initiated by local church-based groups over a five-year period: court action, 9 percent; electoral politics activity, 16 percent; economic boycotts, 25 percent; sit-ins or other forms of direct action, 35 percent; other, 16 percent.[24]

By 1963 SCLC could claim eighty-five southern affiliates and thirty northern affiliates in a total of thirty states.[25] Those affiliates having program responsibilities were restricted to southern states, with the exception of the Western Christian Leadership Conference, based in Los Angeles, which in time also became an activist organization. Initially, however, SCLC West, like its northern counterparts, was organized solely for the purpose of fund raising. This division of labor — and for that matter the affiliate structure itself — was designed in large part to avoid competition with the NAACP, which in a multitude of ways expressed its reluctance to share the civil rights turf with a newcomer organization. But whether North or South, whether action oriented or fiscally oriented, the affiliates, as the grassroots components of SCLC, were the very core of its being.[26] Indeed, according to Morris, the affiliated churches and church organizations "were so central that SCLC leaders referred to them as 'the invisible hand of God.' "[27]

The assessment from the affiliates' perspective was not always quite so charitable. In reality, the quality of relations between SCLC and the local units varied greatly. The affiliates enjoyed substantial autonomy, with minimal top-down control — or even direction. A not unusual complaint was that needed support — in presence, guidance, and information — was not forthcoming from the central staff and board of directors. In part, this circumstance was attributable to the fact that SCLC maintained an ambivalent tension between supporting local initiatives and initiating its own campaigns.[28]

SCLC's major direct action campaigns are well known: Albany, Georgia, 1961–62; Birmingham, Alabama, 1963; St. Augustine, Florida, 1964; Selma, Alabama, 1965.[29] Direct action protest involved a cluster of tactics: marches, rallies, boycotts, sit-ins, civil disobedience, mass arrests — all of them anchored in nonviolence. While for some participants nonviolence was a philosophy — a way of life — for others it was simply a method of social protest. Either way, few participants were immune to the religious character of the campaigns that arose both from the style of the leaders and the hearts of the masses. The typical scenario, once King and his aides responded to a call from a particular community, began with revival-like gatherings in local churches that featured impassioned prayers, civil rights-oriented sermons invoking biblical imagery, and the singing of hymns and movement songs. Then, employing the style of a black Baptist preacher, King would present to the people the "nonviolent way." Describing the joining of King's teaching and preaching with the folk religion of the protesters who were his congregation, Gayraud Wilmore writes: "He was able to elicit from the thousands who flocked to hear him... the old-fashioned religiosity of the folk, converted into a passion for justice. But the passion for justice was already there. Suppressed by years of subjugation and domesticated by the prudence of a mute church, it was nevertheless deeply embedded in the religion of the masses."[30]

If Dr. King and his ministerial compatriots were able to touch the spiritual depths of southern blacks, they were less successful in stirring the souls of whites. King inaugurated his SCLC career with a devotion to the path of moral persuasion, believing that awareness of one's wrongdoing could lead to a transformation in behavior. Invoking the values of democracy and Christianity, he appealed to white liberals in government, churches, and labor unions to create a "coalition of conscience." At the national level, King enjoyed some success. In time, for example, both the National Council of Churches and representatives of the Catholic Church provided an important presence at key civil rights protests. The masses of southern whites — with notable exceptions — proved more recalcitrant. Increasingly, King came to understand the limitations of moral persuasion and began to engage in nonviolent direct action with the dual objective of bringing government pressure to bear on the pernicious structures of brutality that characterized the white South.[31] The extensive media coverage generated by SCLC's more volatile campaigns did cause pressure to be applied in the nation's capital, so that a dialectical relation obtained between the local and national levels of operation. In this manner, SCLC ultimately secured major support for civil rights from Presidents Kennedy and Johnson. Relations with the White House were later severed following King's public expression of opposition to the Vietnam War, but not before two key pieces of legislation — the Civil Rights Act of 1964 and the Voting Rights Act of 1965 — contributed substantially to the achievement of SCLC's objectives.

In between the marching in the streets and the legislative action in the houses of Congress was the more tedious work of educating disenfranchised blacks as to the importance of the ballot, preparing them to exercise their citizenship rights, and instilling in them the courage to confront a vicious, retaliatory system determined to protect white privilege. One of SCLC's most important endeavors was its Citizenship Education Program, taken over in 1960 from the Highlander

Folk School, where the program had been developed by Septima Clark. Through its literacy classes and leadership development training, this program was ultimately responsible for vastly increasing the numbers of black voters. Although much of SCLC's effort was concentrated in Alabama, it joined with COFO, the Council of Federated Organizations, a civil rights coalition including both SCLC and SNCC, to extend its involvement to other states. It was COFO that organized the 1964 Mississippi Freedom Summer and that was instrumental in organizing the Mississippi Freedom Democratic Party. While SNCC was dominant in these projects, SCLC lent its support. After Selma, SCLC launched SCOPE — Summer Community Organization and Political Education — a massive voter registration and citizenship education program initiated to assure utilization of the soon-to-be-secured voting rights.

A program designed to soften the rigidity of local systems was Operation Dialogue, in which white SCLC staff members would seek out dialogue with other white southerners in an effort to improve race relations. Yet another tack taken was Project Vision, a high school tutoring program initiated in 1965 that brought college students to Alabama cities to help prepare black high school students for college. Both programs were modest in scope and had corresponding impact.

Along with direct action protest and voter registration, a third component was added to SCLC's program in 1962 with the creation of Operation Breadbasket. Modeled after the Rev. Leon Sullivan's economic boycott program in Philadelphia, Operation Breadbasket had a dual thrust: organizing boycotts of businesses through local black church congregations to secure jobs for black workers and providing support for the development of black-owned businesses. The principal program was located in Atlanta, with a branch organized in Chicago by Jesse Jackson in 1966. In the early 1970s Jackson's component, which had become the tail wagging the proverbial dog, was severed from SCLC and transformed into Jackson's own organization, Operation PUSH.

Spurred by the violent explosions in major cities of the North and West and by a growing consciousness of conditions in northern urban ghettos, SCLC shifted visibly in the mid-1960s from its agenda of social change (desegregation) and political change (enfranchisement) to a greater emphasis on economic change — part of which was signified by the expansion of Operation Breadbasket. But in addition, SCLC began to focus on the system of economic exploitation and profiteering that accounted for the very existence of the ghettos. A foray into a Chicago-based "War on Slums" contributed greatly to a major redirection of King's thinking and priorities. For the SCLC organization, however, the 1966 Chicago campaign was a challenge that could not be met. If moral persuasion proved ineffective in the South, it was even less adequate in the North. Nor were the finely honed skills of direct action protest and voter registration drives sufficient in the face of the complex configuration of urban ills and evils that Chicago presented. As Fairclough notes, what was needed in the North was the ability to organize neighborhood associations, tenant unions, and consumer boycotts, and while a few SCLC staffers proved up to the task, few of the southern clergy who made up SCLC were.[32] After a frustrated attempt at becoming a truly national organization, most of SCLC's key players prudently reclaimed a regional responsibility. Not so, however, their president, of which more will be said later.

Internal Affairs

Initially, SCLC's organizational structure consisted of its board of directors and conventions, which were attended primarily by affiliate members. Beginning in 1960 board meetings were held twice a year and conventions annually. The administrative committee functioned as the "inner circle" of the board, having primary responsibility for advising King on major decisions. The role of the administrative committee diminished, however, as the executive staff grew in size. And in truth, neither the board nor the staff ever had more than advisory powers, as real authority was unequivocally invested in King himself, who retained veto power over any and all recommendations. More often, it was King who made the recommendations to the board and convention, which in turn rubber stamped his positions. In short, SCLC functioned as what Fairclough describes as a "benevolent autocracy."[33]

King, however, was neither aloof nor arbitrary, but invited open and thorough discussion, insisting on input from staff and aides. Board members and officers engaged in lively debates on policy issues, while the executive staff met frequently to hold forth in animated, argumentative sessions that were mediated by King, whose role was to move the process toward a consensus position. King also convened retreats once or twice a year that served the dual function of providing a needed rest and creating a setting for talking through core philosophical and political issues. Typically, the retreats were attended by senior board members, the executive staff, and some of King's northern advisers. Corollary retreats were also often held for the field staff, providing an opportunity for training in nonviolence and Marxist analysis and for addressing personnel problems and tensions.[34]

SCLC maintained offices in New York and Washington, but the preponderance of the organization's executive staff was housed in the Atlanta office, which, except for a brief foray to Exchange Street in downtown Atlanta, was located on Auburn Avenue in the heart of the black business district. Ella Baker, who, as has been noted, set up the Atlanta office, was also SCLC's first executive director, although she was never granted that title. She was instead designated "associate director," a concession to the preponderance of Baptist ministers on the SCLC board. The first executive director, so titled, was the Rev. John Tilley, who was appointed in April 1958. Upon his departure a year later, Baker was named "acting executive director," serving in that capacity until the second executive director, so titled, was appointed in 1960. The Rev. Wyatt T. Walker remained in that position until 1964, during which time the staff grew from five to sixty, including six regional directors and four field secretaries. Among those joining the ranks in those years were James Lawson, Andrew Young, C. T. Vivian, James Bevel — all ministers — and Septima Clark, Dorothy Cotton, Bernard Lee, and Hosea Williams. These individuals — along with many unpaid, unnamed volunteers — were among those who played critical roles in SCLC's direct action and voter education and registration projects. The staff reached a peak of two hundred in 1965, the year in which Jesse Jackson was added to the roster.[35] Andrew Young succeeded Walker as executive director in 1964, and then in 1967 was named executive vice president (Table 2.2).

Without exception, the executive directors, all of them Baptist but Young, experienced something less than total success in controlling the staff they were charged to supervise. As one observer put it, "The vehicle for carrying [the nonviolent] philosophy into action was a wondrous machine called the Southern Christian Leadership Conference. No one could be certain precisely how it worked.... Beyond the inner circle, SCLC was...an exercise in organized chaos."[36] That SCLC's staff was beset by conflict and competition was explained in part by the fact that so many key players were ministers unaccus-

Table 2.2. SCLC Staff Administration

	Executive Director	Executive Vice President	Administrator
1957	Ms. Ella Baker		
1958	Rev. John Tilley		
1959–60	Ms. Ella Baker		
1960–64	Rev. Wyatt T. Walker		
1964–67	Rev. Andrew Young		
1967–69	Mr. William Rutherford		
1967–70	—	Rev. Andrew Young	
1970–73	—	Rev. Bernard Lee	
1974–76	—	—	—
1977	Mr. Hosea Williams		
1978–79	—	—	—
1980–88			Rev. Albert Love
1988–			Rev. Randel T. Osburn

tomed to functioning in a subordinate role. Each tended to operate out of a minister's worldview — namely, autonomy in decision making and action. The person who surpassed all the others in adopting this posture — and the one person to whom the others deferred — was King himself.[37]

An exception was Ella Baker, who from the very beginning challenged King's leadership style, arguing for a more participatory and less Baptist model and for a more organized and efficient office. But the leadership model of the Black Church — of pastoral charisma and dominance and chauvinism — prevailed.[38] SCLC, of course, preceded the contemporary women's movement, so that it is not surprising that the organization was male-dominated or that the consciousness of its leaders with regard to issues of gender equity was modest. Baker was acutely aware of these issues, though, as were the only other two women executive staff members, Dorothy Cotton and Septima Clark, both of whom remarked on the sexist attitudes of King and of black preachers generally.[39] At the same time, few staff members had the access to King that Cotton enjoyed.[40] But their critique was further validated in the sparse representation of women on SCLC's board of directors — five out of fifty-three in 1967. Only one of SCLC's offices from 1957 to 1967 was held by a woman. Katie Whickham was elected assistant secretary in 1958; in 1967 the same office was filled by Marian Logan.[41]

SCLC reflected the culture of black churches not only in its attitudes toward women and its autocratic leadership, but also in its revivalistic style, which proved both an asset and a deficit. On the one hand, that mode of operation was the key to mobilizing the masses for direct action; on the other, it was obstructive of the rational administration of programs. Consequently, SCLC's relationship to its own programs was sometimes as haphazard as its relations to its affiliates. The early differences between Baker and King regarding management philosophy persisted through the years of King's tenure, with lay staff members arguing for a more structured and disciplined organization, while the clergy held out for spontaneity. The choices were faith-inspired direct action or long-term institutionalized programs, and the former prevailed.

Fairclough suggests that King's style was likely attributable to neither administrative ineptness nor the uncritical manner of Baptist preachers, but at least in part reflected a perceptive insight that the times and the objectives called for maximum flexibility, which bureaucracy would seriously impede.[42] It is a compelling point, but one that does not obviate the frustrations of individuals accustomed to working in a more orderly fashion. The conflict between charisma and bureaucracy persists in contemporary social change efforts, as does the issue of less than humanistic treatment of subordinate staff and workers. In both instances, the transcendent question raised has to do with the consistency of means and ends, a matter that was at the heart of King's devotion to the path of nonviolence.

In fact, King himself moved back and forth between the impromptu style of southern activist clergy and the more deliberate mode of northern supporters. In 1962 King created a northern network of "regional representatives" — all black clergy — who were authorized to speak for SCLC, assist in fund raising, arrange speaking engagements for King, and organize "sympathy demonstrations."[43] As vital to King, if not more so, was a small circle of advisers in New York, at the center of which were Stanley Levison and Bayard Rustin. Both individuals had continued to function in the North as King's consultants on fund raising and political strategy. Along with Jack O'Dell, Levison helped staff the New York office — although he was never on SCLC's payroll — and in that capacity played a critical role as administrator of SCLC's direct mail fund raising program.

In addition to direct mail solicitations, SCLC received income from fees for King's speaking engagements, royalties from his books, offerings from churches and religious organizations, and donations from labor unions. Other than the $25 affiliation fee, local units did not finance SCLC. In fact, most of SCLC's support came from the northeastern states and from Illinois and California.[44] While contributions from individuals, both black and white, were substantial, the larger share of funds came from organizations. Herbert Haines suggests that in 1959 some 60 percent of SCLC's external income came from churches and that the absolute level of church contributions remained constant in succeeding years, although church giving as a proportion of total income decreased.[45] Haines also maintains that in the early 1960s, especially, SCLC, as well as CORE and SNCC, relied heavily on white "conscience contributors" — i.e., white churches and labor unions. Fairclough, on the other hand, contends that dependency on whites increased as SCLC's income grew in the mid-1960s. With yet another appraisal, Morris estimates that in the early years of SCLC, 80 percent of the money that came from organizations came from black religious organizations.[46]

Unlike the more established and more moderate civil rights organizations, the newer ones received little funding from foundations or corporations. In the later 1960s SCLC did receive a few foundation grants, including $230,000 from the Ford Foundation. SCLC's direct mail contributions were funneled through an SCLC-created foundation that began as the organization's legal arm under the name "Gandhi Society" and then was transmuted into the American Foundation on Nonviolence (AFON). In 1966–67 SCLC received three federal grants: $100,000 from the Department of Education; $60,000 from the Department of Labor; and $500,000 from the Office of Economic Opportunity. An important source of support for SCLC's voter registration work was the Voter Education Project (VEP), based in Atlanta. Another major source of revenue was black entertainers, including such personalities as Al Hibbler, Sammy Davis, Jr., Mahalia Jackson, Aretha Franklin, and Dick Gregory. These individuals were joined by white performers such as Joan Baez and Tony Bennett. But none surpassed the efforts of Harry Belafonte, who for years played a crucial role in the movement, particularly through raising bail money for jailed demonstrators. The money King was awarded as the 1964 recipient of the Nobel Peace Prize was divided among the major civil rights organizations.

Fairclough asserts that by 1964–65, over half of SCLC's income was raised by King with his speeches at colleges and universities and at conventions of labor unions, religious organizations, and professional associations.[47] The figures for SCLC's external income, as compiled by Haines, give some indication of this extraordinary effort on King's part. From $10,000 in 1957, the organization's income grew to over $50,000 in 1960; $200,000 in 1961 and 1962; over $700,000 in 1963; and peaked at $1.6 million in 1965. After holding at $1 million from 1966 through 1968, income then fell to half that amount in 1969 and 1970.[48]

Most of SCLC's paid staff members received subsistence wages; King received one dollar a year. Staffing, as might be expected, followed the organization's financial fortunes, with a major drop-off from 1965 to 1966 and early 1967, at which time the staff was reduced to eighty-five.[49] Even as the southern executive and field staffs diminished in size, King's northern advisers assumed ever greater importance. In addition to Levison, Rustin, and O'Dell, the northern-based "research committee," as it was called, included Harry Wachtel, Clarence Jones, and L. D. Reddick. Often joining the group were union representatives Cleveland Robinson and Ralph Helstein, along with Ralph Abernathy and Walter Fauntroy, who headed SCLC's Washington office. These and other advisers met frequently with King to keep him appraised of political, social, and economic issues and developments. In contrast to the theological framework of King's southern clergy aides and colleagues, this group offered a more strictly analytical presentation of current events and dynamics. The research committee had a decidedly northern focus and in particular served as King's link with the northern political left. Consequently, the committee's meetings were not only a forum for exchanging information and testing ideas, but over time were influential in radicalizing King's thought and public posture.[50]

Not surprisingly, the research committee was also the lightning rod for drawing FBI attention. Over the years the FBI succeeded in planting at least one informant on SCLC's staff — Jim Harrison, the organization's comptroller from 1965 on.[51] The vast majority of information gathered by the FBI, however, was from wiretaps and surveillance of members of the committee, especially Stanley Levison. Although King was consistently an independent thinker, as often as not rejecting the advice of committee members, the FBI edited and summarized transcripts of conversations in such a way as to represent him as a pawn of Levison, whom the FBI vilified for alleged Communist ties. In this fashion, King, and subsequently SCLC, were ensnared in the anti-Communist hysteria that J. Edgar Hoover was central in generating and promoting. In 1963 both Levison and O'Dell were compelled to leave SCLC because of allegations of Communist ties, although King renewed contact with Levison in 1965. The FBI campaign against King personally reached its peak in 1964, although the agency continued to attempt to influence fund raising and media coverage of SCLC.[52] King, however, was not to be deterred and persisted in living out his convictions — even when the opposition came to include the majority of national black leadership, as well as many of his closest aides and clerical colleagues.

Transformation

Except for Baker, up to 1967 all of SCLC's directors were ministers. That year, King chose as the new executive director William Rutherford — a management consultant. Far from being incidental, this departure from tradition reflected a deliberate intent on King's part to redirect SCLC. The newly acknowledged need for an organization with solid administrative capacities in turn mirrored a profound change in King's understanding of the nature of the racial crisis in America.

To this day, the most popular image of King, the most common association, is of his "I Have a Dream" speech, delivered on the steps of the Lincoln Memorial in Washington in August 1963. The dream that King put forth so eloquently on that occasion was a dream of integration and equal opportunity — a dream of black and white Americans participating "hand in hand" in the American system. In this he reflected the stated objectives of SCLC in its early years. But by 1967 King's objectives were no longer the same; long before 1967, the "dream" had been put on hold. While King never abandoned his commitment to theologically grounded, nonviolent social change, he did depart from his earlier dream of integration into the American system as it existed. He abandoned that goal because he came to understand that the current system was neither willing to be integrated into, nor worthy. He came, instead, to believe that the very system was corrupt and that participation in that corruption was scarcely a status to which moral Americans ought to aspire.[53]

Central to King's assessment of the system was the matter of economics. That economics, as well as race, entered into the condition of oppression of black Americans was not a new insight on his part, but the extent to which it did so became progressively clearer as the years passed. In 1958 in his first book, *Stride toward Freedom*, King noted, "I was deeply concerned from my early teen years about the gulf

between superfluous wealth and abject poverty, and my reading of
Marx made me even more conscious of this gulf....I had...learned
that the inseparable twin of racial injustice was economic injustice."[54]
In *Why We Can't Wait*, his second book, he speaks of the "two concen-
tric circles of segregation. One imprisons [blacks] on the basis of color,
while the other confines them within a separate culture of poverty."[55]
It was in this book that King proposed for the first time a "Bill of
Rights for the Disadvantaged," a central component of which called
for full employment.[56] The theme of the "richness" of the United
States runs through his writings and speeches, including his acceptance speech upon being awarded the Nobel Peace Prize in 1964.
Gradually, King's perspective also became more global. Whereas earlier in his career he described blacks as living "on a lonely island of
poverty in the midst of a vast ocean of material prosperity," later he
spoke of "the developed industrial nations of the world" as being
"secure islands of prosperity in a seething sea of poverty."[57]

Especially after 1965, the far-reaching implications of the economic
dimensions of racial oppression came into sharp relief and compelled
a new forthrightness on his part. Before that watershed year, King
was no doubt somewhat constrained by his sensitivities as to what
was and was not tolerable public rhetoric. In addition his earlier public posture was consonant with the evangelistic mode of individual
conversion that characterized the church. Thus, in part the change in
King's presentation, both public and private, corresponded to a critical realization that conversion was not adequate to the task of solving
the problem of race — that what was required, instead, was radical
change in the very structure of American society.

In the mid-1960s King was challenged by the anti–Vietnam War
movement and criticized by the spokespersons of the black power
movement — both forces opposing the liberal consensus that kept
America's system of exploitation intact. At the same time, he was
stunned by the explosion of black rage in urban ghettos, dismayed
by the intractability of black impoverishment, and enlightened by the
depths of white resistance to open housing campaigns. Saving the
soul of America was proving to be a far more complex task than King
or the SCLC faithful could have imagined. Processing this collective
social turbulence through the prism of class analysis, King emerged
a pacifist proponent of economic democracy. From the traditional,
liberal commitment to reform, King made a transition to the more
radical way of transformation.[58]

On April 4, 1967—exactly one year to the day before his assassination—King delivered a speech at Riverside Church in New York City, which, far more so than the 1963 "Dream" speech, might be heard as the paradigm of King's aspiration for his country. Declared Dr. King:

> I am convinced that if we are to get on the right side of the world revolution, we as a nation must undergo a radical revolution of values.... When machines and computers, profit and property rights are considered more important than people, the giant triplets of racism, materialism, and militarism are incapable of being conquered.
>
> A true revolution of values will cause us to question the fairness and justice of many of our past and present policies.... True compassion is more than flinging a coin to a beggar; it is not haphazard and superficial. It comes to see that an edifice which produces beggars needs re-structuring. A true revolution of values will soon look uneasily on the glaring contrast of poverty and wealth. With righteous indignation, it will look across the seas and see individual capitalists of the West investing huge sums of money in Asia, Africa and South America, only to take the profits out with no concern for the social betterment of the countries, and say: "This is not just." It will look at our alliance with the landed gentry of Latin America and say: "This is not just." The Western arrogance of feeling that it has everything to teach others and nothing to learn from them is not just. A true revolution of values will lay hands on the world order and say of war: "This way of settling differences is not just."[59]

That same year, in his final presidential address to an SCLC convention, King had this to say:

> The movement must address itself to the question of restructuring the whole of American society. There are forty million poor people here. And one day we must ask the question, "Why are there forty million poor people in America?" And when you begin to ask that question, you are raising questions about the economic system, about a broader redistribution of wealth. When you ask that question, you begin to question the capitalistic economy. And I'm simply saying that more and more, you've got to begin to ask questions about the whole society.... You see, my friends, when you deal with this, you begin to ask the

question, "Who owns the oil?" You begin to ask the question, "Who owns the iron ore?"[60]

King went on to clarify: "I'm not talking about communism."

Communism forgets that life is individual. Capitalism forgets that life is social, and the Kingdom of brotherhood [sic] is found neither in the thesis of communism nor the antithesis of capitalism but in a higher synthesis. It is found in a higher synthesis that combines the truths of both. Now, when I say question the whole society, it means ultimately coming to see that the problem of racism, the problem of economic exploitation, and the problem of war are all tied together. These are the triple evils that are interrelated.

...What I am saying today is that we must go from this convention and say, "America, you must be born again!"[61]

On only one occasion — at the 1965 convention when King asked for support of his position in opposing the war in Vietnam — did he experience direct refusal from those in his closest circle of supporters to follow their leader on his prophetic pilgrimage. The reluctance to endorse his economic analysis and emphasis was generally more subtle — but real, nonetheless. Not even the couching of his analysis in a theology of love — which King consistently did — was effective in convincing his disciples of the veracity of his conclusions. Admittedly, it was not common for conservative black clergy to hear the language of love conjoined with the language of "internal colonialism" and "vicious class system." "Love," to King, in part meant "massive programs that will change the structure of American society so there will be a better distribution of wealth." King refrained from using the word "socialism," recognizing that people were "not ready to hear it yet."[62] And since the "unreadiness" encompassed both the general American public and his ministerial colleagues, he was compelled to carry on the struggle at two levels: confrontation with the system and, at the same time, radicalizing of his fellow clergy.

King's chosen means of midwifing the systemic rebirth of America was to turn to a strategy of pluralism and coalition. Rejecting both integration into the status quo and the extreme separatism of nationalism, King found a middle way in the interim separatism of cultural particularity and the coming together of those racial and ethnic particularities in a united campaign to address circumstances of common concern. "A final challenge," he noted,

> that we face as a result of our great dilemma is to be ever mindful of enlarging the whole society, and giving it a new sense of values as we seek to solve our particular problem. As we work to get rid of the economic strangulation that we face as a result of poverty, we must not overlook the fact that millions of Puerto Ricans, Mexican Americans, Indians and Appalachian whites are also poverty-stricken. Any serious war against poverty must of necessity include them.[63]

The pragmatic expression of this new tack was the Poor People's Campaign, a converging on the nation's capital of the disinherited and dispossessed of all colors to demand of the federal government an Economic Bill of Rights — if necessary, through unprecedented magnitudes of civil disobedience. Out of this effort, King hoped to forge new, inclusive alliances that would move on to engage in long-term organizing of tenants, welfare recipients, the unemployed, and the underemployed.[64]

The "struggle within the struggle" for King was to educate and prepare the cadre of ministers around the country who were needed to organize the proposed Poor People's Campaign. The vehicle for this "radicalization" was a $230,000 grant from the Ford Foundation in support of SCLC's "Ministers' Leadership Training Program." Under this program, 150 ministers from fifteen cities were to be assembled for a series of workshops to prepare participants for the Campaign. The task, in King's view, was to "orient [the ministers] to the values that control SCLC.... We must develop their psyche. Something is wrong with capitalism as it now stands in the United States. We are not interested in being integrated into *this* value structure. Power must be relocated: a radical redistribution of power must take place. We must do something to these men to change them."[65]

The training workshops took place in February 1968. A largely unsuccessful Poor People's Campaign was staged in Washington in the spring of that year. King, of course, was not present. If his fellow clerics and fellow citizens had difficulty hearing him, the powers that be did not.

Ecumenism

The clergy resistance King encountered in the period from 1965 to 1968 was surely nothing new. In his account of the Montgomery bus boycott, King spoke of the fragmentation of the community, not exempting Montgomery's ministers. "The apparent apathy of the Negro ministers," he said, "presented a special problem. A faithful few had always shown a deep concern for social problems, but too many had remained aloof from the area of social responsibility."[66] Far from being unique, Montgomery was typical of black clergy across the South. In Birmingham, for example, estimates of black clergy participation in SCLC campaigns ranged from a mere 10 to 20 percent.[67] As the years passed, King became increasingly strident in expressing his frustration with reluctant members of the clergy. In 1963 southern white clergy received his criticism via the now famous "Letter from Birmingham Jail." Northern white clergy were challenged at the Chicago Conference on Religion and Race. Black clergy were the subject of a sermon from King's own pulpit at Ebenezer Baptist Church in Atlanta. Declared King:

> I'm sick and tired of seeing Negro preachers riding around in big cars and living in big houses and not concerned about the problems of the people who made it possible for them to get these things. It seems that I can hear the almighty God say, "Stop preaching your loud sermons and whooping your irrelevant mess in my face, for your hands are full of tar. For the people that I send you to serve are in need, and you are doing nothing but being concerned about yourself." Seems that I can hear God saying that it's time to rise up now and make it clear that the evils of the universe must be removed. And that God isn't going to do all of it by himself. The church that overlooks this is a dangerously irrelevant church.[68]

If support for King's efforts — and for SCLC's — was limited among local clergy, the situation was no different at the denominational level. Gayraud Wilmore notes that "the national denominations made polite gestures in his direction, but never mounted a strong program that would have thrown their full resources into the struggle."[69] The president during the civil rights years of King's own Convention — the National Baptist Convention, U.S.A., Inc. (NBC) — is perhaps best remembered for his unrelenting opposition to the direct action tactics of the protest movement, the depth of which was evident in his public denouncement of the 1963 March on Washington. In an effort to redirect the Convention, King's supporters sought to oust Joseph Jackson, putting forward Gardner Taylor as their candidate for president. Their failure, and the subsequent banishment of the King family from Convention offices, led the King contingent to organize a schismatic revolt, which culminated in 1961 in the founding of the Progressive National Baptist Convention, Inc.

Taylor Branch maintains that prior to 1957 King had envisioned transforming the multi-million-member NBC into a vehicle for social reform. But Jackson's reversal of his announced intention to step aside as president and the subsequent confrontations between the two factions frustrated that objective. "For the rest of his life," writes Branch, King "would mourn the failure to acquire this institutional base for the civil rights movement."[70]

The stance of the national black denominations and the truculence of so many local pastors make clear that the ministerial leadership of SCLC and its affiliates, along with the churches and church-based organizations that opened their doors to King, constituted a dissenting "remnant" of the Church as a whole. But that SCLC was a church movement is beyond question. Whenever Operation Breadbasket launched an initiative, it was ministers who researched the businesses, developed plans for the employment or promotion of blacks, organized boycotts, and negotiated settlements. In the perpetual voter registration drives, local churches invariably served as the centers of operation. They served, too, as the principal recruiting grounds for participants in the various direct action campaigns. And they did so by *holding* church, in the process generating the spirit-filled atmosphere that moved the people to take to the streets. Scarcely less than the church rallies themselves were SCLC's staff meetings and retreats known for the praying and sermonizing and testifying that enveloped the political and philosophical debates and strategy sessions.

Whatever else he was, King was first and foremost a minister. Expanding the dimensions of the "remnant" was a part of his pastoral charge, and his effectiveness in doing so must be counted among his most significant contributions to the freedom struggle. In the estimation of some, it was never truly appropriate to characterize SCLC as a "civil rights" organization, for what it did was more aptly labeled "Christian social witness."[71] Or in Aldon Morris's view, SCLC was best understood as the "decentralized political arm of the black church."[72] However the movement was named, the pragmatic evidence of its constituent church elements was to be found in the sometimes tragic and always shocking bombings of black churches that dotted the southern landscape.

Beyond being a church movement, SCLC was an ecumenical movement. It was, in Joseph Lowery's words, "the black church coming alive, . . . the black church coming together across denominational and geographical lines."[73] Baptist ministers neither needed the approval of their conventions nor feared their sanctions, and that autonomy undoubtedly accounted in large measure for their disproportionate representation at the national level. Not all of SCLC's members were Baptist by any means — Lowery, for example, is United Methodist and Andrew Young, United Church of Christ — but Baptists did dominate the national board and staff. The local affiliates, in contrast, were quite deliberately ecumenical. The prominent role of heads of Interdenominational Ministerial Alliances — in Montgomery, Tallahassee, Mobile, and elsewhere — has been noted. Even where such bodies did not exist, typically in the early stages of a local movement, two or three progressive ministers would come forward from each denomination. Then, as the local campaign gained in momentum, other more conservative ministers would be drawn in. In this manner, the movement itself had a conversion function — a process greatly aided by the fact that the sentiments of the people were usually more in accord with the progressive pastors than with their conservative counterparts.[74]

That the people sometimes led the way was indicative of a dimension of ecumenism that transcended interchurch cooperation. Early in his career, along with his critique of black clergy, King lamented the passivity of the black population and its characteristic acquiescence to the humiliation and violence of Jim Crow segregation. But as the movement grew and extended over the years, hundreds of thousands of black southerners found a new sense of integrity and self-worth. This change in consciousness and newly gained spirit of pride and purpose was anchored in a positive valuation of ethnicity and so was strongly communal. Thus, the movement sparked by SCLC became ecumenical in the most fundamental sense of the word. Paradoxically, it was this "folk" ecumenism that gave birth to a successor and predominantly secular movement known as "black power," a development that will be taken up in the following chapter.

From Movement to Institution

SCLC is unique among black ecumenical efforts in any number of ways, not least being its longevity. In the decades since King's death the organization has had its ups and downs; yet it endures. If the organization lost its sense of direction in the mid-1960s, that circumstance was greatly compounded with the death of its leader in 1968. At a board meeting in 1965, King had asked for his long-time friend and closest colleague, Ralph Abernathy, to be named "vice president at large," a position that carried with it the provision that Abernathy would succeed King in the event of his death. Accordingly, Abernathy became SCLC's second president. But no one could match the charisma of King, and Abernathy suffered not only from adverse comparisons of their disparate leadership styles, but from the sharp decrease in the level of support extended to SCLC after King's death.

Unlike most of King's advisers and aides who parted ways with him on the issues of peace and economic democracy, Abernathy embraced King's positions on both matters, declaring himself a proponent of "black socialism." But Abernathy's loyalty to King's political agenda collided with the 1968 election of Richard Nixon, which fostered public and media support instead for Jesse Jackson and other new proponents of "black capitalism."[75] In 1971 Jackson left SCLC, taking the Chicago branch of Operation Breadbasket with him and in the process undermining SCLC's role in the North. Without King's mediating presence, internal conflicts intensified, and by 1973 nearly all of the individuals who were on the staff at the time of King's death had left.

A major shift in the emphasis of the civil rights movement was brought about by one of SCLC's most significant achievements — the passage of the 1965 Voting Rights Act. Black political development to a large degree replaced direct action protest as the preferred means of pursuing freedom, so that the traditional role of SCLC was overshadowed by the push to increase the numbers of black elected officials. SCLC protested government cutbacks in social programs and withdrawal of government commitment to civil rights under the Nixon administration; supported the peace movement at home and abroad; continued to conduct voter registration drives; supported black and Hispanic candidates for public office; demonstrated for school integration and labor rights; and addressed such diverse issues as amnesty for Vietnam veterans, political prisoners,

Table 2.3. SCLC Presidents and Chairs

Presidents

Rev. Dr. Martin Luther King, Jr.	1957–68
Rev. Ralph David Abernathy	1968–77
Rev. Joseph E. Lowery	1977–

Chairs of the Board

Rev. Joseph E. Lowery	1967–77
Rev. Walter Fauntroy	1977–

and the farm workers' boycotts.[76] But by the mid-1970s, as it struggled just to keep its national office open, the organization was only a shadow of its former self.

In 1977 Joseph Lowery, who had been chair of the board since 1967 — also at King's behest — became SCLC's third president; he continues to serve in that capacity in the 1990s (Table 2.3). Reflecting modest change, in 1992 the forty-eight-member board of directors included eight women, with half the board members being clergy. Although SCLC had been reincorporated in 1968 as a national organization, most of its chapters — numbering some one hundred — were located in the South, with a relative few in the North and West. SCLC sustained a million-dollar operating budget annually, which supported a staff of from thirty to thirty-five members, approximately one-fourth of whom were clerical and support personnel. In 1992 nine of twenty-four professional staff were women; five were ministers. As with the board of directors, all staff members were African American but one.[77] (See Appendix II for additional information on membership structure and funding.)

Since the early 1990s SCLC has operated out of three buildings in Atlanta, one housing the national office; another SCLC/Women; and the third one of SCLC's larger programs, Wings of Hope, a comprehensive anti-drug program. The organization has focused heavily on program areas involving youth, another example being its nationwide Stop the Killing! campaign. An area of increasing concern has been health care, including the status of the black family and particularly of black males. Ongoing emphases that provide continuity with the organization's past include voter registration, education, and participation, workers' rights, and economic development.

While SCLC has never explicitly predicated its program on class analysis nor engaged in the more radical forms of civil disobedience entertained by SCLC shortly before King's death, Dr. Lowery has kept in the forefront the scope of concerns that engaged King's attention, announcing at SCLC's 1989 convention that "the priority of the organization is economic justice."[78] Under Lowery's direction, SCLC has addressed human rights concerns in Central America, South Africa, the Middle East, Haiti, and Ethiopia. Throughout the Reagan and Bush administrations, SCLC was a persistent advocate for affirmative action, voting rights, black colleges, and housing and employment programs. The organization has addressed issues ranging from black land loss, to discrimination in the criminal justice system, to the resurgence of white supremacist groups, to the disposal of toxic wastes in black impoverished communities — in short, all those issues that bear on the quality of life for poor people and for African Americans generally. One of SCLC's most persistent and lengthiest campaigns — conducted in conjunction with other organizations, most notably the Martin Luther King, Jr., Center for Nonviolent Social Change — was to see its founder's birthday declared a federal holiday.

An adjunct of SCLC, SCLC/Women, organized in 1979 by Evelyn Lowery, has become a vital organization in its own right. SCLC/Women began with a focus on equal rights for women and on the status of the black family, including the issues of teenage pregnancy, drug abuse, and health care. In the 1990s program concerns have included after-school education, suicide prevention, the homeless, and abused women and children. Perhaps its greatest contribution has been in addressing the AIDS epidemic and its disproportionate impact on the black community. Through its National AIDS Awareness Program, ministers and parishioners have been trained to conduct educational and prevention workshops in local church congregations. In groundbreaking work with black churches, the Awareness Program also has provided assistance in addressing the roots of homophobia and the treatment accorded gay men and lesbians.

A highlight of SCLC continues to be its annual convention, held in August of each year. Attendance, which dipped below five hundred in the early 1970s, in the 1980s and 1990s has consistently ranged from two thousand to twenty-five hundred individuals, which represents by far the highest participation rate of all the black ecumenical movements. Not only through the conventions, but in its varied projects, SCLC has continued to perform ecumenical functions — both in reinforcing the ethnic consciousness of African Americans and in fostering cooperative action across denominational lines.

Summary

Like the Fraternal Council of Negro Churches, SCLC underwent a shift in key characteristics of its operation from its earliest years to its later years. Even within the eleven brief years of King's tenure, such a shift is detectable, although the organization itself changed less dramatically in those years than did its leader. Certainly the extreme integrationist and capitalist positions were modified somewhat. The governance model was consistently autocratic, with lay involvement and involvement of women mostly at the local movement level, and ministers predominating at the board and staff levels. Both lay and clergy participants came from the traditional black denominations, as well as from predominantly white denominations; Pentecostals, however, were seriously underrepresented. Further, participation was heavily weighted toward the southern region. If anything, SCLC is the one ecumenical organization in which the imbalance of the spiritual/ political scales was tipped toward the spirituality end — excepting, that is, King's circle of northern advisers. Overall, the profile may be depicted as follows.

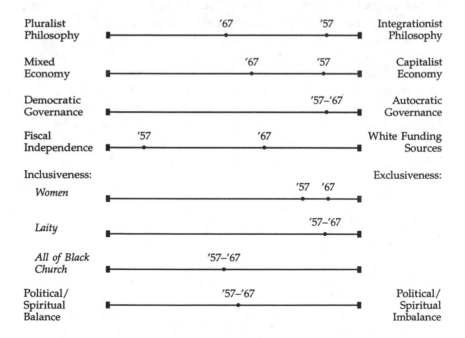

Whatever shortcomings SCLC may have had in the movement years, its gifts to the nation were many and priceless. And they were both tangible and intangible. Among the organization's more concrete achievements are the 1964 Civil Rights Act and the 1965 Voting Rights Act — the one largely responsible for a desegregated South, the other for a black presence in American electoral politics. Many of SCLC's involvements — voter registration; mass demonstrations in Washington; consultations with presidents, Department of Justice officials, and members of Congress — were carried out cooperatively with other organizations, including the NAACP. SCLC also supported projects whose primary sponsors were SNCC or CORE — the sit-in movement, the freedom rides, and Mississippi Freedom Summer among them. These actions, on the other hand, were at least partially inspired by the very existence of SCLC, so that the organization's impact can scarcely be measured by its own programs alone.

Nor are material changes an adequate measure of accomplishments, for SCLC's contributions were as much psychological and spiritual. While SCLC facilitated networking and information exchange, it also provided inspiration and emotional support to local and national activists alike. It provided philosophy and method in its teaching of nonviolence, a renewal of black religion in its preaching of social justice, and rebirth in the transformation of blacks from passive victims of intimidation to self-determining agents of change. And, as one observer reflected, "If the movement that was SCLC [did] nothing else, it made clear that the strength of the Black Church was ecumenical strength."[79]

SCLC gave to the black religious community the insight that the full power of the Black Church is not to be realized in separate denomination or convention units but in interdenominational organizations that affirm the transcendent bonds of ethnicity and serve the agenda of equity and freedom. SCLC was ecumenical in a broader and more inclusive way than other organizations so categorized, largely because of its mass movement dimension. Other groups, including those identified less with the civil rights segment of the freedom struggle than with the black power segment, have been more narrowly confined to institutional components of the Black Church. But all of the subsequent movements, in varying degrees, have been seekers after both spiritual sustenance and political liberation. And that feature of the black ecumenical model was bequeathed by the Southern Christian Leadership Conference.

Chapter Three

TO EMPOWER THE PEOPLE
The National Conference
of Black Christians

Context

The divergence within SCLC in the mid-1960s between Dr. King and many of his southern colleagues and staff actually represented two positions in a three-way split within the larger civil rights community. If many of King's followers found him too radical, others concluded just the opposite. Youthful activists, particularly, who were less closely tied to the church and therefore less beholden to the philosophy of nonviolence, found King's tactics increasingly unpalatable. In 1966 the growing tension exploded in what became known as the black power movement. In northern cities many young blacks embraced the "black pride" and "black is beautiful" slogans of the emergent black consciousness movement. Others found in "burn, baby, burn" an outlet for the frustration that was a product of the discrepancy between the expectations raised by the civil rights movement and the reality of life in urban ghettos. By 1967 the smoke and flames and devastation in lives lost and property destroyed were becoming almost commonplace across the country. And more and more the rhetoric of separatism drowned out the promise of "We shall overcome."

This new, largely secular anti-integrationist movement was not without historical precedents. Throughout the abolitionist movement, the integrationist position as represented by Frederick Douglass vied with the nationalist views put forth by Henry Highland Garnet. From the writings of David Walker and Robert Young, to the emigrationist platforms of Alexander Crummell and Edward Blyden, to the "God is a Negro" theology of Bishop Henry McNeal Turner, nationalism was voiced as a counterpoint throughout the nineteenth century by black leaders, secular and religious alike.[1]

The theme of nationalism, as noted in chapter 1, was sounded in the early decades of the twentieth century by Marcus Garvey, whose exhortations and programs produced the largest mass movement of blacks in the nation's history. Nationalist ideology was preserved in the 1930s and 1940s in movements such as the National Negro Congress and various religious movements, notably the Nation of Islam, which began to achieve prominence in the 1950s and then captured the nation's attention in the early 1960s. Among young people already disillusioned with integration and nonviolence — both those who had been active in SNCC and CORE and those active in the urban unrest of northern ghettos — no one wielded more influence than Malcolm X, the most famous spokesperson for the Black Muslims, as the religio-political movement was popularly known. As the black consciousness movement expanded, a plethora of liberation organizations — US, the Black Panthers, and the New Republic of Africa prominent among them — came into being and increasingly came into conflict with the civil rights movement that was so deeply anchored in the tenets of Christian faith.

For the "remnant within the remnant" — the more radically oriented of the progressive black Christian clergy — the crisis that was generated was this: how to bridge the growing breach in the ecumenicity of grassroots black America. Philosophically and ideologically, the civil rights era, which had begun where the Fraternal Council left off, was ending very close to where the Fraternal Council had begun. As the glitter of integration faded, the insights of the Fraternal Council were resurrected: "[Blacks] cannot hope to cooperate individually, but only collectively. We are of very little power today because we act as individuals. We must act as a body."

The post-integrationist phase of the black liberation movement in fact produced multiple ecumenical bodies. The National Black Evangelical Association and the Black Theology Project, founded respectively in 1963 and 1977, were both products of this new emphasis. So, too, were an array of local movements that emerged from California to Massachusetts. The most significant of these organizations, however, was the National Conference of Black Christians

(NCBC), for in important respects this ecumenical expression laid the foundation for all the others that followed.

NCBC came into being with a threefold agenda: to seek rapprochement with radical activists who had parted ways with SCLC, to interpret black power to an outraged white religious establishment, and to more closely align the institutional Black Church with the sentiments of its more progressively inclined leaders. Both the interpretation and the alignment required a new language, and the language was called "black theology."

It is impossible to talk about ecumenism post-SCLC without talking about black theology. As James Cone, its best-known exponent, recalls,

> [Black theology] emerged as the black clergy was compelled by the urgency of the time to make theological sense out of the struggle for black freedom. To advocate a *black* theology meant that the black clergy wanted the whole world to know that it was searching for a radically new theological starting point that would clearly distinguish its perspective from the alternatives provided by whites and adopted by conservative blacks. Black church leaders sensed the *need* for a new beginning in theology that would affirm the dignity of black persons and expose the racist white churches as unChristian.... In order to give practical guidance to a newly discovered theological idea (namely, that blackness, justice and power were not antithetical to the Christian faith), members of the radical black clergy created ecumenical organizations and black caucuses in white churches.[2]

NCBC, through its Theological Commission, became in effect the "organizational embodiment" of black theology.[3] Black theology, in turn, became the lifeblood of ecumenism.

> With the rise of black theology, it became clear that the denominational identities that black churches derived from the white churches from which they separated were completely irrelevant in our struggle for freedom.... The NCBC was created in order to transcend the denominational barriers that separated black churches. Beyond that they created an ecumenical vision that sought solidarity with the advocates of black power and other radical spokespersons in the black liberation struggle, persons "outside" the churches. NCBC members knew that the only

way to make the black churches a viable vehicle of black liberation was to eliminate division among the churches through
a political commitment as defined by the black consciousness
movement....

   ... Members of the NCBC were not only determined to make
the black church more relevant to the black liberation struggle, but were equally determined to create a black theology that
would be supportive of it.[4]

Ultimately, black theology ended up being neither fish nor fowl —
neither the language of the people struggling for freedom nor the language of conventional academic theologians. Black theology existed in
tension with both worlds and in ambiguity as to whether it would interpret the people to the academy or the academy to the people. That
marginality accounted in part for the relatively short tenure of NCBC
and for its inability to unite more of the diverse segments of the Black
Church. Nevertheless, for a time black theology was potent enough to
infuse a whole array of national and local organizations.

SCLC and NCC: Ties and Disjunctions

In important respects, the disjunctions between SCLC — the ecumenical movement of the civil rights phase — and NCBC — the ecumenical
movement of the black power phase — were never as great as might
at first glance seem to have been the case, or as was projected by
NCBC in its early years. With regard to black theology, Martin Luther
King is now acknowledged to have been "the beginning of it all."[5] In
its strategies and programs, SCLC, as has been indicated, was concerned with empowerment of blacks long before "black power" was
in vogue. Further evidence of convergence is found in the fact that a
number of persons participated in both organizations. The last president of NCBC, Kelly Miller Smith, was a founding member of SCLC;
SCLC staff members, at King's direction, attended NCBC meetings
and several of them became members, including Wyatt T. Walker, who
served on NCBC's board of directors. Further, King called on NCBC
for assistance in training urban black clergy as he prepared for the ill-
fated Poor People's Campaign.[6] But in other respects the differences
between the two movements were marked.

One difference, as noted, was in the language used, an example being the substitution by NCBC of the word "liberation" for the word "freedom," which played so heavily in the songs and sermons and slogans of the earlier movement. The difference, suggests one commentator, was a "reflection of middle-class academia" and its use of a different translation of the Bible than was read by grassroots clergy.[7] Ralph Abernathy, even more than King, had a reputation for speaking the language of impoverished southern black churchgoers. As Andrew Young put it, "You could go into Mississippi and tell people they needed to get themselves together and get organized. And that didn't make much sense. But if you started preaching to them about dry bones rising again, everybody had sung about dry bones. Everybody knew that language."[8]

So Abernathy and his colleagues preached about dry bones and freedom. NCBC leaders talked about oppression and liberation. But NCBC had a different audience; its discourse, to a large extent, was with the church establishment, black as well as white. And that was a significant difference. Another, but related, difference had to do with region. NCBC was based in the North and regarded itself as a northern counterpart to SCLC, although it never became an activist organization in the sense that SCLC was, let alone a mass movement. Finally, NCBC was founded not by southern independent Baptist preachers, but by northern urban ministers, over half of whom belonged to predominantly white denominations, and several of whom were on the staff of the National Council of Churches (NCC).[9] NCBC therefore had a relationship to the white churches and white ecumenical agencies different from SCLC. For NCBC, this relationship was central to its creation and function — and demise.

The 1963 March on Washington was the occasion of the entrance of NCC and a few white denominations into the civil rights movement. The Council was involved in the 1964 Mississippi Summer Project on Voter Registration and the 1965 Selma campaign for voting rights. It endorsed more moderate programs such as Project Equality and the National Urban Coalition and became heavily involved in the Delta Minority and National Farm Workers Ministry. NCC's support of the 1964 Civil Rights Act and 1965 Voting Rights Act was a critical contribution. But the rhetoric of black power and the frightening specter of race riots gave the white churches pause, so that by the end of 1966 their condemnation of and retreat from the new developments in the black liberation movement were well underway. Black ministers in white denominations and church agencies increasingly found themselves being pressured by white colleagues and superiors to denounce the turn of events. In such a climate of polarization and isolation, it was inevitable that they would close ranks. Thus, even as its early promises of genuine integration encouraged the dissolution of one black ecumenical body — the Fraternal Council of Negro Churches — NCC's inability to fully share leadership authority and decision making power gave impetus to two new movements — the National Conference of Black Christians and, later, Partners in Ecumenism.[10]

Origins

An important catalyst for the coalescing of progressive black clergy was provided by the Rev. Benjamin Payton, executive director of NCC's Commission on Religion and Race. The Commission had been created in June 1963 with an unusual license authorizing it to "make commitments, call for actions, take risks in behalf of the NCC which are required by the situation."[11] The trust was short-lived; the Commission was disbanded when it became "too aggressive"[12] — an assessment undoubtedly related to the role of its director in the organizing of NCBC.

In July 1966, five people met in Payton's New York office to discuss the hostile reaction of liberal white clergy to the call for black power sounded by Stokely Carmichael on the Meredith March from Memphis to Jackson the preceding month. Present at the meeting in addition to Payton were his associate, Anna Arnold Hedgeman, J. Oscar Lee, H. R. Hughes, and Gayraud Wilmore. At that meeting, "the decision was made to form an ad hoc group called the National Committee of Negro Churchmen (NCNC) and to publish a carefully worded statement of black power that would clear the air, clarify the position of northern (black) church leadership, and point to some theological implications of the concept of power."[13]

Payton, acting as the interim national coordinator of the group, drafted a statement that was revised and adopted at a meeting of forty-seven churchpersons held July 22 at Bethel AME Church in Harlem. A third meeting was held at Mother Zion Church. Then, on July 31, 1966, NCNC's statement was published as a full-page ad in the *New York Times:*

As black men who were long ago forced out of the white church to create and to wield "black power," we fail to understand the emotional quality of the outcry of some clergy against the use of the term today. It is not enough to answer that "integration" is the solution. For it is precisely the nature of the operation of power under some forms of integration which is being challenged.... Without [a] capacity to *participate with power* — i.e., to have some organized political and economic strength to really influence people with whom one interacts — integration is not meaningful....

America has asked its Negro citizens to fight for opportunity *as individuals* whereas at certain points in our history what we have needed most has been opportunity for the whole group, not just for selected and approved Negroes.... Power today is essentially organizational power.... Getting power necessarily involves reconciliation. We must first be reconciled to ourselves.... We must be reconciled to ourselves as persons and to ourselves as an historical group....

We must not apologize for the existence of this form of group power, for we have been oppressed as a group, not as individuals. We will not find our way out of that oppression until both we and America accept the need for Negro Americans as well as for Jews, Italians, Poles and white Anglo-Saxon Protestants, among others, to have and to wield group power....

We must...rest our concern for reconciliation on the firm ground that we and all other Americans *are* one. Our history and destiny are indissolubly linked. If the future is to belong to any of us, it must be prepared for all of us whatever our racial or religious background. For in the final analysis, we are *persons* and the power of all groups must be wielded to make visible our common humanity. We must organize not only among ourselves but with other groups in order that we can, together, gain power sufficient to change this nation's sense of what is *now* important and what must be done *now*.[14]

The statement was signed by forty-eight prominent black church leaders, over half of whom were identified with predominantly white denominations. Key participants in this early activity, in addition to the five persons present at the initial meeting, included Dr. Nathan Wright, United Methodist Bishop Charles F. Golden, the Rev. Horace

Sharper, the Rev. M. L. Wilson, and the Rev. J. Metz Rollins.[15] Neither these early participants nor subsequent members acted as official representatives of their denominations. Nor, for that matter, were they representative of all black ministers. Rather, they were the "ecclesiastical renegades, denominational radicals, and mad preachers"[16] who perceived most keenly the betrayal of the trust that members of the earlier Fraternal Council of Negro Churches had placed in NCC and the mainstream white churches.

If the "Black Power Statement" did not completely "clear the air," the response to it did encourage the ad hoc group to continue their alliances. In the fall a group of thirty church leaders met with Rev. Payton to draft a statement on "Racism and the Elections." On November 3, 1966, nearly 150 ministers, clad in clerical robes, processed to the Statue of Liberty where the statement was read publicly by Payton. On November 6, this statement, signed by 172 church officials, was also published in the *New York Times*. Once again, the authors emphasized the theme of group power, asserting that "integration is not an aesthetic goal designed to add token bits of color to institutions controlled entirely by whites. Integration is a political goal with the objective of making it possible for Negroes and other Americans to express the vitality of their personal and group life in institutions which fundamentally belong to all Americans."[17] A significant shift in representation occurred at this event, with over half the participants coming from the historic black denominations. In contrast to SCLC, however, the majority of those from the black denominations were not Baptist, but Methodist.[18]

These early NCBC statements are particularly notable for the effort they represent to formulate a model of relationships that would stand as an alternative both to the traditional conception of integration and to the extreme separatism of nationalism. What emerges is a model of pluralism — an assertion of the sanctity and celebration of group identity, conjoined with the desire, indeed, the imperative, of pursuing relations among the various groups on a basis of equal power. The parallel with Dr. King's critique of integration and his advocacy of a multicultural coalition is striking and argues a larger conversation that enveloped both King and NCBC clergy in the years from 1966 to 1968.

In March 1967 a hundred members of NCNC attended a one-day meeting in Durham, North Carolina, at which the decision was made to form a permanent organization. Two additional meetings were held — one in Boston in May and the other in Washington in August — prior to the official organizing convocation in Dallas, in November 1967.[19] At that meeting bylaws were adopted and an election of officers held. Bishop Herbert Bell Shaw became the first president and Rev. M. L. Wilson the first chair of the board of directors[20] (Table 3.1). NCNC was incorporated in the State of New York in 1967. At the second convocation, in 1968, the name of the group was changed to the National Committee of Black Churchmen.

By 1972, after five brief but intense years, NCBC was on the downturn. In 1973 the name was changed to the National Conference of Black Churchmen, but thereafter NCBC's primary activity was the convening of annual convocations as a forum for church representatives who wished to continue addressing the concerns that had brought them together originally.[21] The last convocation was convened in 1982, although the last election of officers was held in 1978. In 1983, in response to the insistence of women members of the steering committee, the name was once again changed, to the National Conference of Black Christians. The organization became completely inactive, however, following the death of its president, Kelly Miller Smith, in 1984.

Organizational Identity

At its peak, NCBC had some twelve hundred members, while attendance at its convocations fluctuated from over seven hundred in 1967 to scarcely a hundred in 1974. The membership ratio of clergy to laity was approximately five to one. About 40 percent came from white denominations and 60 percent from black denominations, with many of the latter being younger, seminary-trained ministers. A few women were members, among them Catholic sisters, but their numbers were never substantial. The heaviest concentration of members was from the Northeast, followed by the Midwest, then the South and the West.[22] While officers and board members came disproportionately from the black denominations, the strategists, theologians, and commission heads were mostly from the white denominations.[23] From 1967 to 1982, NCBC had a total of five presidents — two African Methodist, two Baptist, and one United Church of Christ — and four board chairs — one African Methodist, one United Methodist, and two Baptist. The original 1967 board had one woman

Table 3.1. Original NCNC Board of Directors, 1967

Rev. M. L. Wilson, Chair	NBC, USA, Inc.
Bishop John Bright, Vice Chair	AME
Bishop Herbert Bell Shaw	AMEZ
Rev. Robert H. Wilson	NBCA
Rev. Bryant George	Presbyterian
Rev. Gilbert Caldwell	UMC
Bishop Charles Golden	UMC
Rev. Benjamin F. Payton	NBC, USA, Inc.
Rev. Donald O. Wilson	Baptist
Rev. Charles L. Warren	UMC
Rev. Horace P. Sharper	Baptist
Rev. Tollie Caution	Episcopal
Rev. Harold A. L. Clement	AMEZ
Rev. Isaac Green	NBC, USA, Inc.
Rev. Mance Jackson	CME
Rev. Herbert T. Miller	ABC
Rev. Gayraud Wilmore	Presbyterian
Rev. James Breeden	Episcopal
Rev. William McKee	ABC
Rev. Reuben L. Speaks	AMEZ
Rev. Stephen P. Spottswood	AME
Bishop E. L. Hickman	AME
Rev. Lucius Walker	ABC
Rev. Charles Spivey	AME
Rev. Calvin Marshall	AMEZ
Rev. Edler Hawkins	Presbyterian
Rev. James Forbes	United Holy Church
Rev. Wyatt Tee Walker	NBC
Rev. Leon Watts	AMEZ
Rev. Willis C. Tabor	Presbyterian
Rev. Joseph C. Coles	CME
Bishop Norris S. Curry	CME
Rev. Lawrence W. Bottoms	Presbyterian
Rev. Timothy Mitchell	NBC, USA, Inc.
Bishop George W. Blakely	AME
Rev. John Sass	NBC
Rev. W. L. Wilson	NBC
Ms. Anna A. Hedgeman	UMC

member, Anna Hedgeman; subsequent boards never had more than two women members[24] (Table 3.2). Administrative tasks were shared with an executive committee and various standing committees, while the program was organized in three commissions: Theological, African Relations, and Urban Mission and Crisis (also referred to as

Table 3.2. NCBC Board of Directors, 1974–76

Elected Officers

Rev. Charles Cobb
President
New York

Rev. Muhammed Kenyatta
Appalachian Regional V.P.
Chester, Pa.

Rev. Kelly M. Smith
Vice President
Nashville

Mr. Owen Brooks
South Atlantic Regional V.P.
Greenville, Miss.

Rev. Mance Jackson
Executive Director
Atlanta

Rev. Sterling Cary
Midwest Regional V.P.
New York

Rev. Lynwood Walker
Secretary
Seattle

Rev. Donald Hunter
Plains States Regional V.P.
St. Louis

Rev. Eldridge Gittens
Treasurer
Hollis, Long Island

Rev. Raymond Hart
South West Regional V.P.
Dallas

Rev. Gilbert Caldwell
Chair of the Board
New Haven

Bishop Charles Golden
Rocky Mountains & Pacific S.W.
    Regional V.P.
Los Angeles

Rev. Carrol Felton
Vice Chair of the Board
Chicago

Rev. Will Hertzfield
Mid-Pacific Regional V.P.
Oakland

Rev. Virgil Wood
North Atlantic Regional V.P.
Milton, Mass.

Rev. Gil B. Lloyd
Pacific N.W. Regional V.P.
Seattle

Rev. Timothy Mitchell
Mid-Atlantic Regional V.P.
Flushing, N.Y.

Members at Large

Rev. William Howard
New York

Rev. Leon Watts
Larchmont, N.Y.

Rev. Nathaniel Grady
Yonkers, N.Y.

Ms. Mary Kinnard
Newton Centre, Mass.

Rev. Calvin Marshall
Brooklyn, N.Y.

Mr. Marty Gool
St. Louis

Ms. Mary Jane Patterson
Washington, D.C.

Rev. John Satterwhite
Princeton, N.J.

Rev. Cameron Byrd
Newton, Mass.

Rev. Maynard Catchings
Montclair, N.J.

Mr. Robert Washington
Teaneck, N.J.

Bishop Herbert Bell Shaw
Wilmington, N.C.

Rev. David DeRamus
San Diego

Rev. George Daniels
New York

Rev. I. Leroy Brown
Seattle

Rev. Gayraud Wilmore
Rochester, N.Y.

Economic Development). An Education Commission was added later. (For additional organizational information, see Appendix II.)

In the first year of its official existence, NCBC had an acting director, the Rev. Leon Watts. In 1968 the Rev. J. Metz Rollins became executive director and served until 1972. Rev. Watts remained as the associate director from 1968 to 1969. The staff also included a secretary. NCBC offices were first established at Convent Avenue Baptist Church in Harlem, pastored by M. L. Wilson, and later moved to 125th Street. At the time NCBC was organized, Rollins was an associate director of the Presbyterian Commission on Religion and Race (later, Council on Church and Race), for which Gayraud Wilmore was the executive director. Through Wilmore's intercessions, Rollins was assigned to NCBC in 1968 and his salary paid for a year by the Presbyterian Church as part of their contribution to NCBC. From 1969 to 1972, his salary was paid by NCBC. When financial resources were exhausted, the office was moved to Atlanta, where Mance Jackson, a CME minister and faculty member of the Interdenominational Theological Center, took over as the volunteer executive director.[25] Jackson continued in that capacity until NCBC became inactive (Table 3.3).

In its best years NCBC's annual budget was in the range of $150,000 to $200,000. In addition to membership dues, numerous small grants of from $5,000 to $10,000 were received from the racial and social concerns agencies of the various denominations. The most substantial contributions were "in-kind," however, such as travel expenses for agency and denominational representatives to attend NCBC's convocations and board meetings.[26]

NCBC's formal structure was not always indicative of how the body actually functioned. Late in 1971 an observer speculated that NCBC might "indeed be making the transition from a volatile movement to a strong and stable organization of black liberation" — a prognosis that proved to be optimistic.[27] NCBC's organization never quite matched its vision. In spite of NCBC's fluid character, in spite of the fact that it represented a small minority of black clergy and had no official standing in relation to the black denominations, it defined itself emphatically as an ecumenical organization. Its ecumenical understanding was distinctively "black," however, in contrast to the more conventional church definition of ecumenism. Thus, in 1971 Metz Rollins wrote: "Long separated from each other by racial and sectarian divisions not of their making, taken less than seriously by white denominational leaders, black churchmen have

Table 3.3. Chronology, National Conference of Black Christians

Year	President	Board Chair	Executive Director	Annual Meeting
		National Committee of Negro Churchmen		
1967	H. B. Shaw	M. L. Wilson	L. Watts (acting)	Dallas
1968	"	"	J. M. Rollins	St. Louis
		National Committee of Black Churchmen		
1969	H. B. Shaw	M. L. Wilson	J. M. Rollins	Oakland
1970	J. A. Bright	H. B. Shaw	"	Atlanta
1971	"	"	"	Chicago
1972	G. B. Lloyd	"	"	New York
		National Conference of Black Churchmen		
1973	G. B. Lloyd	H. B. Shaw	M. Jackson	Memphis
1974	C. Cobb	G. Caldwell	"	Seattle
1975	"	"	"	Atlanta
1976	"	T. Mitchell	"	Washington
1977	"	"	"	St. Louis
1978	K. M. Smith	"	"	Nashville
1979	"	"	"	Birmingham
1980	"	"	"	Los Angeles
1981*	"	"	"	New York
1982	"	"	"	St. Louis
1983	"	"	"	—
		National Conference of Black Christians		
1984	K. M. Smith	T. Mitchell	M. Jackson	—

*The last election was held in November 1978 for the 1978–80 term of office. Officers elected at that time continued to serve until the organization ceased functioning in 1984.

been hammering out a unity based on the uniqueness of the black experience in America and a determination to respond to the revolutionary ferment taking place in the black community." He further described NCBC as "an organization that reflects the renaissance of the black religious experience in America."[28] Leon Watts voiced a similar sentiment, but stressed the goal of liberation:

Black ecumenicity must not be simply contrived interdenominationalism, as with church mergers or the integration of Methodism's Central Jurisdiction into its mainstream, or the building of a superstructure called the Church of Christ Uniting (COCU). It must be more dynamic, realistic and potent than any of the fore-going could ever hope to be. The central thrust must be Black liberation. Anything that does not serve that purpose does not demand serious commitment from Black churchmen.

The NCBC is not an ecumenical organization alongside others. It is a movement of Black churchmen committed first to the Church of Jesus the Christ, then to the liberation of the Black community. It may save Christianity in the Western world by giving it back to the people.[29]

Program

NCBC's 1970 constitution further defined its purpose in this manner:

To bring the strength of the black religious leadership in the nation to the forefront of American life, with special emphasis on public issues growing out of the problems of black people as a racial and cultural minority;

To lift the level of the black community economically, socially and morally, by every means appropriate to, and in unison with, the spirit of the Christian Gospel;

To unite black churchmen throughout the nation in order to effect strategies related to the empowerment of their communities; and

To enhance the contribution of black churches and church-men to, and their participation in, the larger Christian fellow-ship across racial denominational lines.[30]

The most immediate task of NCBC in pursuit of its goals of black unity and liberation was to render black ethnicity theologically legitimate — that is, to interpret the black power movement in Christian terms. Accordingly, much of NCBC's activity was centered around *thinking about* social action, as opposed to *engagement in* social action. Of its four commissions, the Theological Commission was by far the liveliest and most fruitful.

Initially, NCBC was made up of "movement-oriented church lead-ers and church executives; community organization and urban church specialists; Pan-Africanists, social activists, social radicals"; and, most particularly, "young, black pastors hungry to break out of the stul-tifying structures of black denominationalism and get involved in a whole new movement within the Black Church." The "theology professors and seminary scholars" came later,[31] and they came under the auspices of the Theological Commission at the invitation of the Commission's chair, Gayraud Wilmore. James Cone, Major Jones, Henry Mitchell, Deotis Roberts, Joseph Washington, Preston Williams, and others were among those involved in the dialogues of the Committee on Theological Prospectus, as it was called in the early years. The Committee produced numerous reports and statements on black theology, culminating in 1969 in what became the normative statement:

> Black Theology is a theology of black liberation. It seeks to plumb the black condition in light of God's revelation in Jesus Christ, so that the black community can see that the gospel is commensurate with the achievement of black humanity. Black Theology is a theology of "blackness." It is the affirmation of black humanity that emancipates black people from white racism, thus providing authentic freedom for both white and black people. It affirms the humanity of white people in that it says No to the encroachment of white oppression.
>
> The message of liberation is the revelation of God as revealed in the incarnation of Jesus Christ. Freedom IS the gospel. Jesus is the Liberator! ... [32]

In 1971 many of the theologians and other professors in NCBC became involved in a new undertaking, the Society for the Study of Black Religion (SSBR) organized by C. Shelby Rooks. SSBR functioned as an academic society or guild rather than a social change organization.[33] Accordingly, under its oversight black theology entered into what Wilmore characterizes as the second stage of its development, a progression that entailed a shift "from the streets to the academy."[34] In 1976, after a silence of seven years, NCBC reasserted its role in the black theology movement by issuing a statement that reaffirmed the 1969 statement, but that went even further in that it provided a critique of capitalism and affirmed the "exploration of socialistic alternatives." This statement is also significant for its position on black ecumenism:

> Black Theology is the theology of the Black Church. It seeks the reunion of all Black Christians, Protestant and Roman Catholic, in one Church encompassing the totality of the Black religious

experience and the history and destiny of all Black people. All efforts to reunite and renew the Black Church serve the ultimate purpose of confirming the catholicity, apostolicity and holiness of the whole church of Jesus Christ in which every race and nation joined together, each contributing properly and equally, upbuilds the One Church of Christ in love and justice. Black Theology does not deny the importance of the interdenominational and ecumenical efforts toward church unity with White and other Christians. Rather it asserts the operational unity of all Black Christians as the first step toward a wider unity in which the restructuring of power relations in church and society and the liberation of the poor and oppressed will be recognized as the first priority of mission.[35]

If unity with white Christians was not an immediate priority, unity with African Christians was. Even before the Commission on African Relations was formally established, NCBC was involved in Africa. NCBC representatives attended the All Africa Conference of Churches meeting in September 1969. Subsequent meetings led to the creation by NCBC of a Pan-African Skills Project, which recruited black Americans to work in Tanzania. This project, in turn, led to the first dialogue of black and African theologians, held in Dar es Salaam in 1971.[36] NCBC was also involved with South African church representatives seeking to alter the repressive circumstances in that nation.

In the area of education, the executive director, Metz Rollins, worked with student members of NCBC to increase black faculty representation at major seminaries.[37] The Commission on Urban Mission and Crisis never implemented a systematic program, although among NCBC's most ambitious proposals were a National Renewal and Development Corporation and an Economic Development Bank.[38] These projects presumed federal and industrial involvement and were abandoned when the Great Society era of President Johnson's administration came to a close. As Wilmore recalls, "The irony did not pass unnoticed in the board of directors that, its pretensions to black power notwithstanding, it had neither the expertise nor the financial resources necessary to launch a national ghetto development scheme without wide private-sector and government support."[39] On a more modest scale, however, the securing of funds from white churches, as well as both NCC and COCU, to address the problems of urban blacks was the focus of some of NCBC's most important statements and involvements.

The concern with the "urban crisis" and economic empowerment was closely related to two principal components of NCBC's "program" that transcended the formal commission structure. The first had to do with the relations of black churchpersons to the white denominations and ecumenical bodies. Specifically, the issue was relationships of power. NCBC sought not only to develop a theology of black power, but to actually secure power within the white church structures through control of urban mission programs and appointments to policy-making positions. The second component involved consciousness raising and dialogue among NCBC's own members and, through them, with the hierarchies of the black denominations. Both of these areas of activity — confrontation with the white churches and renewal of the black churches — are best understood in the larger context of the time.

The black power and black consciousness movements, as noted, ignited an explosion of ecumenical activity among black churchpersons at the local level. Many of the leaders of these local groups were also active in NCBC; indeed, in certain respects, NCBC was the national counterpart of the local ecumenical phenomenon. But as a national body, it experienced the tensions within the collective Black Church on a grander scale. Part of NCBC's function was to serve as a forum for addressing those tensions and working out internal differences.

In an era of intense black pride and militancy, NCBC was the site of sometimes anguished discussions regarding whether black members and ministers in the predominantly white denominations could justify remaining there. Members of the historic black denominations questioned those in the white churches and invited them to "come home." The members of white denominations themselves entertained doubts as to the appropriateness of their church alliances and talked of disengagement. On the other hand, the NCBC members from the white denominations were critical of the black denominations for being too conservative and questioned whether they therefore constituted an adequate alternative to the white denominations. Creation of an entirely new church structure for all blacks was suggested, but received little serious consideration. There were tensions, as well, within the black denominations' contingents — between older, establishment-oriented members and younger, more radical members — that reflected the state of the black denominations generally as their leaders and members underwent the transformation in consciousness that attended the black power movement.[40]

Much of the discussion within NCBC was an extension of discussions that took place among blacks within the white denominations through the medium of black caucuses and race-related commissions. In fact, the racial commissions and black caucuses were a major source of NCBC membership and, conversely, were NCBC's point of access to the denominations. The commissions had been created following the National Conference on Religion and Race held in Chicago in January 1963 and attended by representatives of sixty-seven religious bodies — Protestant, Roman Catholic, Orthodox, and Jewish — in commemoration of the hundredth anniversary of the Emancipation Proclamation. At that time, the white denominations were called upon by NCC to establish commissions on religion and race to serve as the mechanisms through which the churches — coordinated by NCC's Commission on Religion and Race — would participate in the civil rights movement. By the mid-1960s most of the mainstream denominations had established such bodies.[41] They were joined in the late 1960s by the formation or reactivation of black caucuses, which were given impetus not only by the black power movement, but by the death of Martin Luther King, Jr., and the ineffectual responses of the white denominations to the resulting urban disorders.[42]

The caucus movement was fueled by events at an NCC-sponsored conference on the urban crisis held in September 1967, two months prior to the formal organizing of NCBC. The black delegates at the conference, most of whom were participants in the ad hoc forerunner of NCBC, refused to meet with the white delegates, instead withdrawing into a separate caucus and thereby initiating a confrontation with white churchpersons that was to intensify over the next two years. The statement prepared by the black caucus at the conference not only called upon white churches to enlarge their investments in the black community and develop collaborative relations with black churches, but also addressed "Black Churchmen of the Black Church" and "Black Churchmen of the Non-Black Churches," calling upon both entities to support the emerging NCBC and challenging the former to "insure the return of the Black Church to an expression of its original reason for being."

We confess that in recent times we have not lived up to our heritage, for we have not celebrated, preserved, and enhanced the integrity of Blackness. Rather we have fallen prey to the dominance of white Society.... The Black Church has unwittingly become a tool for our oppression, providing an easy vehicle for escape from the harsh realities of our own existence. This of necessity makes it impossible for us to be instruments of liberation which is our calling as Christians and particularly Black Christians....

... We call upon Black Churchmen everywhere to embrace the Black Power Movement, to divest itself of the traditional churchly functions and goals which do not respond to the needs of a downtrodden, oppressed and alienated people.[43]

The statement specifically called upon the Black Church to establish freedom schools, foster black family solidarity, train lay leaders in community organizing, and provide financial support to black groups pursuing self-determination. But the search for funds to carry out this program was directed primarily toward white church bodies. The following spring — on April 4, 1968, the very day of King's assassination — NCBC's board of directors, meeting in Chicago, issued a statement called "Urban Mission in a Time of Crisis." At the heart of the statement was a challenge to white churches to funnel their mission resources to urban ghettos by way of NCBC's proposed Economic Development Corporation, which in turn would fund projects proposed by black churches, church groups, and caucuses. The statement was drafted by AME Bishop John H. Adams, who later became the founder and first chair of the Congress of National Black Churches.[44]

Meanwhile, a federation called IFCO — the Interreligious Foundation for Community Organization, Inc. — had been created in 1966 and become operational in September 1967. Originally a coalition of ten mission agencies of white denominations that came together to fund minority community organization and development projects, member organizations ultimately numbered twenty-three, including SCLC and other black and Hispanic social change oriented groups.[45] The executive director of IFCO, the Rev. Lucius Walker, Jr., as well as controlling members of its board of directors, were members of NCBC, so that NCBC representatives were intimately involved in the organizing of the IFCO-sponsored Black Economic Development Conference held in Detroit at Wayne State University in April 1969. That conference was the occasion of James Forman's presentation of the

Black Manifesto, which called for reparations in the amount of $500 million to be paid to black Americans by white churches and synagogues to finance a program of black empowerment and liberation. The Manifesto was presented to the religious establishment on May 4, 1969, when Forman disrupted services at the prestigious Riverside Church in New York City. Three days later, NCBC's board of directors expressed its support of the Manifesto, which Wilmore speculates was influenced in the first place by NCBC's 1968 "Urban Mission" statement.[46]

In responding to the Black Manifesto, NCBC once again assumed the role of translator between the more secular young nationalists, whom Forman represented, and the white church establishment. In his own individual response, Wilmore once again strove to speak to his white clergy brethren in a language that they might hear:

> There has always been, at least among Christians in the United States, a misapplication of theology to the concept of integration.... American theologians, both Black and White, have been interpreted as teaching that the Christian understanding of brotherly love, social progress and the unity of mankind in the family of God required the disappearance of all ethnic and racial identity and separateness....
>
> Liberal theologians in the United States never calculated the extent to which the infusion of God's love for others is related to the freedom and ability to affirm and esteem oneself. They neglected to state the extent to which the achievement of authentic personhood (which is a prerequisite of discipleship) is related to the need for a positive sense of historic community and group experience. Such self-esteem based on group identity precedes and supersedes, at least for people who have known segregation, a satisfying experience of koinonia in most interracial churches.[47]

Once again, the theological unacceptability of integration was asserted and the theological soundness of ethnicity, particular historical experience, and pluralism affirmed. Paradoxically, it was NCBC's steadfast allegiance to this middle way that ultimately prompted radical nationalists such as the Rev. Albert Cleage to leave NCBC. They departed, leaving behind contributions of great merit but having failed to win over their fellow clergy to their degree of separation.

The circumstance was lost on white church leaders, which caused to be lost as well the opportunity for genuine dialogue and partnership with NCBC.

Following the issuance of the Manifesto, the Black Economic Development Corporation (BEDC) was established as an ongoing organization, independent of IFCO. Because of Forman's alienating tactics, none of the denominations would consent to fund BEDC directly. NCBC initially presented itself as an alternative to BEDC and sought to work with the black caucuses, encouraging them to solicit funds from their respective denominations, but to accept a coordinating role by NCBC in administering the funds. Shortly thereafter a member of the NCBC board of directors, Calvin Marshall, was elected chair of BEDC. With their interlocking directorates, NCBC and BEDC were functionally the same organization.[48] Although no denomination was willing to allocate funds designated as "reparations," the funding to black caucuses dramatically increased once BEDC was perceived to be under the control of NCBC rather than Forman. Scarcely any of those funds found their way to either BEDC or NCBC, however, as the caucuses gave priority to sustaining their positions within their denominations rather than addressing in a collective fashion the problems common to all of their constituencies. The monies that BEDC did receive came through IFCO and through NCBC, which acted as the conduit for a single grant of $200,000 from the Episcopal Church.[49]

Demise

If the Manifesto served to infuse the caucuses with life, that development in turn ultimately was the undoing of NCBC. As the caucuses grew stronger and more active, hiring their own staffs and convening national conferences, participation in NCBC declined. Of critical significance was the dependency of NCBC members on the white denominations for payment of travel and lodging expenses to attend NCBC meetings. When the denominations began funding the caucuses in substantial amounts, those resources were no longer available to NCBC.[50] But most debilitating of all was the caucuses' failure to pool their funds in support of a coordinated program. The consequence of the "lingering and divisive effects of denominationalism," writes Wilmore, "was the inability of the new interdenominational body to produce the infrastructure of a national movement: regional offices, membership drives, fund raising, educational and action programs, and the integration of black laity into what continued to be a clergy-dominated movement."[51] Instead, the solidarity of NCBC was shattered and a rare moment of ecumenical possibility lost.

The mood of the Manifesto and the church establishment's typical liberal response to it prompted NCBC to threaten a takeover of NCC. When NCC's General Assembly convened in December 1969, Leon Watts and Albert Cleage were offered — unsuccessfully — as candidates for president and general secretary.[52] That incident marked the pinnacle of confrontation with white churchpersons, however. Thereafter, NCBC began shifting its emphasis to self-sufficiency, calling upon the resources of the black community and black churches. In 1972 an observer of NCBC's annual convocation wrote: "While the organization continues to reserve the right to speak out on social issues to the white world, it now sees as its major goal the establishment of genuine communication within the black Christian community for the purpose of galvanizing it for action."[53]

But by 1972 NCBC's activist days were already over. Unable to sustain a paid staff, the office was closed and the headquarters transferred to a post office box in Atlanta, where the organization was separated from its strong northeastern base. Other factors contributed to NCBC's decline as well — including its successes. Some of its members were appointed to high-ranking positions in the white denominations' agencies, where they were isolated from one another. The more scholarly inclined became involved in publishing books on black theology, which meant less investment in the Theological Commission.[54] Framing all of these factors was the dramatic shift in the national climate that attended the 1968 election of Richard Nixon. By the early 1970s the Vietnam War had diverted attention from the black freedom movement, and the plight of urban blacks was no longer a priority. Not only was NCBC's agenda out of sync with the times, but it made the movement a ready target for the Nixon administration's campaign of repression against black leaders and organizations — radical and otherwise.[55] Reflecting the new conservatism, by the mid-1970s the white church establishment had drastically reduced funding even to its own black caucuses.

Summary

If NCBC's tenure was brief and its impact on societal structures minimal, it was nonetheless immensely significant for the development of black ecumenism. Certainly, it played a critical role in the metamorphosis from the philosophy and ideology of the civil rights movement to the theologically grounded pluralistic model that would give rise to later efforts at institution building. In its last years it began to appreciate anew the celebratory and healing dimensions of the black religious tradition and to move toward a more balanced affirmation of the political and the spiritual.

Internally, NCBC offered no new lessons, save in a negative way, regarding reliance on fiscal resources that, while including significant contributions from black congregants, came through predominantly white agencies. As much as any organization, it did involve representatives from the various components that make up the Black Church, at least at the ministerial level, and, however tenuously, it began to engage the question of the role of women. Even in its talking left and walking right where economic issues were concerned, it further cracked the door for other groups to entertain economic democracy or a mixed economy. In general, then, NCBC takes on this profile:

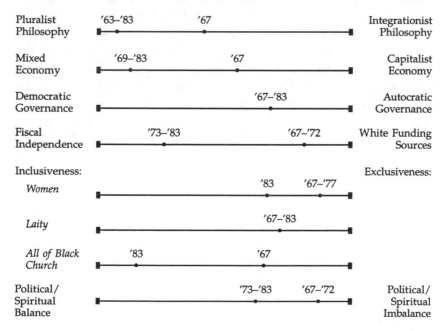

In 1977 Gayraud Wilmore's own assessment of NCBC was this:

On the occasion of our 10th Anniversary we are humbler and
soberer than we were in those heady days.... It is not that we
have retired from the struggle or given up hope. We are just
more aware than we were ten years ago that the movement for
the indigenization of Christianity in the culture of Black America and the liberation of both the mind and the body from
the oppression of White racism is a thousand times more difficult than we had imagined when we made that barnstorming
Northeastern invasion of Dallas, Texas, in the fall of 1967.[56]

NCBC continued to meet, but it faced competition from newer
movements such as the National Black Pastors Conference.[57] Many
of NCBC's participants became involved in the mid-1970s in the
Black Theology Project, which inherited the theological emphasis of
NCBC and filled the vacuum created for New York–based theologians,
educators, and pastors when NCBC moved to Atlanta. Other participants were drawn to Partners in Ecumenism, which most notably
assumed NCBC's dual functions of challenging the National Council of Churches and the white denominations to be more responsive
to black concerns, and of providing a forum for black churchmen and
churchwomen to come together to consider these same concerns. Before turning to NCBC's successors, however, it is appropriate to visit
some of the local organizations that gave ecumenism meaning at the
grassroots level.

Chapter Four

GRASSROOTS PROPHECY
Local Models of Ecumenism

The honest fact about the American Christian religion is that it is a "creation" of white society. This religion has been promulgated to the advantage of white society both in the good it has secured for whites as well as the inhuman acts it has rendered against Black people since 1619. However, the reality of the Christian religion has been contrary to the teachings of its source, Jesus Christ. His life symbolizes what the Christian expression is supposed to be. His ministry was almost a complete contrast to the practice of the Christian religion in the Western World following the second century. He served the poor, alienated, dejected, rejected, and the oppressed people of His society...

It is well to establish that the white Christian religious expression is status-quo oriented. The Black expression has an opportunity to be the religious arm of Black people that reflects the source of the Christian religion. Black people are the oppressed and alienated of American society. This is where the Black church and Black churchmen must stand to be representative of Jesus Christ and His teachings.[1]

So reads a 1968 position paper of the Philadelphia Council of Black Clergy. If the words sound reminiscent of the theological formulations of the National Conference of Black Christians (NCBC), that is in part because several of the members of the Philadelphia Council were among the most active and vocal members of NCBC. Conversely, NCBC — then NCNC — committed itself in its early years to supporting "local groups set up to deal with problems arising from urban

90

tensions in their area." The rationale offered for these relationships by NCNC's executive director, Metz Rollins, was this: "Black churchmen need to consciously come together to reflect ecumenicity, lift up issues which the Black Church must speak to, and devise strategies to bring about local involvements and change."[2]

These words capture precisely the agendas of the local organizations that came into existence in the 1960s in response to the civil rights and black power movements and to the unrest in America's urban areas. Beyond these general features, however, each local movement had its own character, for each came into being in the context of the peculiar circumstances and particular history of its own city. Some movements involved only a cluster of neighborhood churches coming together to organize one project or speak to one crisis and then dissolve. Others engaged the depressed conditions of the entire ghetto area of a city for an extended time. Still others organized citywide to take on the downtown establishment of city hall, police, board of education, and corporate entities. Some movements were committed to theological development and education, some to social action, others to both. And they varied in their structures as much as in their programs.

In the early 1960s, particularly in the South, a number of conventional interdenominational ministerial alliances were transformed into fulcrums of local civil rights activism, some of which then became SCLC affiliates. In other locales — in the South as well as the North and West — ministers and lay people inspired by the example of Martin Luther King, Jr., came together for the first time across denominational lines with the express intent of forming SCLC chapters in order to effect the SCLC agenda of desegregation at the local level. Yet another model, exemplified in Seattle, was that of black clergy providing leadership for an interfaith, interracial assault on racial inequities.

The Central Area Civil Rights Committee was called into being through the efforts of the Rev. Mance Jackson, who subsequently became the director of the National Conference of Black Churchmen, and the Rev. John Hurst Adams, who later founded the Congress of National Black Churches. By 1962 the civil rights struggle had reached even the far northwest corner of the country. In Seattle Rev. Jackson, the pastor of a small CME congregation, was the leading voice of protest. In that year, Rev. Adams — later Bishop Adams — was appointed to pastor First AME Church, a congregation that

counted among its members many of the influential black citizens
of Seattle, including the president of the local NAACP chapter and
the director of the local CORE chapter. In 1963 the pastors of half-a-
dozen other major churches and the heads of Seattle's various human
rights and civil rights organizations came together with Rev. Jackson
and Rev. Adams to form the Central Area Civil Rights Committee —
the "Central Area" being the inner city where most blacks resided.
Adams was chosen to chair the fifteen-member Committee, which
included representatives from the Urban League, NAACP, CORE,
the Anti-Defamation League, the Council of Churches, major black
denominations, and a Catholic parish.

The Committee became the heart of a powerful civil rights coalition, calling for and coordinating the demonstrations that led to open
housing and school integration and that helped create the political climate that ultimately enabled the election of a black mayor — in spite
of a black population base of only 10 percent. For years the Committee met every Saturday to assess the events of the past week and to
plan the happenings of the coming week. Nothing transpired in Seattle in the arena of civil rights activism that did not first go through
the Central Area Committee.

Rev. Jackson left Seattle early in the Committee's tenure, while
Rev. Adams departed in 1968. The Committee continued to function
into the 1970s, though with a less aggressive agenda. In retrospect,
the organization modeled a unique but effective blend of charismatic
leadership and coalition politics.

With the emergence of the black power and black liberation theology movements in the mid- to late 1960s, the tone and character of
local black ecumenical efforts shifted notably. Reflecting the changed
national mood, local groups concerned themselves with the further
development of black theology, the theological retraining of fellow
clergy, and forms of activism that called into question the values
and practices of established structures and systems. Prominent among
these organizations were the Philadelphia Council of Black Clergy,
Chicago Black Churchmen, Alamo Black Clergy, and the Black Ecumenical Commission of Massachusetts — the only statewide effort of
its kind.

Few records of these movements, of either the civil rights or
black power eras, are extant today. Documentation for the sake of
historical memory was not high on the list of priorities of activist
churchpersons or grassroots theologians responding to the urgency

and intensity of the 1960s. Many of the participants are still living, however; many of them are still active. They are the persons who can tell their organizations' stories in full.

Nor are the stories merely a matter of history. Beginning in the late 1970s and continuing through the 1980s, a second generation of local organizations came into being to address the problems current in their day. Many of these have continued to function in the 1990s. From The Gathering in Los Angeles to Concerned Black Clergy in Atlanta to the Church Association for Community Services in Washington, local clergy have taken upon themselves the ecumenical mantle. Even a cursory look at the two generations provides some indication of their variety as well as their common purpose.

Movements of the 1960s

Alamo Black Clergy. Journeying from Seattle to Oakland, California, Mance Jackson emerged as a participant in the formation of a group in the East Bay area known as Alamo Black Clergy. The initiative for this organization came from the Rev. Hozaiah Williams, who in 1966 was the staff person for the Religion and Race component of the Oakland Council of Churches. Rev. Williams brought together twenty-five or so black ministers from the East Bay who met weekly at a retreat center known as "The Alamo." There plans were formulated and strategies developed for carrying on the kinds of social protest and social change activities reminiscent of both SCLC and NCBC. In fact, the Alamo Black Clergy became the nucleus of the SCLC arm in the Bay Area.

In addition to Rev. Williams and Rev. Jackson, the core group of Alamo Black Clergy included the Rev. J. Alfred Smith, Bishop Will Hertzfield, and the Rev. Gene Farlow. They came from both the traditional black communions and predominantly white denominations. Like most groups of this period, this one included no women and no lay representatives. A major focus was the raising of funds from churches and businesses to support community projects, provide seed money for starting small businesses, or provide assistance to existing small businesses. But in keeping with the emphasis of the National Conference of Black Christians — in which several of the Alamo Black Clergy members participated — theological education was also a top priority.

In one of its most successful undertakings, the group challenged the character of the theological education being provided black students by Graduate Theological Union (GTU) in Berkeley. Ultimately, negotiations with the board of directors of GTU led to the creation of a Center for Urban Black Studies, with Rev. Williams retained as the first director. For a number of years the Center offered courses through the various seminaries in Berkeley, including the Pacific School of Religion. As the Alamo Black Clergy became less active and ultimately ceased to function, the scope of the Center was also diminished, although it still existed in the early 1990s.

Chicago Committee of Black Churchmen. Of the local efforts closely associated with the National Conference of Black Christians, the Chicago group was among the smallest. It consisted, in fact, of the dozen or so local clergy who were members of the national organization and never expanded to become a local movement or larger network. Reflecting the early composition of NCBC, the Chicago members came exclusively from predominantly white denominations. From 1966 until the mid-1970s, the local delegation was convened regularly by the Rev. Philip Harley. Along with theological discussions, the group engaged in social action protests and lobbied their respective denominations to support social programs to address the needs of the black community. The most ambitious undertaking of the group was the development of a proposal for a religio-cultural center to train and retrain black clergy along the lines of black liberation theology. The center offered courses for about a year and a half and developed informal relationships with several area seminaries, but never secured sufficient funds to become viable on a long-term basis.

Philadelphia Council of Black Clergy. Theological education was very much at the core of the program of the Philadelphia Council of Black Clergy (CBC), a reflection of the significant role played by the Philadelphia contingent in the theological work of the national organization. Indeed, one member of CBC characterized the Philadelphia group as the "most radical contingent of NCBC" and as being on the "cutting edge of black theology."[3] That commitment to the development and dissemination of black theology was institutionalized in the "Council of Black Clergy's Institute for Black Ministries at the Conwell School of Theology" — commonly referred to as the Institute for Black Ministries.

The Conwell School of Theology at one time was a part of Temple University. When the school merged in the 1960s with another entity to become Gordon-Conwell Theological Seminary, its constituency became largely suburban. CBC then offered to carry on an urban emphasis, proposing that they develop a program predicated on black theology. The negotiations between CBC and Temple University proceeded in the climate of the Black Manifesto, issued in April 1969, and the resultant reparations movement. Temple's response was to lease Conwell's building to CBC for $1 a year for purposes of operating a black seminary program.

Vaugn Eason, the staff director of CBC from 1968 to 1978, served in a dual capacity as the academic dean of the Institute from 1969 to 1977. Archie Allen, Ronald Peters, and O'Neil Mackey were among those who served as dean of admissions, dean of practical studies, or dean of students and, in those capacities, as members of the Institute's management team. Among the ministers who taught at the Institute over the years were Leon Watts, Calvin Marshall, M. Lorenzo Shepard, James Woodruff, Archie Allen, Alfred Dunston, and John Satterwhite. Other ministers served as the Institute's librarians. Rev. Allen, who also was an administrator at Temple University, was instrumental as well in helping to develop funding proposals to support the work of the Institute.

In addition to theology, the course offerings of the Institute included church history, pastoral care, religious education, and community organizing. The program, which offered a three-year master of divinity degree and could accommodate up to eighty students, was designed to serve three constituencies: pastors interested in continuing education, laypersons not involved in vocational ministry but active in the liberation movement, and laypersons interested in entering the ministry. In addition to the regular course offerings, from 1970 to 1977 the Institute convened annual convocations whose participants included leading personalities of the black theology movement as well as top officials of the historic black denominations.

The Institute was an authentically ecumenical venture, with six black denominations recognizing it as a "jointly run seminary for the preparation of their clergy." Those denominations were the CME Church, AME Church, AME Zion Church, National Baptist Convention, Progressive National Baptist Convention, and Fire Baptized Holiness Church. Noted Rev. Eason on the occasion of the formal announcement of the denominations' involvement: "The larger ideal here is to promote union among the black denominations. Should they agree to take over the Institute jointly, it would be the first thing that they have ever owned jointly and worked together on. We would hope that this would be just the first step toward further coopera-tion."[4] The denominations never "took over" the Institute, although they did underwrite operating costs. Support was also provided by Gordon-Conwell and by several white mainline denominations, including the Racial Justice office of the United Church of Christ and the Restitution Fund Commission of the Pennsylvania Episcopal Diocese.

An effort by the AME Zion Church to buy the building housing the Institute was foreclosed when the building burned to the ground. Relocated twice in the nearly ten years of its existence, the seminary ceased to function in 1978, a year after Rev. Eason left to attend Union Theological Seminary in New York. Shortly thereafter Eason became the director of the Black Theology Project, succeeding Muhammed Kenyatta, who also had been an active member of CBC.

The Philadelphia Council of Black Clergy was more than just the Institute for Black Ministries. It was a politically astute social activist organization that functioned as the watchdog of the community, a clearinghouse for airing problems, an advocate for the people, a thorn in the side of the establishment. From issues of police brutality to ed-ucational inequities to economic development and prison reform, the CBC acted where individual churches could not. The thirty-member board of directors, consisting of the pastors of the larger churches, met monthly to hear community concerns and to strategize responses. Among the objectives cited in its Statement of Purpose were these:

- To affirm the cultural contributions of black people to America.

- To create a community power to eliminate problems within the educational system.

- To work for the redistribution of wealth so black people get their fair share.

- To organize the black community for the selection, development and preparation of black political leadership.

- To eradicate slums.

- To rid the black community of police harassment, intimidation and brutality.

- To rediscover and develop a way of life that is meaningful to oppressed people and true to the teachings of the Gospel.[5]

The Council had antecedents in the selective patronage movement of the early 1960s, which became known as the Philadelphia Four Hundred. Itself a remarkable ecumenical effort, this campaign was devoted to breaking through employment barriers and opening up jobs to blacks in Philadelphia's businesses and industries. Each Sunday four hundred black ministers would speak from their pulpits encouraging their congregants to boycott those companies that had been singled out for their discriminatory practices. Out of this movement, which was led by Baptist minister Leon Sullivan, came the Opportunities Industrialization Centers established around the country to provide job training and vocational skills to inner city residents.[6]

In 1968 many of the ministers who had been involved in the selective patronage movement were galvanized by the assassination of Martin Luther King, Jr., and the resultant urban disturbances into joining the Council of Black Clergy. The Council began with a meeting of a small group of clergy that included the Reverends Jesse Anderson, Gene Turner, Clarence Cave, James McIntosh, George Simms, O'Neil Mackey, Archie Allen, M. Lorenzo Shepard, and Vaugn Eason. Represented were AME, AMEZ, Baptist, Presbyterian, Episcopal, and UCC churches. Ultimately, this core group was joined by one of every three black ministers in Philadelphia, for a total membership of some 300, representing a constituency of 250,000.

The organization began operating with an initial grant from the local presbytery, subsequently becoming self-supporting through the contributions of pastors and church congregations. As it developed, however, most of the Council's membership came from the black denominations, while more of its fiscal resources came from churches in predominantly white denominations. The tension introduced by this configuration was never overcome and accounted in part for the movement's decline as the 1970s progressed.

Rev. Anderson served as the first president of CBC and then was succeeded by Rev. Shepard, who in later years became chair of the steering committee of Partners in Ecumenism as well as a prominent member of the Congress of National Black Churches. Rev. Simms served, for most of its tenure, as chair of the board of directors of the Council's Institute for Black Ministries. By the late 1970s, the Council, for all practical purposes, had merged into the Institute, foregoing its activist focus. That it had had an impact was confirmed when it was learned that one of the Council's secretaries had functioned in a dual capacity as a police informant.[7] Both the police and the FBI were no doubt gratified to see the movement die — and equally disconcerted when a successor organization emerged a few years later.

Black Ecumenical Commission of Massachusetts. In 1966 the Massachusetts Council of Churches (MCC) established its Commission on Church and Race, appointing the Rev. James Breeden as the executive director. In July of 1968, Ms. Ann Petett became the Commission's metropolitan field director, with part of her responsibility being "to relate in a meaningful way to the churchmen, both clergy and lay, of the metropolitan area."[8] On September 18, 1968, Ms. Erna Ballentine Bryant and the Rev. Earl Lawson, in their capacities as co-chairs of the Steering Committee for the Proposed Local Black Churchmen's Organization, sent a letter to black clergy who had agreed to be on the steering committee, inviting them to a forthcoming meeting. The letter, printed on MCC stationery, read in part: "We are desirous of uniting all Black Churchmen in our region in a structure based upon the objectives of the National Committee of Negro Churchmen and our local stated needs and concerns." The letter further indicated that Metz Rollins, executive director of NCNC (later NCBC), would be in attendance. Present at the meeting, in addition to Rollins, Bryant, and Lawson, were Ann Petett, Mrs. Clarence Elam, six other ministers — Charles Adams, Vernon Carter, Ted Lockhart, William McClain, Warner Traynham, and Virgil Wood — and Professor Preston Williams from Harvard Divinity School.

Subsequent meetings of the steering committee in 1968 and early 1969 led to the creation of an organization called the Metropolitan Boston Committee of Black Churchmen (MBCBC). In April 1969 the Black Manifesto was adopted by the National Black Economic Development Conference in Detroit. A month later MBCBC issued its own demand for reparations, which prompted the formation of the White Reparations Caucus of Metropolitan Boston to help facilitate a response to the demand. Also that month the steering committee of MBCBC formally proposed to MCC that "the Commission on Church and Race be reconstituted as a Black Ecumenical Commission of the Massachusetts Council of Churches."[9] MBCBC then offered itself as the vehicle for working with black churchmen throughout the commonwealth to design such an entity. The following month, in June

1969, the Commission on Church and Race itself submitted a proposal to its parent body, MCC, calling for the creation of a Black Ecumenical Commission responsible to MBCBC and funded by the Council of Churches.[10] Stated the proposal,

> BEC (1) is created and designed to develop relationships in Black communities throughout Massachusetts, to lead to empowerment, unity and self-determination of the Black people in these communities; (2) is the means through which MCC can develop the strongest possible link to the prophetic life of the Black community in Massachusetts, particularly: a. Black Churchmen in Black denominations and Black Caucuses, b. Black Churchmen in predominantly White Churches, c. Black Seminarians and Faculty, d. Black communities generally — including Black Youth; (3) is an interdenominational strategy through which Churches can develop strategies to deal with the problems in Black Communities and to promote meaningful relationships between Black and White Churchmen.[11]

In August 1969 MCC officially dissolved its Commission on Church and Race in favor of a Black Ecumenical Commission, pledging minimum funding of $35,000 annually for a period of five years.[12]

MBCBC immediately began planning a statewide consultation for Black Churchmen to "come together to explore dialogue and share with one another their understanding, ideas and thinking about a model and structure for the Black Ecumenical Commission."[13] The consultation, the theme of which was "Towards a Relevant Black Church," was held in November 1969. Professor Preston Williams chaired the consultation planning committee. Rev. Thomas Kilgore, Jr., was brought in as the consultation resource person, while Dr. James Cone gave the keynote address.

The Black Ecumenical Commission (BEC) was actually incorporated a month prior to the consultation, with the officers and steering committee members of MBCBC also being the official incorporators of BEC. For the remainder of the year Ann Petett served as the staff coordinator of the new organization, while Warner Traynham served as the interim chair of the board of directors. In January 1970 the Rev. G. Wesley Raney III became chair of the BEC committee on structure, and the Rev. William McClain began a six-month term as the interim executive director. That same month BEC was the recipient of the first $250,000 installment on a one million dollar pledge made by the Massachusetts Conference of the United Church of Christ, the largest of the Protestant denominations in the commonwealth.

The action of the United Church of Christ (UCC) was explicitly a response to the reparations demands of the Manifesto. It was also the cause of a storm of controversy, not only within the ranks of the UCC Conference, but between the Conference and the national office of the NAACP, which denounced UCC's action as an endorsement of separatism. The newly elected president of the UCC Conference, the Rev. Avery Post, stood by the decision, remaining a staunch advocate of BEC and of the goals of black self-determination and empowerment. Read the pastoral letter issued by Rev. Post: "I do not regard black self determination as ideological separatism, but as a glorious and overdue chapter in the life of an oppressed and unbelievably patient people.... The whole society is on the way to a quality of humanness and a sense of wholeness that black people alone have known deep in their hearts is not expressed by pursuing integration in an unrenewed society."[14] Joining in the defense of UCC — and of itself — was the Massachusetts Council of Churches, which issued a statement declaring that "the establishment of the Black Ecumenical Commission is consistent with the patterns of decision-making which prevail in the Council, but, more than that, the establishment is consistent with the obligation we have as fellow Christians to set our priorities, that ancient injustices can be redressed and future hopes brought to life."[15]

The beginnings of BEC were thus auspicious on several counts: first, for the prominent role played by women in its creation; second, for the degree of interaction between black clergy and a statewide council of churches; and third, for the response of white churches to the demand for reparations. The prophetic voices within the UCC Conference and MCC were both white and black. But the real work of building BEC fell to local black churchmen and churchwomen who had the commitment to see their vision realized.

The issue areas defined for BEC at the statewide consultation included Black Theology; the Black Church in Mission; Economic (Human) Development; Organized Church Ministries; and Church, Seminary and Community Cooperation. In order to serve its seventy-five thousand constituents across the state, BEC proposed the creation of eight regional area groups, each having its own administrative council and coordinator. Four of the area groups became functional, while the established Interdenominational Ministerial Alliance in

Boston functioned as the regional group for that area. The first annual meeting of BEC was held in June 1970, at which time the Rev. Jefferson Rogers came on board as the first permanent executive director. In 1971 BEC became fully independent of MCC, operating out of an office at 14 Beacon Street in a building owned by a subsidiary of UCC. At that time MBCBC became inoperative as a separate entity.

In addition to setting up the area groups, one of Rev. Rogers's primary emphases was the creation of a publication called *The Black Church*. Started as a quarterly journal and later redesigned as a magazine, the publication included on its board of contributing editors Lerone Bennett, Benjamin Mays, Howard Thurman, Metz Rollins, Charles Spivey, then the general secretariat for the World Council of Churches Programme to Combat Racism, and Robert Chapman, executive director of the National Council of Churches Department of Social Justice. Following the issuance of the first three issues, Gayraud Wilmore, who at that time was a professor at Boston University, took over the editorship. Three additional issues later, the magazine folded, largely because Wilmore's pleas for financial support met with insufficient response to put the project on an independent footing. *The Black Church* stands as a unique effort on the part of an ecumenical movement to create a print forum for theological reflection and discussion of the role of the Black Church in relation to the community as a whole.

BEC was also a social activist organization, participating under Rogers's leadership in protests and rallies with SCLC and other civil rights organizations. The years from 1974 to 1977 were a particularly volatile period in the Boston area, with racial conflict over school desegregation regularly escalating to incidents of overt violence. In 1974 BEC called for a freeze on the bussing of black children into white schools pending the development of a genuine two-way plan. It also became involved in opposing the reelection of Governor Sargent Francis on account of his stance on school integration.

In 1975 and 1976 BEC moved to institute educational and service programs of a more structured nature. One of these efforts was the Black Women Seminarians Project conducted through Harvard Divinity School with the objective of involving more black women in ministry. Field education opportunities involving community programs and projects were also provided for both men and women seminarians from area divinity schools. A youth program providing academic tutoring, social services, and family counseling was operated in Springfield. Local churches were engaged in statewide voter education and registration campaigns. An effort was made to increase the number of black chaplains employed at state institutions, in part through the filing of law suits. For a number of years BEC operated a federally funded Foster Grandparents program in Cambridge. It was also instrumental in securing state grants for social service programs in local communities. BEC supported the development of a black church curriculum for children that included holiday observances and rites of passage. From 1974 to 1979 statewide annual meetings were convened that were attended by three hundred to four hundred individuals, including both clergy and laypersons. And while the statewide programs were being implemented, the area groups initiated their own projects. One area founded a new nondenominational black church. Others attempted to act as catalysts for housing and economic development programs. These efforts met with only marginal success, however, and ultimately the portions of BEC's endowment that had been deposited in area banks were reverted to a centralized fund.

Throughout BEC's history, its leadership came primarily from predominantly white denominations, although its constituency was predominantly from the traditional black denominations. All of BEC's staff directors were affiliated with the United Church of Christ, except that Rev. McClain was United Methodist and Rev. Rogers later became Presbyterian. Two of the directors — Erna Bryant and Ron McClean — were laypersons, although McClean sought ordination in later years.

BEC's board of directors, known as the Covenantal Council, consisted of one to two representatives from each of the functioning regional councils and one representative from each of the fourteen member organizations, which included the AME Church, AME Zion Church, a state black Baptist Convention, the black caucuses of five white denominations, and several Pentecostal groups. The chair of the board from 1970 to 1972 was a Pentecostal minister, the Rev. J. P. Morgan. Episcopal Bishop John M. Burgess was chair from 1973 to 1975, followed by United Methodist Bishop Edward G. Carroll from 1976 to 1981. Other officers who served prominently for most of the 1970s included Episcopal Canon Ed Rodman and UCC minister Clyde Miller. Bishop Carroll was succeeded by AME Zion minister Warren Brown, who remained as chair of the board from 1982 to 1985.

Erna Bryant, who received her doctorate from Harvard in 1974, was the executive director from 1974 to 1979. Like her predecessor, for most of her term, BEC employed a total staff of four or five individuals. While BEC intermittently received annual dues of $25 from the 120 member black churches in the commonwealth, its basic operating budget of $60,000 to $70,000 came primarily from interest generated by the $1.5 million endowment established with reparations payments. Ultimately, those payments came not only from the UCC Conference, but from Methodists, Baptists, Episcopalians, and Unitarians as well. Even in its early years BEC drew on the principle of the endowment to support its program; by the 1980s, the principle was being used for operating costs as well.

Mr. Ron McClean took over from an interim director in 1980 and remained as executive director until 1986. At that time, he moved to the position of chair of the board, convening the last board of directors meeting in the fall of 1988. The area groups had ceased to function in 1982, however, so that the board was no longer representative in the way that it had been in the 1970s.

In spite of its longer than usual tenure for black ecumenical movements, many observers of BEC consider that it never fulfilled its potential. In part that failure is attributed to BEC's inability to generate more resources in order to sustain a strong presence in the community; in part to an unresolved tension between members from white denominations and those from black denominations over whether the primary emphasis should be theological reflection and political activism, or social service delivery. Corollary to that disagreement was the question of whether the endowment principle should be used to pay for social services. The conflict was further compounded by denominational differences in doctrine and polity, which BEC never addressed in a direct way.

BEC's statewide structure posed a problem, with participants from communities outside of Boston often feeling they were treated as less than full members. Another difficulty was presented by the turnover among clergy, with the early participants moving to other assignments and younger clergy coming in who had no organizational memory. BEC was also weakened by a year-long investigation by the IRS of charges of failing to comply with its 501 c. 3. status. Although BEC ultimately won the case on appeal, its resources were diminished by legal costs and the attention and energy of its staff deflected from other activities. Given the patterns of government interference that developed in the 1960s and 1970s, BEC might have found validation in its perceived threat to the powers that be.

No doubt each of these circumstances was a factor in BEC's over-all performance. But success or failure must be measured against the extraordinarily high expectations held of the organization at the time of its creation. In fact, BEC did generate dialogue and operate a variety of programs for an extended period that had both tangible and intangible consequences not only for the metropolitan Boston area but for other communities in the state as well. Furthermore, the entire process of bringing the Black Ecumenical Commission into being remains an instructive chapter in the history of black and white relations within the larger ecumenical movement.

The Second Generation

The Gathering. As the Philadelphia CBC was closing down, a new ecumenical group was just coming into existence in Los Angeles. Concerned that the established Interdenominational Ministerial Alliance was giving little attention to social and economic problems, the Rev. Thomas Kilgore, Jr., in the spring of 1978 contacted the Alliance's 500 members inviting them to attend a strategic planning conference. The 130 ministers who responded determined to form an activist organization and began functioning as The Gathering, having designated Rev. Kilgore as their president.

A few months later the organization joined in the public outcry that met the January 1979 police shooting of Eulia Love, a black woman and mother of three daughters who was killed when two officers went to her home to investigate a dispute involving an unpaid gas bill. As a result of The Gathering's negotiations with the Los Angeles Police Department, the agency's policy on the use of handguns was changed. Upon learning of a series of citizen deaths from police choke holds, The Gathering then successfully negotiated for use of the choke hold to be officially prohibited.

For the next three years, The Gathering remained involved in police-community relations while it responded on an ad hoc basis to various community crises. In 1981 a $25,000 planning grant was obtained from the Lilly Endowment, Inc., in an effort to put the organization on more solid footing. Out of that process came three specific projects: one to monitor police actions, a second to investigate housing conditions and make recommendations to housing development agencies, and a third to become involved in community conflict resolution as demographics changed with the influx of Korean residents and businesses.

The years 1982 and 1983 were the most active for The Gathering, the membership of which had settled into a core group of fifty-five clergy, including two women and a few white ministers. The organization functioned with membership dues of $25 per year, supplemented by periodic assessments for special projects. Rev. Kilgore, a Baptist, was succeeded as president by United Holy Church Bishop Ralph Houston, who served in 1983 and 1984. Bishop Houston, in turn, was succeeded by the Rev. Cecil Murray, pastor of First AME Church. Upon his election, The Gathering was merged back into the Interdenominational Ministerial Alliance, thus bringing to a close the brief life of a potent clergy action group. Rev. Kilgore subsequently was involved in organizing other local ecumenical efforts while also serving as an active member of the board of directors of the Congress of National Black Churches.

Organization of African American Clergy. Police-community relations were a central concern for a New York–based group as well. The Organization of African American Clergy (OAAC) — a play on Malcolm X's Organization of Afro-American Unity — came into being in late 1979 and early 1980 in response to the beating of a black seminary student by New York police. Organized by the Rev. Calvin Butts, pastor of Abyssinian Baptist Church, OAAC had a membership of some fifty Baptist, Methodist, and Pentecostal clergy. Police brutality was a singular focus during the early years of the 1980s, until attention was turned to a boycott of the *New York Daily News*. The organization became relatively inactive around 1988 but then was revitalized in 1993 as grievances with the *Daily News* again prompted clergy protests.

Black Clergy of Philadelphia and Vicinity. By 1982 the ministers of Philadelphia had regrouped, naming themselves "Black Clergy of Philadelphia and Vicinity" (BCPV). This successor to the earlier CBC emerged out of the efforts of black clergy to settle a public school teachers strike in 1981. With a grant from Pew Charitable Trust, the clergy surveyed some two thousand black churches to assess priority needs for programmatic action. Four key areas emerged — education, economic development, social outreach, and evangelism — to which was added the fifth area of electoral politics.

From 1983 to 1990, the ecumenical movement of some four

hundred clergy launched a diverse array of initiatives. BCPV's Political Action Committee was heavily involved in Wilson Goode's mayoral campaigns, taking credit for his elections. The Committee not only provided forums for electoral candidates, but engaged in fund raising efforts as well, contributing some $300,000 to Goode's campaign. The organization developed an "Adopt a School" plan, urging each pastor and congregation to take responsibility for a neighborhood school. Its "Save Our Children" anti-drug campaign had the active involvement of fifty churches. BCPV protested economic discrimination, held seminars on the black family, entered into dialogue with the Jewish community, and reached out to the Hispanic clergy and community to work cooperatively on issues of common concern.

The group's third president, Rev. William B. Moore (the first two were Rev. James S. Allen and Rev. O. Urcille Ifill, Sr.) was centrally involved in the creation of a minority-owned bank. Forty percent of the initial investors in United Bank — also known as "The Bank the People Built" — were clergy and parishioners, most of them affiliated with BCPV.

The Philadelphia movement of the 1980s was anchored less overtly in a black theology orientation than had been the case with the 1960s movement, for which black theology very much set the agenda. But the later group did also have an interest in theological education and training and in 1989 began offering six-week courses through two area seminaries. In the 1990s the educational effort was expanded to offer equivalency certificates as well as master of divinity and doctor of ministry degrees through three seminaries and two schools of theology. As part of the consortium, BCPV assumed major responsibility for recruiting students while also being involved in making recommendations on curriculum and faculty and staff to the various schools.

Under the leadership of the Rev. Jesse Brown and the Rev. Ralph Blanks — the fourth and fifth presidents respectively — BCPV significantly expanded its operations in the 1990s, becoming the most comprehensive local ecumenical endeavor in the nation. BCPV continued to function as an advocacy group, but in 1991 created a new component — Black Clergy, Inc. — to function as the service delivery arm. As a nonprofit entity, Black Clergy, Inc., was able to receive grants from foundations and businesses to underwrite new programs in the areas of education, evangelism, economic development, and health and human services. In addition Black Clergy, Inc., acted as the conduit for church contributions and annual membership fees of $50. Beginning in 1993 Black Clergy, Inc., received free office space from a major bank in downtown Philadelphia.

At that time, Black Clergy, Inc., was administered by a fifteen-member clergy board of directors, representing eleven denominations — including the traditional black denominations as well as United Methodist, Lutheran, Presbyterian, and Episcopal bodies — plus the independent Baptist churches and the Pentecostal network. The entity also worked with a twelve-member advisory committee composed of lay academicians and other professionals from the community. The board of directors was chaired in 1993 by Rev. Moore, while the Rev. John Wesley Mosley, Jr., served as the full-time executive director.

Once established, Black Clergy, Inc., assumed primary responsibility for BCPV's involvement in the educational consortium. In the area of economic development, it assisted several local churches to create credit unions, became involved in capital fund raising, provided investment counseling, and initiated a housing program. Under health and human services, involvements ranged from the provision of day care to working with the homeless to assisting uninsured individuals obtain coverage. The organization worked with the public school districts to provide tutorial programs and continued to address the issues of violence and drug abuse.

In a marked departure from other ecumenical movements, Black Clergy, Inc., gave high priority to evangelism. Under their auspices, as of 1993, some sixty ministers had been trained to work with congregations in church growth and at the same time to tie the churches into the citywide social services network. In its first two years the group also worked with the Billy Graham Crusades, which resulted in the Philadelphia Crusades having minority co-chairs for the first time in their history, and produced evangelistic literature for use by pastors and churches in their outreach efforts.

The scope of Black Clergy of Philadelphia and Vicinity's concern extended beyond the boundaries of its own community. Following a briefing on their activities by a Philadelphia minister to a group of clergy in Atlanta, a new ecumenical effort was initiated in that city. In the mid-1990s interest was being expressed by clergy in Los Angeles, Chicago, and other cities in transplanting the Philadelphia model to their communities. The appeal of this model inhered in large part in its two-pronged emphasis of "empowering" and

108

Grassroots Prophecy

"equipping." The mission of BCPV, noted the director of Black Clergy, Inc., was to "resource the community and develop leadership" to "empower and equip the people to become spiritually and economically self-sufficient."[16] Certainly this statement of purpose aligns the Philadelphia movement with the core tradition of black ecumenism. It departs from that tradition in explicitly ranking spiritual empowerment alongside of social and economic empowerment.

Concerned Black Clergy of Metropolitan Atlanta, Inc. The beginnings of Concerned Black Clergy (CBC) may be dated to 1983, when a group of pastors came together to address the issues of homelessness and hunger in the city of Atlanta. A year later the organization was instrumental in launching Odyssey III, a nonprofit organization devoted to providing meals, transitional housing, and counseling to trainable and employable men. While homelessness remained a central concern, the scope of Concerned Black Clergy's involvement expanded substantially over the next ten years.

In the early 1990s CBC described itself as an "interfaith, interdenominational, inclusive, nonpartisan organization which consciously pursues justice for all of God's people." CBC, reads its statement of purpose, "educates the masses relative to legislative policies which threaten the stability of working class neighborhoods, establishes programs that speak to the plethora of needs and concerns in African American communities, and creates opportunities for relationship building between clergy and lay, males and females, Blacks and Whites."[17]

CBC established a practice of meeting every Monday in an open forum to which anyone could bring issues and concerns and solicit the aid of CBC in redressing circumstances of social injustice. A monthly meeting was then held for CBC members to plan the organization's strategy and programs. In 1993 two of its major programs were Mission Uplift, an effort to empower the community economically through business growth and development, and Keeping in Touch (KIT), a mentorship program for young African American men. CBC also served as a clearing house on programs for youth operated by various churches, in turn making the information available to churches interested in initiating programs through its "CBC Youth Excel Network." CBC was involved with the Carter-Atlanta Project, enabling churches to become conduits for federally funded services to impoverished communities.

Through its Political Action Committee, CBC involved itself not only in educating its constituencies regarding the political process, but served as a critical forum for political candidates, which then became the point of access to individual congregations. Networking with agencies involved in job placement, emergency assistance, housing placement, human relations, and civil rights activity was an equally significant aspect of political engagement. In the early 1990s CBC also became involved in advocating for Haitian refugees.

CBC's financial base, which was erratic over the years, occasionally enabled a paid staff, but more often called for reliance on a volunteer staff. In the 1990s that role was assumed by Ms. Marla O'Hara. Two major sources of funding were the Annual Salute to Black Fathers Awards Banquet and the Annual Salute to Black Mothers Awards Banquet. In 1993 CBC moved to institute a sponsorship program in which member churches were asked to donate $100 per month. Some 120 churches and mosques were members of CBC, along with another twenty representatives of non-church organizations. Fifty individuals were also members, a category that allowed for lay membership. Other membership categories included students and senior citizens. The twenty-member executive committee included four women, two of whom served as secretary and treasurer. The president of the organization was the Rev. J. Allen Milner, who succeeded the Rev. McKinley Young. Rev. Young, in turn, had succeeded the founding president, Dr. Cornelius L. Henderson. CBC is notable for its governing structure, which includes three vice presidents, one for administration, one for missions, and one for programs. Notable, too, is the broad base of potential membership and support created by its self-characterization as an interfaith, interracial endeavor.

African American Clergy Action Network. The Chicago effort known as AACAN — African American Clergy Action Network — was the dream of the Rev. Carrol Felton. Rev. Felton had served as the head of mayoral candidate Eugene Sawyer's Ministerial Committee following the death of Mayor Harold Washington, while fellow clergy members were actively involved in the campaign of Sawyer's opponent. Following the election, forty ministers came together at a retreat where Rev. Felton proposed a coalition organization to address community issues on a united basis. The strategy was to move from the language of electoral politics to the language of theology in order to enable the participation of ministers who would not otherwise be politically active. "Prophetic ministry" was the phrase adopted for political action as a means of transcending the differences in doctrine, training, and ideology that characterized the 402 ministers brought into the new network.

By mid-1989, AACAN had assembled a 115-member board of directors and 45-member executive committee that included judicatory officials from both black and white denominations — Roman Catholic, mainstream Protestant, Apostolic, Pentecostal — as well as representatives from twenty-seven different ministerial organizations. A 125-member organization of women clergy was represented on AACAN's board and executive committee, with one of seven vice presidents being a woman. AACAN began with contributions of $100 each from a hundred congregations, with member churches subsidizing printing and computer costs.

The thrust of AACAN was education toward the end of developing people's political awareness and involvement. The vision was two-tiered: first, to train the network of clergy around seven issue areas in order to establish a common ground of information and awareness; second, to initiate a series of workshops in the same seven areas in which all of the 250,000 constituents of AACAN would be invited to participate. The issue areas were Education, Political Action, Current Issues, Foreign Affairs, Government Funding, Health, and Economic Development.

The promise of AACAN was cut short with the untimely death of Rev. Felton, but the plan and the vision stand as a unique contribution to the varied expressions of black ecumenism.

Church Association for Community Services. The Church Association for Community Services (CACS) began in 1989 when a group of some thirty-five clergy from the Washington, D.C., and neighboring Maryland areas came together around issues of drug abuse and violence. Building on efforts already underway by several individual churches, and borrowing from the Project SPIRIT model developed by the Congress of National Black Churches, CACS developed a multifaceted program to respond to the needs of families and youth.[18] An evening program for youth from ages twelve to twenty provides mentoring, tutoring, and athletic and martial arts opportunities, as well as workshops on health care and self-esteem. A crisis intervention center works both with individuals and families. Parenting education classes and support groups are offered as part of the agenda of strengthening the family. Once a month a group of clergy from the member churches meet with representatives of social service agencies, the school board, the police department, and other community service entities in a collective effort to address community problems. In addition CACS initiated a program called "Reclaim Our Youth," which provides mentoring and supervision as an alternative to incarceration.

Structurally, the programs of CACS are offered at a minimum of two locations in each of the eight wards of the District, with clusters of five to six churches relating to each program site. Altogether, some 120 churches participate in the ecumenical effort, which in 1993 was administered by a forty-five-member board of directors chaired by the Rev. Frank Tucker, pastor of First Baptist Church. Initially the organization was funded by membership fees of $1000 each from some thirty-five to forty churches; subsequently, it has relied on contributions from the member churches.

Summary

Long before the civil rights movement, interdenominational ministerial alliances had become a familiar ecumenical configuration in most cities having a significant black population. Particularly in the South, such networks of black ministers often functioned in times of crises as the intermediary between black citizens and the city establishment, and not a few of the leaders of these ministerial groups, as noted, became influential civil rights leaders. More commonly, however, the functions of such alliances tended toward fellowship and mutual support of their members, a characterization not significantly altered in the 1980s and 1990s.

Formal ministerial alliances aside, estimates are that in the 1980s, nearly 60 percent of all black churches were engaged in some type of interdenominational cooperation. But two-thirds of that activity took the form of fellowship or evangelistic campaigns with other black churches, while some 10 percent involved joint cooperation with white churches. Less than 15 percent of the interdenominational cooperation involved joint efforts to provide community services or to address community problems.[19]

The local ecumenical efforts profiled in this chapter can thus make two claims. First, like ecumenical movements at the national level, they constitute a prophetic remnant of the whole of the Black Church. Second, they point to a model of local interdenominational cooperation that departs from convention in its emphasis on social change and in the motif — expressed sometimes overtly, sometimes implicitly — of black liberation theology. Within the larger model are any number of sub-models, for local ecumenical movements evidence a striking range in longevity, complexity of structure, and diversity of programming. What they share is the common goal of improving the quality of life of their constituents.

Local ecumenical movements arguably face a greater challenge than do most national movements in that they are engaged in a direct and immediate way with the people whose needs they seek to alleviate; they are, in a word, on the frontline of the urban battle for the sanctity of human life. Collectively, local ecumenical movements constitute an immensely significant component of the overall story of black ecumenism. Not only are they their own justification for being, but they make a compelling case for national movements being more attentive to the development of local chapters and affiliates.

Chapter Five

PRAXIS AND REFLECTION
The National Black
Evangelical Association
and the Black Theology Project

Context

In addition to the array of local ecumenical groups and in addition
to the National Conference of Black Christians (NCBC), the ferment
of the 1960s gave life to a second national ecumenical effort and to
yet a third that emerged a decade later. The National Black Evangelical Association (NBEA), which represented the segment that had
historically least identified itself as part of the Black Church, actually predated NCBC by three years. Indeed, it predated the black
power movement both in its founding and in its own embryonic
formulations of black theology.

NBEA was organized initially simply because white evangelicals
and their institutions — including the National Association of Evangelicals — did not concern themselves with the black community.
Until the 1960s conservative black Christians who called themselves
"evangelicals" had difficulty accepting as theologically and doctri-
nally sound the pronouncements and actions of their more liberal
brethren. The mood of the times proved too compelling to deny,
however, as black consciousness overtook even the prodigal evangelicals. While the theological conservatism of much of its membership
precluded joining forces with the radical NCBC, the tenets of black
liberation theology nevertheless generated a decided shift in their

113

attitude toward both social activism and ethnicity. The revitalization of black religion inaugurated by the leaders of SCLC ultimately
reached — however tenuously — into the least accessible crooks and
crannies of the Black Church.[1]

Entering into a new stage of its development, black theology re-
emerged organizationally in 1977 — the tenth anniversary of NCBC —
in the Black Theology Project of Theology in the Americas (TIA). Although some members of NCBC initially viewed the Black Theology
Project (BTP) as a rival movement, it is more aptly characterized as
one of the progeny of NCBC.[2] Devoted to black theological development, dialogue, networking, and coalition building, BTP, like NCBC,
sought to provide a forum for reflecting on the empowerment of the
African American nation.

National Black Evangelical Association

In one major respect NBEA and NCBC stand on common ground.
Reporting on the state of NCBC at its 1974 annual convocation, a
participant remarked: "We sought to return to our roots as black
churchmen. Thus, worship was a central part of our experience. We
have finally moved from a position of apology for the black church
style to one of affirmation. For me, that is a positive statement about
our coming of age."[3] The implicit, if unwitting, confession of this
statement is that at least some NCBC members were renewed by the
Black Church as much as the Church was renewed by them. An important aspect of the ecumenical character of NCBC was the new
unity created by "the sense of a common historical heritage which
some of the churchmen from white denominations [came to] share
with their fellow black clergy."[4] It was through the black power movement — and the cultural and historical celebrations that attended it —
that black clergy in white denominations rediscovered the radical tradition of the Black Church and, with the proverbial enthusiasm of
new discoverers of the faith, sought to initiate a reformation within
the black church establishment.

The National Black Evangelical Association never arrived at the
"reformation" stage, but in its awakening to the radical tradition —
and, for that matter, to the evangelical and mission traditions — of
the Black Church, it was not so dissimilar from NCBC. Just as black
clergy affiliated with the liberal white denominations comprising the

National Council of Churches had been cut off from the heritage of the Black Church, so too had the black clergy who identified with the fundamentalist white denominations and sects comprising the National Association of Evangelicals been cut off from the heritage of the Black Church — only more so.

The Rev. Dr. William Bentley, who is regarded as the "father" of NBEA and who was one of the organization's most creative thinkers, wrote of this separation:

> *Black evangelicalism as a distinct phenomenon* — and so identified — is of very recent origin, and developed out of the same forces which reacted with a new burst of orthodoxy to the issues of the unresolved "Fundamentalist-Liberal" controversy of the late 1920s and 1930s....It adopted therefore the same stance toward the traditional Black church in Black structures, which it regarded as empty of Gospel proclamation, and the Black church within white structures — which it regarded as apostate — as white fundamentalism did toward the major denominations....
>
> The often condescending attitudes which many a white evangelical has toward the Black church was shared by much of our earliest leadership.... This simplistic thinking shows obliviousness to the fact that the Black church existed in major dimension almost two centuries before there was such a thing as a self-identifying group of Black believers referring to themselves as "evangelicals." Had this been understood we would have been in a position to see that evangelicalism is not new and did not originate in the sixth decade of the twentieth century! There is and always has been a significant evangelical presence within mainline Black Christianity even from the first....
>
> Here was a strange thing! We were seeking to reach people, our people, but we had little awareness of the resources to be found within our own religious tradition, resources that had been forged in the fires of affliction and had not been exhausted by the mere passage of time. We could not draw on these because we hardly recognized their existence.[5]

Recognition of their mutual separation from and rediscovery of the black church heritage resulted in explorations of collaborative possibilities between NCBC and NBEA. But while black theology as it was developed by NCBC became a key point of discussion and debate within NBEA, merger of the two movements was recognized as a pragmatic impossibility on account of both structural[6] and doctrinal[7] incompatibilities. Some fifteen years later, Gayraud Wilmore was less certain of the perceived incompatibilities, writing that "there certainly was an impulse to come together. And I have long felt that we made a mistake in not recognizing that the theological differences were not that wide. There may have been some differences between [the leaders of the two groups]. But for the ordinary pastor there was no great disjunction between their understanding of Protestant evangelicalism and our more liberation-oriented understanding of theology."[8]

Wilmore may have overstated the case, however. NBEA participants did make a leap of considerable magnitude in putting aside the fundamentalist versus liberal debate that so occupied white evangelicals' attention. Indeed, it was that preoccupation — and the concomitant exclusion of social concerns — that gave black evangelicals impetus to separate into their own organization. And the black theology developed by NBEA certainly embraced the liberation motif. But it insisted, too, on a rigorous biblical grounding and on inclusion of the spirituality that was so much a part of the evangelical tradition. These features, Bentley and his colleagues perceived, were lacking in the theological endeavors of NCBC members, who relied more exclusively on the black experience as their source.[9]

If there could be no rapprochement with other organizations, NBEA was nevertheless ecumenical in its own fashion. In certain respects, NBEA was a counterpart of the various black caucuses in the white denominations. The difference was that white evangelicals did not comprise a single denomination, but instead represented a theological orientation cutting across an array of denominations and segments of denominations and independent churches. If NBEA was a "black caucus" within the evangelical wing of American Protestantism, it was an interdenominational caucus, drawing members from independent, Bible, Holiness, and Pentecostal churches, as well as Methodist, Baptist, Presbyterian, Mennonite, and Quaker bodies. NBEA itself chose not to use the term "ecumenical" to describe itself, however, preferring the phrase "umbrella concept" to characterize its organizational and philosophical approach. The phrase connotes inclusiveness of diverse political perspectives ranging from the apolitical to the nationalistic, from conservative to radical.[10]

NBEA was organized to be a refuge for black pastors who had termed themselves evangelicals, embraced white evangelical perspectives, attended white evangelical schools — and then found themselves left to minister to African Americans with white evangelical models bereft of any sensitivity to the cultural accoutrements, social circumstances, or religious experience of the black community.[11] Its initial purpose was fellowship — the provision of a supportive environment where black evangelicals, regardless of background or training or denominational affiliation, could know acceptance, share frustrations, and collaborate with fellow clergy, as well as lay persons, in designing ministries appropriate for urban black communities. What emerged was a corollary purpose, namely, the definition and implementation of a holistic ministry inclusive of social concerns as well as spiritual affairs. From the perspective of its founders, to "be in Christ" also meant to be "in fellowship with one another"; "evangelism" came to mean "commitment to God and to community."[12]

NBEA had its origins in a group in Los Angeles called the Evangelical Action Committee. In 1963 the Committee convened a leadership conference of black evangelicals out of which came the National Negro Evangelical Association (NNEA), which was incorporated in California in 1964 and again in New York a few years later.

The founders of NNEA included William Bentley (United Pentecostal Council of the Assemblies of God, Inc.), Aaron Hamlin (Evangelical Friends), Marvin Prentis (Presbyterian), Dessie Webster (National Baptist), Charles Williams (Christian and Missionary Alliance), Bishop William Holman (Church of Christ Holiness), Theodore Banks (United Holy Church of America), Ralph Bell (Christian and Missionary Alliance), Jeremiah Rowe (United Brethren), Ruth Lewis Bentley (InterVarsity Christian Fellowship), Walter Whittingham (Harlem Evangelistic Association), and Tom Skinner (Harlem Evangelistic Association).[13] Their motivations were threefold: (1) a desire to embrace their own heritage and express themselves as blacks so far as music and worship styles were concerned; (2) a commitment to address the needs of the black community; and (3) a perceived responsibility to challenge white evangelical institutions to respond to the black community by appointing blacks as teachers and administrators and by supporting the ministries of black graduates of their schools.[14] The official objectives as they were later defined were "to promote and undergird a dynamic Christian witness among Afro-Americans and to help all evangelicals to find involvement with vital

social issues."[15] By that black evangelicals had in mind not the issues
of drinking, dancing, smoking, and pornography that preoccupied
white evangelicals, but such matters as hunger, poverty, and racism.[16]

Not all the evangelicals who came into the Association shared the
progressive views of the founders, however. For the first five years
the conservative end of the membership spectrum dominated. As the
1960s progressed, some of the members — led by Dr. Bentley — became increasingly adamant in advancing a pro-black stance. Others
in these years declared the notions of black power and black pride
to be anathema. In 1968 the radical wing gained power, and tensions
were intensified accordingly. In 1973, at their tenth anniversary convention, the organization's name was changed to the National Black
Evangelical Association, but the change came only after years of internal dissension regarding the theological legitimacy of the concept
of black ethnicity. Before the change was accomplished, NBEA experienced an exodus of many of its conservative and radical members,
although most of those individuals ultimately returned.[17] Black activism, black theology, and black power provided fodder for ongoing
conflict throughout the 1970s and into the 1980s, however, as black
evangelicals engaged in a perpetual consciousness raising process.
Even in the 1990s not all the divisiveness of the earlier years has been
healed.[18]

The traditional integrationist and radical separatist extremes had
moderated significantly by the early 1990s, however, although enough
advocates of each view remained to hold the continuum intact — a
circumstance that in part defined the uniqueness and the strength
of NBEA. One of their more notable self-ascribed achievements was
the creation of "unity in diversity without enforced conformity."[19] A
point of near consensus for NBEA members became the rejection of
a conventional understanding of integration, but with an openness to
cross-cultural and cross-ideological relations. Thus, just as NBEA in-
ternalized a model of pluralism in the organization itself, so it leaned
toward a pluralistic model in its view of society at large. In 1988
Dr. Bentley articulated his understanding of NBEA in this fashion:

> Changing the times by changing ourselves...means making a
> major contribution to the dynamic development of our own in-
> dividual and group identity. And it means using that group
> unity as a viable bargaining instrument in persuading the larger,
> controlling community to address the basic issues that relate to a

truly open society. In so doing, we will be fellow-travelers with every other ethnic group as it faced the issues of a truly open society, for American political and cultural history has shown that the individual enters the open society in direct proportion to the prestige and political power of the group that he is a part of. NBEA recognizes that until black people, as a group, come to terms with this, and begin to seriously address itself to the intra-group unitive forces which lead to a healthy group self-concept, it will always have to discuss progress in terms solely of favored individuals....

... Dedication to the carrying out of the dictates of the gospel, with priorities centered on a specific group, need not be divisive of the unity of the One Body! Two truths must be clearly and simultaneously held in mind: One, that restriction to a specific group must be recognized as valid, and two, that the alternative truth of the universality of the body must be maintained with equal force. The prioritizing of one part does not in any manner deny nor detract from the universality of the whole. We unconditionally, therefore, accept the fact that God may well work in a particularizing situation, but at all times His unerring and unswervable purpose is the salvation of all parts of mankind.[20]

The struggle of NBEA had a parallel in the later years of the civil rights movement in that it involved not only embracing blackness, but disengaging from whites. Approximately one-third of the founding membership consisted of whites who had responded to the invitation extended to "those within the white community who were thought to possess genuine interest in the evangelization of the Black community." Many of those individuals left at the height of the black consciousness movement, but a few remained and were subsequently joined by other whites — some no doubt affiliating for symbolic purposes, but others, who were "re-thinking their own white ethnic identity," because they were genuinely committed to NBEA's concept of holistic ministry.[21] At no time were there more than two whites on the board of directors, however, so that leadership was always vested in black members. The larger dilemma was NBEA's dependency on funding from white evangelical agencies such as Campus Crusade, the National Association of Evangelicals, and World Vision, which then sought to control NBEA's positions and programs.[22]

At its peak, around 1980, NBEA's budget was approximately $60,000; by the end of the decade it had dropped to under $40,000. In addition to the white agencies, NBEA received revenues from membership fees, individual churches, small foundations, and general gifts and contributions. The largest benefactor was Evangelical Friends, which, over the years, through local yearly meetings, contributed more than $100,000; the most unlikely contribution came from the National Council of Churches, which for two years provided free office space in New York City. In the early 1990s NBEA affiliated with World Relief, which became an additional source of support.

For a number of years NBEA's office was housed in a private home and moved with the president. The first staff person, Aaron Hamlin, began as the field director in 1968, at which time NBEA also had a volunteer executive secretary. In the early 1970s the two positions were combined and Hamlin became the executive director; he has remained the mainstay of the organization as of the mid-1990s. From 1967 to 1981, NBEA maintained an office in Atlanta, which Hamlin staffed on a full-time basis. Subsequently, the office was moved to Portland, Oregon, and until mid-1993 was housed in the church Hamlin pastored while he served one-third time with NBEA. At that time, Hamlin again became the full-time executive director.

In the early 1990s NBEA had some five hundred members and maintained a mailing list of four thousand individuals. Approximately half of the members were clergy and half laity; one-third were women; one-third were white. Day-to-day administration of the organization was the responsibility of the executive director and executive board. The full twenty-five-member board — the majority of whom were ministers — made major policy decisions, with substantial input from members. Generally, four to six members of the board were women, and one or two white (see Appendix II).

NBEA's commissions — which included Theology, Social Action, Family, Development, Evangelism, Missions, Education, Communications, Women, and Youth — functioned primarily at the annual conventions as workshops. Assistance was then provided for replicating the content of the various workshops in local churches. The national convention also provided a forum for sharing involvements in social concerns, thereby encouraging social outreach at the congregational level. Attendance at the conventions in the 1990s has varied from six hundred to a thousand after dipping to the four hundreds in the 1980s. Local congregants who attend the national conventions

Table 5.1. NBEA Conventions

1963	Founding Conference, Los Angeles	1979	Atlanta
1964	Baltimore	1980	Dallas
1965	Detroit	1981	Chicago
1966	Cleveland	1982	Kansas City, Mo.
1967	Philadelphia	1983	Atlanta
1968	Chicago	1984	Atlanta
1969	Atlanta	1985	Kansas City, Mo.
1970	New York	1986	Philadelphia
1971	Los Angeles	1987	Philadelphia
1972	Jackson	1988	Pasadena
1973	Pittsburgh	1989	Dallas
1974	Dallas	1990	Chicago
1975	New York	1991	Portland, Ore.
1976	Chicago	1992	Detroit
1977	San Francisco	1993	Jackson
1978	Atlanta	1994	Memphis

From William H. Bentley, *National Black Evangelical Association: Evolution of a Concept of Ministry*, rev. ed. (Chicago: Wm. H. Bentley, 1979), Appendix, 146.

generally come with either a traditional evangelical orientation or a primary focus on social matters; NBEA, through this forum, seeks to bring the two perspectives together (Table 5.1).

NBEA's Twenty-fifth Anniversary Conference was held in Pasadena, California, in 1988 while the thirtieth was observed in 1993 in Jackson, Mississippi. Both events served to stoke NBEA's hopes of once again establishing a national office with a full-time staff to support the ministries of black evangelicals nationwide. A major thrust in the 1990s has been fund raising efforts to develop a regional structure, a plan designed both to reduce the cost of attending national conventions — which would be held every other year rather than annually — and to increase the level of participation through regional conventions. Expansion of local chapters also is planned, with chapters already operative in Dallas, Chicago, Portland, Philadelphia, San Francisco, and Jackson.

The local chapters have total autonomy in designing their respective programs and accordingly reflect the diversity of views and values within the national membership. Certainly evangelism remains a priority. Their common goal, however, is to assume "total responsibility for the community's needs" — a prominent NBEA theme. Thus, social concerns addressed by the chapters, as well as local churches, encompass such matters as homelessness, low income housing, unemployment, status of black men, single parents, hunger, and electoral politics. In the early 1990s health issues such as drug abuse were added to the agenda both nationally and locally, although the AIDS epidemic received only nominal attention.

The national body continued to systematically foster the concept of holistic ministry and assigned high priority to training and leadership development for such ministries at the local level. Closely related was the networking activity in which NBEA engaged in an effort to integrate the full range of resources within the African American community into indigenous urban ministries. Over the years NBEA also spun off separate entities with specialized functions, such as the National Black Christian Students Conference, the National Association of Christian Communicators, and United Gospel Outreach, the last an organization based in Los Angeles whose activities included a bookstore, counseling services, and feeding program.[23]

Significantly, little NBEA energy was invested in issues that were at the core of conservative white evangelical concern, e.g., abortion, homosexuality, and the role of women. That did not mean that the personal positions of NBEA members were significantly different from conservative white evangelicals, particularly on the issues of abortion and homosexuality — only that corporate social issues took precedence for the organization. On the issue of the role of women, the membership was more divided, with many being fully supportive of women's ordination and leadership. As noted, two of the original founders were women, and women served on the board of directors from the early years on. Women also held key offices — except for president and board chair. But while the trend was in the direction of being more affirming in the 1990s, much of the membership still objected to women in those positions. In contrast, in the late 1980s and into the 1990s, NBEA made racism in white evangelical churches and organizations a priority item for action. Joint consultations of the social action committees of NBEA and the National Association of Evangelicals were held in 1989 and 1990, resulting in a resolution on racism that both bodies subsequently adopted. In 1991 NBEA initiated an ongoing program of bringing black and white congregations together through what were termed "Reconciliation Sundays." Economic philosophy, on the other hand, was not a part of the NBEA conversation; nor did NBEA programs evidence

Table 5.2. NBEA Presidents and Chairs

	President	Board Chair
1963	Rev. Marvin Prentis	Rev. Marvin Prentis
1964–66	"	Dr. Howard Jones
1966–68	Dr. Howard Jones	Rev. Charles Williams
1968–70	Rev. George Perry	"
1970–72	Rev. Dr. Wm. Bentley	Rev. Tom Skinner
1972–74	"	Rev. Mel Banks
1974–76	"	Rev. Willie Jemison
1976–78	Dr. Ruben Conner	Rev. Dr. Wm. Bentley
1978–80	"	"
1980–82	Rev. Benjamin Johnson	"
1982–84	"	Rev. Eddie Lane
1984–86	Rev. Eddie Lane	Rev. Clarence Hilliard
1986–89	"	"
1989–91	Bishop George McKinney	Rev. Eddie Lane
1991–93	Rev. Lloyd Lindo	"
1993–	"	"

any critique of capitalism and its relationship to the economic status of African Americans.[24]

In one sense, by the 1990s NBEA had come full circle from where it started. While the original participants were products of white evangelical colleges and were affiliated predominantly with independent, Bible, and small Holiness and Pentecostal church groups, in the 1980s and 1990s more and more members came from the traditional black churches — Methodists, National Baptist Conventions, and Church of God in Christ. By and large, these were individuals with a well-developed social consciousness who also were among the more evangelical of their colleagues and who found in NBEA a blend that accommodated their need for a balance of social and spiritual concerns.[25] Indicative of this trend was the election in 1989 of George McKinney, a COGIC bishop, as president of NBEA (Table 5.2).

The creation of an atmosphere in which black evangelicals could depart from white traditions, embrace the black heritage, engage social concerns, *and* honor a tradition of spiritual expression — all this free from fear of dogmatic judgment and reprisal — remained NBEA's most basic function. Toward that end, the group designated "fellowship" as its highest priority — much as it was at the very beginning. Not least among NBEA's contributions was its role in raising the consciousness of individual white evangelicals and altering the employment profiles of white evangelical agencies and institutions.[26] NBEA's most important achievement, however, undoubtedly was its appropriation of "evangelicalism," producing, through redefinition and indigenization, a distinctly black evangelicalism that, in affirming the black religious tradition, allowed those black evangelicals who chose to do so to take their place as part of the Black Church.

Overall, NBEA's profile contrasts in significant ways with its ecumenical contemporaries:

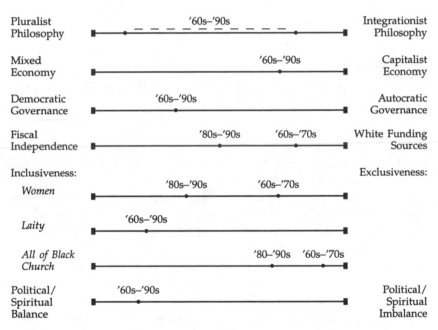

Pluralist Philosophy	'60s–'90s	Integrationist Philosophy
Mixed Economy	'60s–'90s	Capitalist Economy
Democratic Governance	'60s–'90s	Autocratic Governance
Fiscal Independence	'80s–'90s '60s–'70s	White Funding Sources
Inclusiveness: Women	'80s–'90s '60s–'70s	Exclusiveness:
Laity	'60s–'90s	
All of Black Church	'80–'90s '60s–'70s	
Political/ Spiritual Balance	'60s–'90s	Political/ Spiritual Imbalance

Certainly no group has been more determined or more faithful in pursuing its mission than NBEA. Some thirty years after its founding, the leaders of the organization remain undeterred, notwithstanding that the surface has scarcely been scratched in their outreach to and redirecting of black evangelical ministries. What will become of this tenacity when the executive director, Aaron Hamlin, is compelled to step down is a question of some moment. But if the organization succeeds in institutionalizing a regional structure and if the trend of affiliation by evangelicals from more mainstream black denominations continues, then the notion of another thirty years of "doing the Lord's work" seems a prospect undeserving of skepticism.

Black Theology Project

Among nonevangelicals, the black power phase of ecumenism found renewed expression in the 1970s in an effort known as the Black Theology Project (BTP). BTP defined itself as "an Afro-American Christian group devoted to the discovery, development, and promotion of historic and contemporary Black religious thought and action."[27] This self-description locates it somewhere between the academic formality of the Society for the Study of Black Religion (SSBR) and the political inclinations of the National Conference of Black Christians (NCBC). BTP, whose initial agenda was research and education,[28] functioned in the 1980s much as a national reflection group, exploring the relations between theology and the realities of life in the African diaspora. In the 1990s the organization has acted more as a network and clearing house for black theological activity occurring around the country and internationally.

NCBC was one progenitor of the Black Theology Project, but it had others as well. John Satterwhite, for example, traced its ancestry to the "Fellowship of Teachers of Religion in Black Colleges, Universities, and Theological Seminaries" which met in the 1940s. Headed by Benjamin Mays, the group included persons such as Harry Richardson, Frank Wilson, Carleton Lee, Stuart Nelson, and Howard Thurman. The Fellowship was responsible for founding the *Journal of Religious Thought* and the Institute of Religion at Howard University and served generally as a forum for exploring "the black experience, and how to incorporate it in living a theology."[29]

The most direct catalyst for the creation of BTP, however, was an endeavor called Theology in the Americas (TIA). TIA was the project of an exiled Chilean priest, Sergio Torres, who in 1975 was instrumental in the convening of a dialogue on liberation theology between Latin American and North American theologians. The conference, called "Theology in the Americas: 1975," was held in Detroit and attended by some two hundred delegates, approximately thirty of whom represented ethnic minorities in the United States. Angered at the presumptions and domination of white theologians, the minority delegation, led by Dr. James Cone, pressed for a restructuring of TIA in which the concerns of ethnic minorities would be more prominent in the organization's agenda. The result was the formation of several "affinity projects," which included the Black Theology Project, the Hispanic Project, the Asian American Project, the Indigenous

Peoples' Project, the Women's Project, the Church and Labor Dialogue, and the Alternative Theology Project — the last consisting of
white males.[30]

Even prior to the convening of TIA: '75, black theologians and
interested churchpersons in the New York area had begun holding
discussion sessions on the direction black theology should take. In the
words of AME minister Charles Spivey, there was "a ferment already
going on."[31] When the Projects were formally identified, TIA designated Muhammed Kenyatta, who earlier had been active in NCBC, to
provide staff support to BTP. Rev. Kenyatta, a Baptist, subsequently
became the executive director of the Project, and Shawn Copeland, a
Catholic sister, became the program director. In 1976 BTP began planning for a TIA-sponsored national black theology consultation on the
theme "Black Church and Black Community: Unity and Education
for Action." A meeting convened in New York in preparation for the
event brought together the TIA staff and members with the participants of the earlier discussions. Rev. Spivey was elected to chair the
meeting; he subsequently chaired the black theology consultation as
well, and then served as chair of BTP's board of directors until 1981.
In addition to the New York meeting, regional meetings were held
around the country and hundreds of local contacts made in an effort
to assure grassroots participation in the consultation.[32] "Atlanta '77,"
as it came to be called, was held at the Interdenominational Theological Center in August 1977; it proved to be the most eventful moment
of the Project's existence.

The ecumenical character of the consultation was never matched.
Among the two hundred and more participants were Protestants
and Catholics, Christian Nationalists and evangelicals, representatives from the historic black denominations as well as mainstream
white denominations, secular activists and radical Marxists. Writes
Gayraud Wilmore:

> Unlike any previous meeting since the Detroit IFCO conference
> in 1969, the Atlanta conference included not only the famil-
> iar church leaders and theologians, but the so-called "street
> people" and representatives of left-wing political organizations.
> It was less dominated by professional theologians and less con-
> cerned simply to react to what was or was not happening
> in the white churches. This meeting was more political and
> more international than any previous conference of either the

Black Churchmen's group or the Society for the Study of Black Religion.[33]

Out of the conference came the "Message to the Black Church and Community," which Wilmore characterized as "the most significant statement on Black Theology since 1969."[34]

> Black Theology is "God-talk" that reflects the black Christian experience of God's action and our grateful response. Black Theology understands the "good news" as freedom and Jesus Christ as the Liberator.
>
> Black Theology is formulated from our reading the Bible as we experience our suffering as a people. Black Theology moves between our church and our community: the church proclaims the message and the message reverberates back upon the church, enhanced by the religious consciousness of black people, including those who stand outside of the institutional church but are not beyond God's grace and His revelation. . . .
>
> In our day, the blackness of Jesus is a religious symbol of oppression and deliverance from oppression; of His struggle and victory over principalities, powers and wickedness in high places of this age.[35]

Wilmore also dates the beginning of the third stage of black theology from this conference, the first having been the initial development by radical, activist churchpersons in NCBC and the second the academic stage under the aegis of SSBR. The characteristics of the third stage, made manifest at Atlanta '77, included renewed criticism of the conservatism of the black denominations, criticism of the black middle class for its abandonment of urban ghettos, a stronger expression of alliance with African and other Third World peoples, the recognition of sexism as an aspect of oppression, and an explicitly Marxist critique of capitalism.[36]

> Exploitative, profit-oriented capitalism is a way of ordering life fundamentally alien to human value in general and to black humanity in particular. Racism and capitalism have set the stage for despoliation of natural and human resources all around the world. Yet those who seriously challenge these systems are often effectively silenced. We view racism as criminality and yet we are called the criminals. We view racism as a human aberration, yet we are called the freaks. The roots of our crisis are in

social, economic, media and political power systems that prevent us from managing the reality of our everyday lives.

It is this intolerable, alien order that has driven us to Atlanta seeking a word from the Lord out of the wellsprings of black theological tradition.[37]

Although its beginnings were auspicious, BTP sustained neither the grassroots flavor nor the radical posture. Younger members, as well as more women, were brought into the Project after 1980, but the membership as a whole shifted toward theologians, seminary professors, and clergy with "status" appointments in churches or denominational agencies. In short, it became more middle class and less daring — which undoubtedly reflected in part the overall mood of the times. The black theology movement generally has been criticized for its lack of connections to social transformation processes and for its failure to sustain a clear ideological posture with regard to political and economic analysis.[38] As critical as any factor for BTP, however, has been its organizational instability.

At the 1977 Atlanta Conference, BTP "formulated a detailed two-year follow-up agenda," which was to include "development and dissemination of televised and videotaped documentaries on Black theology; printed and electronic media materials for Christian education programs in local churches and for pastors' continuing education; an album recording liberation sermons and songs for popular audiences; and a one-day seminar package including a guest lecture supplemented by printed and audio-visual learning aids...[to] be made available to seminaries, regional church conferences, denominational assemblies and colleges."[39] A second national consultation was to be held in 1979 to evaluate the two-year follow-up. That consultation never materialized, for shortly after the 1977 meeting, BTP suffered a schism caused by differences between Kenyatta and the board of directors regarding purpose, structure, and lines of authority,[40] as well as by BTP's difficulty in paying its staff. Kenyatta and the largely Philadelphia-based faction that departed BTP with him were not reconciled with the Project until 1983.

Charles Spivey was succeeded as chair by UCC minister Yvonne Delk, who served from 1981 to 1982. Vaugn Eason, then a graduate student of Cone's at Union Theological Seminary — formerly executive director of the Philadelphia Council of Black Clergy — became executive director of BTP in 1978 and remained in that capacity until

Table 5.3. Chronology, Black Theology Project

	Chairs/Co-chairs	*Director/Coordinator*	*Meetings*
1976	Rev. Charles Spivey	Rev. Muhammed Kenyatta (Executive)	New York Planning
		Sr. Shawn Copeland (Program)	Meeting
1977	"	"	Atlanta
1978	"	Rev. Vaugn Eason	—
1979	"	"	—
1980	"	"	Detroit (T.I.A. II)
1981	Rev. Yvonne Delk	Dr. Cornel West	—
1982	Dr. Howard Dodson	Dr. Howard Dodson	—
1983	"	"	—
1984	Dr. Jualynne Dodson/ Rev. Gayraud Wilmore	Dr. Jualynne Dodson	Washington
1985	Rev. Olivia Pearl Stokes/ Dr. William Watley	"	"
1986	"	"	"
1987	Dr. William Watley/ Rev. Yvonne Delk	"	Atlanta
1988	"	"	—
1989	"	—	Newark, N.J.
1990	Rev. Yvonne Delk	Dr. Iva Carruthers	—
1991	"	"	—
1992	"	"	—
1993	"	"	—

1980. He was succeeded briefly by Cornel West. In 1982 Howard Dodson became the third chair of BTP and served simultaneously as staff director until 1984. At that time Jualynne Dodson and Gayraud Wilmore assumed the roles of co-chairs, and in 1985 William Watley and Olivia Pearl Stokes were elected to those offices. In 1987 Yvonne Delk again assumed office, serving as co-chair with Rev. Watley (Table 5.3). From 1984 through 1988, Jualynne Dodson functioned as the administrative coordinator in a volunteer capacity.[41]

BTP regrouped for the second TIA conference — known as Detroit II — held in 1980 and attended by six hundred delegates, half of whom were ethnic minorities.[42] BTP issued a second major theological statement at this conference, entitled, "Black Theology 1980: A Statement to the Theology in the Americas Conference in Detroit, Michigan." The 1980 statement reiterated many of the themes of the Atlanta '77 statement, but with even greater emphasis on the need

to eliminate sexism in the Black Church and classism in the larger
society. The latter was to be accomplished through "a system of production [that] will look something like a socialist configuration in
which there is class equality and a relative egalitarian distribution
of wealth." The 1980 statement also added a new dimension in its
emphasis on the black family — defined as "the center of black life
in Africa and in the western hemisphere" and therefore critical to
the "cultural revitalization of the black community."[43] In bringing the
black family into the reflection-action paradigm, BTP was instrumental among black ecumenical organizations in establishing the subject
as a legitimate part of the radical liberation endeavor, in the process appropriating it from the exclusive domain of conservative white
evangelicalism.

But in spite of the calls for action, for the two years preceding
and following Detroit II BTP functioned only marginally, with a few
members meeting on an ad hoc basis and acting in the name of the
Project. From 1981 to 1983 BTP functioned primarily as a participant
in the program of interethnic dialogue among African Americans,
Hispanics, Asians, and Native Americans, which was an outgrowth of
Detroit II.[44] Ultimately, the weakness of the other TIA affinity projects
caused BTP to withdraw from that wider ecumenism and concentrate
on the black churches. A revitalization of BTP occurred in 1984, with
the convening of an annual convocation in Washington, D.C., in cooperation with Howard University Divinity School, the remnants of
the National Conference of Black Christians, and the Congress of National Black Churches. Spurred by the continued setbacks occurring
under the Reagan administration and by the presidential candidacy
of Jesse Jackson, subsequent convocations addressing the social, economic, and political issues of concern to African Americans and to
other Third World populations were held in Washington in 1985 and
1986. During this time the Project also reached out to liberation theology efforts in Cuba and the Philippines. The tenth anniversary
conference returned to Atlanta in 1987.

Even after its revitalization, BTP continued to function on a largely
informal, ad hoc basis, with business being transacted by an executive committee. The first board meeting and elections in several years
were held in 1985, at which time its membership was estimated to be
130 persons; attendance at the annual convocation was around 100. In
1986 the Project moved toward strengthening its organizational structure by reducing the size and clarifying the membership of its board

of directors, electing officers to function as the executive committee and steering committee, adopting bylaws, and seeking incorporation as an entity independent of TIA.[45]

At that time, TIA, while still maintaining offices in New York City, was only marginally functional. BTP itself — whose records had been impounded by the National Council of Churches for nonpayment of rent — was operating from a post office box address in New York. Nevertheless, participants were hopeful of future growth, including more systematic cultivation of a constituency to participate in and support the Project, as well as decentralization — i.e., expansion beyond the persisting concentration in the New York area through development of a regional structure. Those efforts met with only marginal success and its Black Theology and Black Church Conference held in Newark, New Jersey, in 1989 was the Project's last national effort. By the early 1990s formal membership and governance structures had been largely abandoned in favor of an umbrella approach in which BTP acted as an advocate for the institutionalizing of black theology in other organizations around the country.[46] The office relocated to Chicago at the beginning of the decade, with Rev. Delk continuing as the chair and Dr. Iva Carruthers assuming responsibilities as executive director on a volunteer basis. Sustained by contributions from individuals and churches, the chair and a core group of BTP supporters continued to act in the name of BTP in various capacities.[47] (See Appendix II for additional organizational information).

In part, BTP has come to see the fulfillment of its mission in the emergence of theological reflection groups in local churches in major urban areas and in the incorporation of black theology courses in the curriculum of many seminaries and religious studies programs. Equally significant has been the renewal of participation in international theological dialogues that were first initiated by NCBC. In the 1990s BTP has been a presence at conferences in Latin America and Africa sponsored respectively by the Latin American Council of Churches and the All Africa Conference of Churches. In addition BTP has joined in a three-way African American–Caribbean dialogue, held in Cuba, that involves representatives from Canada, the United States, and the Caribbean. In these and other activities, the goals of BTP have continued to be pursued — not so much through the direct efforts of a centralized organization, but through the seeds planted by countless individuals who identify with and affirm the vision that BTP seeks to keep alive. Among the elements of that vision are these:

- To elevate Black theological dialogue within the academy and the Church as an on-going process of the Christian experience; To do so locally, nationally and internationally;

- To explain the nature and mission of the Black Church. The sources of this endeavor must be the contemporary Church community, as well as scripture, tradition, Black historical and cultural experience and revelation;

- To assess how the Black Church presently ties in beliefs and actions (praxis) in light of its nature and mission;

- To bring to light contemporary sociopolitical issues and the ultimate liberation and justice concerns of faith;

- To challenge the Black Church to engage in an on-going process of self-evaluation and transformation; and

- To contribute to the intellectual and political process of creating a theological vision and praxis of fundamental social transformation in the world society.[48]

Because of its erratic operation over the years of its existence, BTP is somewhat difficult to assess. In the 1980s the continued ecumenical character of the membership was apparent in the range of denominational affiliations, which included Baptist, Methodist, Presbyterian, United Church of Christ, Lutheran, Episcopalian, Disciples of Christ, and Catholic, as well as some Pentecostal groups and non-denominational churches. The scales were tipped, especially among the leadership, toward the predominantly white denominations, but traditional black denominations were represented as well. Women were less well represented, holding only seven out of forty seats on the national board of directors. The intentionality of ecumenism was evidenced, however, in BTP's revised self-definition: "We are an African American Ecumenical Christian organization, dedicated to the enhancement, growth and understanding of the theology and action for justice of the Black religious experience."[49]

Certainly BTP's relational philosophy remained pluralistic and its economic ideology open to a more socialist arrangement, although both were moderated over the years. For the most part, its administration continued to rest in the hands of a few people, but generally exceeded other organizations in the level of participation of women. If theology was its *raison d'être,* an intentional spiritual focus was scarcely manifest. A distinguishing feature of BTP, reminiscent of NCBC, was the level of participation of academicians, particularly seminary faculty and administrators.

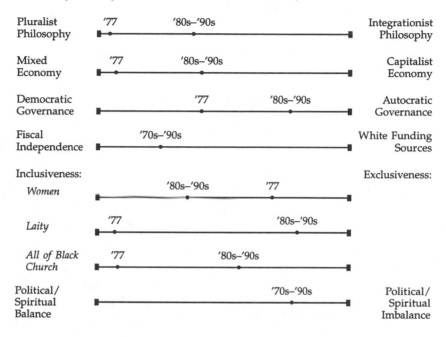

Summary

As the decade of the 1970s progressed, the echoed refrains of the civil rights and black power movements grew increasingly dim; the 1980s brought near total silence. Black ecumenism suffered accordingly. For a time, many local groups became inactive. NCBC shut down. NBEA faltered, regrouping as that decade came to a close. BTP struggled to keep the reflective endeavor alive. But even as the focused theological and protest phases of black ecumenism were waning, a new form of ecumenism had emerged. Partners in Ecumenism, founded in 1978, attended less to theological development and more to the task of enlisting black and white churches in actively addressing urban ills. The Congress of National Black Churches, Inc., organized the same year, also adopted as its intention the alleviating of urban community problems. With the emergence of these two organizations, the project of institution building became the new foreground of black ecumenism, while black theology took its place as the contextual background.

Chapter Six

THE ECUMENICAL DIALECTIC
Partners in Ecumenism

Context

The key social descriptor for the 1970s was "white backlash" — words that signified the reaction of middle America against not only the black freedom movement, but against the peace movement and the emergent women's movement as well. Symbolized in the reelection of Richard Nixon and actualized in the repressive tactics of federal and local law enforcement agencies, the white backlash succeeded in extinguishing much of the vitality of the radical social change movements that for a moment had threatened to undermine the power and authority of the white establishment. Not until the mid-1970s, however, did the far-reaching implications of this reversal for black America become apparent. Indeed, not until the Reagan years of the 1980s was the full scope of the reversal played out in sordid and excruciating detail.

The reactionary backlash fostered a withdrawal of white churches from involvement with black churches and the issues that concerned them. Finances and membership statistics too often took precedence over justice issues — justice, that is, for African Americans. The safer issues became ecology, hunger, and women's liberation. Black churches were thrust back upon their own resources. If they did not attend to the needs of the black community, who would? As had happened so often before when entry into American society as full partners was frustrated, African Americans resorted to strategies of self-containment and self-sufficiency. It was this climate and mood that in 1978 brought into being the independent Congress of National Black Churches (CNBC).

It is this climate and mood that make Partners in Ecumenism such a paradox. For in the same year that CNBC was born, Partners in Ecumenism emerged out of the very bowels of the National Council of Churches (NCC) and the local white ecumenical movement, declaring that it would settle for nothing less than full partnership. And to confirm the resoluteness of its purpose, the organization ensconced itself within the structures of NCC itself.

The unlikelihood of such an arrangement was attested by a telling summation of NCC's posture toward the social events of the 1960s and early 1970s, provided by the Council's own historian:

> No one can adequately describe the 1960s. The decade was the culmination of 100 years' neglect of basic social issues unresolved since the Civil War.... The crisis in the nation was not in our cities but in official Washington, state capitols, city halls and the minds of all those who would not face the issues that caused the problems and cause them still: racism, injustice, oppression and poverty.
>
> All institutions were challenged and were caught up in this, including the National Council of Churches. Sometimes the NCC was courageous and useful.... Other times it was not.... There was a tremendous loyalty from the member churches throughout this period. It went roughly through three phases:
>
> 1. In the early 1960s there was a committed enthusiasm for social change directed mainly at eliminating poverty, racism and oppression.
>
> 2. By 1966 there was a growing resentment in the churches against minority use of confrontation which was finally and most dramatically symbolized by the Black Manifesto's demands for "reparation" ... for the violence of racism perpetrated against the black community for so long.
>
> 3. Following 1969 there was a period of readjustment, consolidation, retreat, fence-mending, reorganization.[1]

It was in the discomforting atmosphere intimated in this account of the last phase that this audacious new black ecumenical movement came into existence. The organization's very name was as if to say: "Notwithstanding NCC's failure to effect the integration that was the dream of the Fraternal Council; notwithstanding NCC's failure to honor the pluralist alternative proposed by NCBC — let us try being partners; let us make one last effort to work together in a spirit of mutual respect and common cause." Partners in Ecumenism — or PIE, as it was known — was very much a product of the conciliar movement and was unique among black ecumenical organizations in actually being located within a white ecumenical body. It nevertheless claimed the same hopes and aspirations as its predecessors: that the white ecumenical movement would respond to black concerns and that the Black Church would be accorded a place in the universal Church as a full and equal "partner."

Origins

The first president of PIE was the Rev. George Lucas, long-time executive secretary of the Fraternal Council of Negro Churches who, as early as 1969, in proposing a merger of the Fraternal Council and the National Conference of Black Christians (NCBC), had expressed his discontent with NCC. Colleagues recall Rev. Lucas remarking at the time he became president of PIE on the irony, nearly thirty years after his service began with the Fraternal Council, of the necessity of forming yet another organization to pressure the National Council to take black churches more seriously. His career, Lucas felt, had come full circle.[2]

Members of the Fraternal Council had entered into NCC in the early 1950s expecting to be received as equals. Instead, they found themselves submerged in a white-controlled organization where decision making, program planning, and resource allocation were anything but participatory. While the dissatisfactions with NCC were multiple, an irritating symbol of NCC's disinclination to fully incorporate the agenda of the black churches into its own agenda was provided by the failure to elect a president from a black denomination. A black president was elected in 1972, and a second in 1978 — the year of PIE's official formation — but both came from predominantly white denominations. Their election thus failed to assuage the feelings of representatives of the black denominations that they were not counted as full members and participants.[3]

In spite of the years of disappointment and disillusionment and even in the face of NCC's inability to respond to the critique provided by NCBC, there were persons within NCC unwilling to relinquish the vision of an ecumenical movement embracing both blacks and whites. Accordingly, rather than soliciting resources from the white churches that black churchpersons would then control, PIE sought to enter into a configuration of partnership. Its strategy was neither assimilation nor separation, but a pluralistic and coalition approach from within the church establishment.

The boundaries of PIE's involvement were not confined to NCC, however. In fact, the impetus for creating PIE came from the local level of the conciliar movement, which was also the primary focus of PIE's program. Throughout the United States there exist some seven hundred state and local councils of churches and community ministries, approximately half of which are staffed to some degree and all of which are completely independent of the National Council. Memberships of the state councils usually consist of judicatories: synods, presbyteries, dioceses, etc. Local councils are more often congregationally based. Most of the councils engage in some form of social ministry: legislative programs, chaplaincies to hospitals and prisons, public information, or programs addressing hunger, poverty, migrant workers, and the like. Thus, in theory at least, the councils provided a point of access to white churches at the local level for purposes of enlisting their involvement in issues of concern to the black community.

Staff members of the various councils and ecumenical agencies are affiliated with one another through an organization called the National Association of Ecumenical Staff (NAES), which in the 1970s and 1980s received support from an office of NCC called the Commission on Regional and Local Ecumenism, or CORLE.[4] In the early 1970s, the black caucus within NAES called for a program to increase the involvement of both black and white churches in local ecumenical bodies and to direct their attention to the problems of the cities.[5] At the same time, members of NAES had been complaining among themselves that they were generally excluded from leadership positions both in local councils and in NCC — in short, that they were not treated as "partners."[6] In 1974 the first black president of NCC, the Rev. Sterling Cary, gave the keynote address at the Annual NAES Conference, using the occasion to criticize the retreat of the white churches from civil rights involvement.[7] Inspired by Cary's speech, a small group of persons within NAES took steps to create a "Partners" project. Among the group were the Rev. Maynard Catchings and the Rev. Lucius Walker, both of whom were members of NCBC;

the Rev. Horace Mays, director of the Southern California Council of Churches; and the Rev. Donald Jacobs, director of the Greater Cleveland Interchurch Council.[8] In addition Rev. Jacobs was secretary of NAES from 1974 to 1976. Also involved in the early discussions were the Rev. Joan Campbell, then associate director of the Greater Cleveland Interchurch Council, who subsequently became president of NAES, and Rev. Lucas. Sterling Cary, however, is regarded as the "father" of PIE.[9]

The original plan was for the proposed project to be located in the CORLE office with a full-time paid director. When funds were not forthcoming, an agreement was reached with the general secretary of NCC, Claire Randall, to assign Rev. Catchings, then Randall's Special Assistant for Interpretive Relations, to CORLE to work half-time on the Partners Project. The agreement between the general secretary and Catchings stipulated the following activities:

1. To explore with local ecumenical bodies ways by which Black churches and denominations in their area may become more fully involved in ecumenical life and work.

2. To work with Black churches to stimulate greater understanding and involvement in the ecumenical movement.

3. To find ways that Black churches working ecumenically can link with community programs in their area toward greater service to the needs of people around them.

4. To find the ways by which Black ecumenical life can be fully related to the total ecumenical efforts in a given community.

   It is understood that members of NAES will constitute a small advisory group to work with this project.[10]

With this mandate, Catchings initiated a two-year schedule of visitations to local communities, meeting with state and local councils and church bodies to advocate the "ecumenical imperative."[11] In time NCC's Governing Board formally accepted sponsorship of the project, the name "Partners in Ecumenism" was adopted, and the program was officially located under CORLE. In the meantime, from 1975 to 1978, the formulators of the project continued to hold discussions at NAES meetings and to press NAES members to employ more African Americans in local ecumenical agencies. Black chief executives of state and local councils did increase from two to eight, but then subsequently declined in number once again.

Organization and Development

The first public event of PIE, marking the beginning of its systematic program, was a conference held in May 1978, which is regarded as PIE's official founding date.[12] In the same year, PIE began to develop an organizational structure. Rev. Campbell was named national coordinator of PIE in 1978 and held that title until 1980. Meanwhile, in 1979 she became the assistant general secretary of NCC for CORLE.[13] Also in 1978, Rev. Jacobs was named national director of PIE, although he functioned on a part-time basis for several years while continuing to direct the Cleveland Council. The PIE office moved from Cleveland to New York in 1983, at which time Jacobs assumed full-time responsibilities as director.[14] In 1986 he returned to a part-time basis while also pastoring an AME church in Ohio.[15] Also that year, the Rev. Henry Carnes joined the staff as program coordinator on a two-thirds time basis. Rev. Carnes served as the national director for a brief time in 1987 before leaving PIE; Rev. Jacobs became director emeritus that year. After 1987 PIE no longer had a paid staff, and by 1990, for all practical purposes, had ceased to function.

The initial "advisory group" that was to work with PIE ultimately became the steering committee. According to Campbell, George Lucas was asked to become the first president of PIE in 1978. Lucas, Jacobs, and Campbell then designated the initial members of the steering committee. Subsequently, new members of the committee were selected through its nominating committee, who were then affirmed by the general membership.[16] The first annual meeting of the "National Board," as the committee was called, was held March 11–14, 1979, in Washington, D.C., at which time Lucas was formally elected president.[17] Rev. Lucas, a member of NBC, USA, Inc., remained as president of the committee until 1981. He was succeeded by AME Bishop Frank Madison Reid, Jr., who served from 1981 to 1984. The third president, elected in 1984, was the Rev. M. Lorenzo Shepard. Rev. Shepard was succeeded by the Rev. Jewett Walker, who remained in office until 1990 (Table 6.1).

The steering committee of PIE had significant representation by women, including, from 1984 to 1986, the vice president at large

Table 6.1. Chronology, Partners in Ecumenism

	President	Director/Coordinator	Conference
1976–77	—	Rev. Maynard Catchings	—
1978	Rev. George Lucas	Rev. Donald Jacobs (Director)	Cleveland
		Rev. Joan Campbell (Coordinator)	
1979	"	"	—
1980	"	Rev. Donald Jacobs	Washington
1981	Bishop Frank M. Reid, Jr.	"	"
1982	"	"	"
1983	"	"	"
1984	"	"	"
1985	Rev. M. Lorenzo Shepard	"	—
1986	"	"	Cleveland
1987	Rev. Jewett Walker	Rev. Henry Carnes	Atlanta
1988	"	—	
1989	"	—	Washington
1990	"	—	—

for national program, one of six regional vice presidents, one of six regional representatives, and four of twenty-two at-large members. The committee consisted almost entirely of clergy, however, with little lay representation. Furthermore, as it happened, PIE's elected officers always came from the historic black denominations (Table 6.2). (See Appendix II for additional information on the structure of PIE.)

The May 1978 conference, held in Cleveland, had as its theme "Urban Crisis and Black Survival." At that time, the movement presented itself as "a grassroots program of the National Council of Churches of Christ and the National Association of Ecumenical Staff." A 1979 fact sheet described PIE as "an attempt to strengthen the role of the Black Church in addressing *today's crisis facing Black America*. PIE strives to unite black congregations at a local level with one another and, through local ecumenical bodies, with white churches."[18] The word "partnership" clearly assumed multiple meanings as PIE adopted an agenda of (1) interdenominational action among black churches at the local level, as well as (2) increasing the involvement of blacks both individually and as a body in white ecumenical agencies at the local and national levels, in order that (3) the programs and resources of those agencies could be effectively brought to bear on the living conditions of urban blacks.

Table 6.2. PIE Steering Committee, 1984–86

President	Rev. M. Lorenzo Shepard	(PNBC)
Vice President at large for National Program	Ms. Allie Weeden, Esq.	(PC USA)
Vice President at large for Regional Organization	Bishop Cecil Bishop	(AMEZ)

Regional Vice Presidents and Representatives

Southeast	Rev. Jewett Walker	(AMEZ)
	Rev. Mary Bellinger	(AME)
South Central	Rev. Doyle Allen	(UM)
	Rev. Clyde Carroll	(NBC)
Southwest	Rev. Cecil L. Murray	(AME)
	Rev. Algae Rousseau	(Disciples)
Northwest	Rev. William G. Mitchell	(CME)
	Rev. Edsel Goldson	(UM)
Midwest	Ms. Rebecca Redman	(Episcopal)
	Rev. Otis Moss	(PNBC)
Northeast	Rev. Melvin A. Hoover	(UU)
	Mr. Henry Carnes II	(Friends)

Secretary	Rev. Landrum Shields	(PC USA)
Treasurer	Rev. Henry C. Gregory III	(NBC)
Immediate Past President	Bishop Frank Madison Reid, Jr.	(AME)

At-large Members

Dr. Charles Adams	Christian Methodist Episcopal
Rev. Georgia Allen	United Methodist
Dr. Barbara King-Blake	Independent
Rev. Raymond Campbell	Christian Methodist Episcopal
Rev. Ellis H. Casson	African Methodist Episcopal
Rev. Arthur Renfro Crowell	United Methodist
Rev. William W. Easley	African Methodist Episcopal
Rev. Ernest R. Gibson	National Baptist
Ms. E. Terry Hamilton	Roman Catholic
Rev. William Hannah	Christian Church (Disciples of Christ)
Bishop J. Neaul Haynes	Church of God in Christ
Mr. Herbert A. Johnson	Roman Catholic
Rev. Thomas Kilgore	Progressive & American Baptist
Rev. Adam Kittrell	American Baptist
Rev. Archie LeMone	Progressive Baptist
Dr. Pearl McNeil	American Baptist
Rev. K. L. Moore	National Baptist
Rev. Lonnie Simon	Progressive National Baptist
Rev. Maxie Turner	National Baptist
Dr. William D. Watley	African Methodist Episcopal
Rev. Jeanne B. Williams	African Methodist Episcopal
Rev. Randall Jelks	Presbyterian Church (USA)

The initial step in implementing this agenda was the building of a national network, and the means for constructing the network was a series of regional conferences, held over a period of two years, for which the Cleveland conference served as a model. Stated PIE's literature at the time: "PIE is a grassroots program being developed through a series of regional conferences. Participants in these regional conferences identify key problems for black Americans, especially those in the inner cities. Its goal is to build a network of key black church persons across the nation who, through concentrated cooperative action, will address the social problems of this country through the political process."[19]

The success of these conferences — in Durham, North Carolina, in March 1979; Columbus, Ohio, in June 1979; Los Angeles in September 1979; Philadelphia in January 1980; and Dallas in February 1980 — encouraged PIE participants in their intentions to develop permanent regional structures with local chapters and full-time staff. Local support for such an undertaking was high, particularly in half-a-dozen areas identified by PIE as "urban clusters" — Philadelphia, New York, Cleveland/Columbus, Houston/Dallas, Los Angeles, and Seattle — but lack of resources and staff to provide follow-through from the national office precluded implementation of the regional design. By 1985 PIE's network, which at one time had reached a peak of six thousand individuals, had declined to some two thousand. Despite these setbacks, PIE continued to work toward its objectives, engaging in other types of program activity consonant with its purpose.

The movement's statements of purpose underwent modest change from time to time. In 1982, for example, its objectives included development of "an action agenda in the urban communities of the United States that focuses ecumenical energies and resources on the elimination of racism [and on achieving] economic justice and the empowerment of minorities."[20] In 1985 PIE described itself as "a movement of Black Church leaders, clergy and lay, cooperating across denominational lines to inspire, inform and organize us so that we can provide viable solutions for the problems caused by racism, sexism, and classism."[21] But if the official language was modified to encompass issues of class and gender, the pragmatic activities continued to address the initial and fundamental concerns of networking, political action, and partnership.

The first national conference of PIE was held in September 1980 in Washington, D.C. Annual meetings were held in the same city and the same month through 1986, except in 1983 when priority was once again given to regional conferences. Two such conferences were held that year, one in Greenville, South Carolina, and one in Dallas, with over a hundred participants at each. Attendance at the early national conferences was around four hundred, but from 1984 to 1985 it was closer to two hundred, a decline attributed to restricted finances and reduced communication from the national office. In 1987 the national conference was held in Atlanta and then returned in 1989 to Washington for what proved to be its final national meeting.

In addition to tending to organizational matters, the conferences provided an occasion for assessing the status of black Americans, sharing information and resources, and addressing current national and international issues. Concerns addressed at the 1987 conference, for example, included economic development, education, drug and alcohol abuse, needs of the black family, and teenage sexuality. Workshops were also held on regional development, and time was set aside for worship and Bible study.

Delegates to the conferences came from fifteen to twenty different denominations and from some thirty states. In the mid-1980s, they were about evenly divided between black denominations and predominantly white denominations, a shift from the early years when three-fourths of the conference participants came from the historic black denominations. PIE made a concerted effort to include the laity, resulting in close to 25 percent of the participants being laypersons, which Jacobs counted as the "most enthusiastic contingent." That emphasis also accounted for a higher participation rate of women — some 20 percent — than has characterized most black ecumenical movements. A number of women participants were ministers. In fact, PIE maintained a national list of five hundred women who were pastoring black churches. A few whites attended PIE conferences, most of them representing church agencies, and in 1985 a proposal — albeit short-lived — was put forth to begin including Hispanics in the "partnership" plan. For the most part, however, PIE conferences remained noteworthy for the fact that they constituted the sole forum in which African Americans from both black and white denominations who were committed to ecumenical action and who were still willing to explore cooperative interracial efforts could come together with like-minded individuals. Overwhelmingly, they were not the bishops, denominational officers, or pastors of the more prestigious churches, but representatives of grassroots churches, ministerial alliances, and local councils of churches who had an interest in social ministry.[22]

PIE also maintained communications with its locally based network through a semi-annual newsletter, although NAES was the primary structure through which PIE disseminated information about its program and vision. Based on this information, some local and state councils of churches then initiated local "partnership" projects to bring black and white churchpersons together in dialogue. In turn, many African Americans who went to PIE meetings heard about the movement from local council members who attended NAES meetings.[23] Three local PIE chapters received impetus from such exchanges — one in Columbus, Ohio, which subsequently became inactive, and two others in Cleveland and Minneapolis.[24] A fourth chapter was formed in Atlanta in 1987.

Program

Through NAES channels PIE also encouraged collective political action on issues indigenous to local communities. Indeed, Jacobs described one of his long-range goals for the movement as "PIE chapters in regions all over America, working for political objectives, registering people to vote, and getting involved in local campaigns."[25] But the most significant political involvement of PIE took place during the annual conferences held in Washington, when "a day on the hill" was set aside for participants to visit Capitol Hill to meet with their representatives and lobby for legislation responsive to the social and economic needs of impoverished and oppressed populations. In this, PIE was reminiscent of the Washington Bureau, the lobbying arm of the Fraternal Council of Negro Churches.

In 1982, as part of the strategy for increasing black involvement and leadership in the ecumenical movement, PIE instituted an internship program in cooperation with the Interdenominational Theological Center in Atlanta.[26] Later expanded to include other schools, the Summer Intern Program each year placed up to fourteen black seminary students with local, state, national, and international ecumenical agencies for a period of ten weeks, in exchange for which the students received a stipend, transportation, and living expenses. Interns placed at the local level, in particular, were challenged to encourage cooperative action among black congregations and to increase involvement by black churches in the ecumenical movement, as well as to sensitize the predominantly white councils to the agenda of the black community. In the mid-1980s, due to limited funding, applications for the program exceeded by as much as four times the number of positions available.[27] In the latter part of the decade, sponsoring agencies were asked to cover the cost of placement. When PIE ceased funding the Intern Program, it was taken over by NCC and has continued to operate in the 1990s under the auspices of the office of Ecumenical Networks. In 1993 the program was renamed the Donald Jacobs Ecumenical Internship Program.

In a less formal fashion, PIE continued its "consciousness raising" activity toward the end of ecumenical partnership through NAES, steadily pressing the need for increased black representation in local agencies. By 1983 twenty-seven local and regional councils of churches were reported to have black presidents — a significant increase, but still less than 4 percent of all councils.[28] Progress in the numbers of executive staff was nil; in 1988 the members stood at seven.[29] Throughout the 1980s PIE staff provided technical assistance to more than a dozen state councils interested in increasing the involvement of black churches. PIE officials also noted increased participation by black denominations — particularly NBC, USA, Inc. — in NCC, and by African Americans in the WCC, after PIE was founded.[30] An ongoing activity of PIE was advocacy for increased representation of blacks on both NCC and WCC committees and commissions.

In 1984 PIE received a grant from the Ford Foundation to conduct a feasibility study for developing four pilot projects in urban neighborhoods for the delivery of human services "using black church clusters as the base and local ecumenical bodies as partners." The objective of the program was to "inject new life into ventures to which black churches have historically committed their resources" — i.e., "providing emergency clothing and food, day care, aid to senior citizens, voter registration, personal counseling, and after-school tutoring and recreation programs." The innovation of the proposed program was that it would "boost the efforts of these churches — which work largely alone and with limited resources — by building cooperation among black clergy and by finding new avenues of support for their work through local ecumenical agencies."[31] The pilot projects were never implemented, but the model remains one worthy of consideration as black churches address the issue of "urban crisis and black survival," which dominated the agenda of PIE's first meetings.

At the same time PIE sought to become more action oriented, it also incorporated a reflection component in its overall program. Beginning in 1984 the organization enlisted James Cone as a consultant to conduct a series of workshops on theology, the Black Church, and PIE's agenda. Jacobs himself forthrightly declared that "PIE is based on black theology; it is based on the gospel and teachings of Jesus Christ."[32] The intention of a dialectic of praxis and reflection was never brought to fruition, however, foundering instead on the shoals of financing. A renewed effort was made in 1987 to expand PIE's network: In cooperation with the African Desk of NCC and the Black Theology Project, PIE was represented at the Fifth Assembly of the All Africa Conference of Churches, and the National Conference of Black Seminarians was welcomed as an official affiliate of PIE. But a deficit incurred earlier in the decade severely hampered PIE's ability to endure, let alone expand.

PIE was a semi-autonomous organization at best. Program planning was largely the responsibility of the staff, and policy making the province of PIE's forty-member steering committee, which met twice a year and provided oversight between annual conferences. In addition to reporting to the steering committee, however, the director was accountable to the head of CORLE, which was administratively responsible for PIE. In 1986 CORLE and two other units of NCC — Faith and Order, and Justice and Liberation — were brought together in a new configuration called the "Cluster on Unity and Relationships and Office of Ecumenical Development." CORLE itself consisted of forty-six members, nine of whom represented black denominations, so that PIE was technically accountable to a white-controlled body of NCC. Further reorganization in 1989–90 replaced the Unity and Relationships unit with Ecumenical Networks, housed in the office of the general secretary.

From 1981 to 1985, PIE received $20,000 a year from NCC. For the remainder of the decade, NCC's Ecumenical Commitment Fund was PIE's major source of financial support. For three years PIE was awarded $10,000 annually from the WCC Programme to Combat Racism. Throughout the decade PIE received contributions from various denominations — mostly the larger white denominations, little from the historic black denominations — sometimes totalling $30,000 to $40,000 annually.[33] PIE also received $3,000 a year from NAES and was the recipient of support from some local councils of churches — e.g., the Minneapolis Council of Churches — for grassroots activities.

In addition local and state councils absorbed the costs for approximately one-third of the delegates attending the annual conferences.[34] The $50,000 grant awarded PIE in 1984 by the Ford Foundation resulted in a total budget that year of $110,000. Two years later, however, the budget had declined to approximately $85,000, and in 1989 was reduced to $27,000.[35]

Funding was a source of particular consternation for PIE because of its peculiar situation. Many black ecumenical movements have suffered because of their dependence on white funding sources; for the most part, these other movements sought to be independent and found that independence compromised by the fact of white agencies having control of the sources of funding. PIE, on the other hand, precisely because of its function and role as a "mediator" and "bridge-builder," logically qualified as the organization most appropriate to receive funds from both black and white sources. Unable to secure adequate resources or to cultivate ownership on the part of the historic black denominations,[36] the options for PIE ultimately became either to seek alternative sponsorship or to become completely independent. Although the latter option was viewed by many participants as a contradiction of PIE's very reason for being, in 1989, a few of PIE's more stalwart supporters did join in an attempt to initiate a new movement. Black Ecumenical Advocacy Ministries (BEAM) proposed to enlist congregational memberships in a national lobbying network to bring the influence of local churches across the nation to bear on policy issues affecting the black family and community. As the midpoint of the 1990s approached, the prognosis for BEAM remained uncertain.

NCC Relations

That there was room for improvement in relations between blacks and whites within NCC throughout the 1980s was hardly contestable. Evidence to that effect is to be found in reports such as this one on the November 1984 meeting of the Governing Board of NCC:

> The gathering erupted occasionally with the expression of internal tensions, some dealing with equality of lay/clergy and male/female representation, but even more frequently with racial difficulties that longtime participants described as new to Governing Board meetings. At several points black delegates

expressed displeasure with the racial balance of various committees and with the method of their membership selection.
In some cases the black delegates did not count among their
number the black representatives of "nonblack communions"
(i.e., churches other than, for instance, the African Methodist
Episcopal Church). Many participants expressed pain at these
developments, and seemed somewhat discouraged concerning
their resolution. It is matters such as this that will prove whether
the National Council is truly a community of communions. It
has demonstrated that it can creatively engage its external critics; but it must even more creatively address any divisiveness
within its own family.[37]

The National Council of Churches has been challenged more than
once to rectify the racial inequities that persist in society and church
alike. If the messages of the Fraternal Council, SCLC, and NCBC ultimately went unheeded, perhaps it will be argued they were too
distant, too strident, too oblique — too much in the wilderness. But
PIE was a voice in the establishment's very midst, and one scarcely
vulnerable to criticism on grounds of being either immoderate or
enigmatic. At the same time, the movement's ultimate intentions, expressed in the words of one of its presidents, might well have made
some uncomfortable and been construed by others as subversive.

Black churches are not an extra for the ecumenical movement,
not an afterthought. We are an essential element in making
whole the ecumenical movement.... The black church continues
to give strength and solace to black people, but it must be much
more. It must challenge all people, black and white, to serve
human need and to build partnership with those who would
walk beside the black churches in the historic striving to end
oppression.
   Both white and black churches must take initiative in building the partnership. There has been a history of hesitancy on
both sides that has created distrust and even disinterest....
Partnership between those who too often see each other as oppressed and oppressor does not come easily, and it will not
happen unless it is someone's job to broker and nourish that
partnership. PIE is in place to be such an instrument. Let us
utilize and support it.[38]

Ultimately, Bishop Reid's plea went unheeded. When NCC's reorganization was completed in 1990, PIE was nowhere to be found. Not that NCC was unchanged by PIE's decade-long presence: both in consciousness and in program emphases, most notably through NCC's Prophetic Justice unit, the spirit of PIE continued to exert itself. And the intent of PIE was partially actualized in local ecumenical councils, where cooperative efforts between black and white churches, if not the norm, were also not uncommon. But the holistic program of PIE, presented futilely to NCC as a proposal for survival, languished. It bears preserving, however, both as a summary of PIE's endeavors and as a creative plan of action.

PARTNERS IN .ECUMENISM
PROPOSAL

In order for the ecumenical movement to begin to rectify the current status of too few Blacks involved in the broad stream of ecumenism, PIE proposes a strong creative program designed to constructively engage the Historic Black Churches and other NCC member churches in working together. It also proposes to link human and technical resources to strengthen and empower the NCC, the Black Church, as well as Black constituents in predominantly White denominations, and to address and work toward resolving problems that impact the Black community. PIE will enunciate from its own cultural milieu NCC's policy formulations and projections.

The National PIE program will function in the role of a facilitator rather than a service provider. As a facilitator, PIE will develop a network and link valuable resources from the Black religious community to the wider ecumenical movement. Its goals are:

A. To relate to denominational and ecumenical leaders at state, local, regional and national levels for program visibility and network development; to engage these leaders in support of the PIE program and PIE fund-base development.

B. To create a network of Black Church persons across the United States to build a membership base for PIE.

- to develop and share model program designs that have had a positive effect in major inner-city communities,

- to promote and develop ecumenical linkages among local congregations and within communities,

- to assist in the formulation of local and regional PIE Chapters.

C. To help facilitate internship programs for Black seminary students to gain experience in working relationship with ecumenical agencies by working cooperatively with the National Association of Ecumenical Staff for the placement of seminary students in effective internships.

D. To convene individual local and regional chapters and other supporters in a national conference every other year

- to focus on ecumenical cooperation

- to identify social problems and strategies

- to focus on economics and political issues

- to review program accomplishments

- to facilitate goal setting

- to build regional PIE support

E. To provide opportunities for theological reflection (within Black Churches) for both clergy and lay persons

F. To provide technical assistance in leadership and resource development for:

- the PIE membership

- clusters of Black Churches seeking funding from private and public sources for neighborhood/community improvement projects

- strategies of national and local empowerment for public policy formation.

Summary

For all their planning and meeting, PIE's leadership never succeeded in developing either a broad-based constituency or a broad base of support. Although it became more inclusive in membership, governance and decision making remained in the hands of a relative few. A clear political-economic philosophy was never articulated, which meant that PIE's lobbying efforts were by default mainstream. But in spite of its moderate political stance, the organization failed to engage the historic black denominations at an institutional level. In part this circumstance was no doubt attributable to the conception and development of the Congress of National Black Churches, Inc. — an organization that operated precisely as a cooperative body of the various denominations — during the very years that PIE was functioning. But another factor may have been involved as well.

PIE was unique in that it sought to function simultaneously at two levels of ecumenical activity — not just in theory, not as a projection of the future, but as a practical matter for the present day. First, PIE was intent on fostering self-determination — that is, on enhancing the power, resources, and self-sufficiency of the black particularity. But even as it was engaged at that level, it also sought to work cooperatively with the white particularity. Indeed, in the dialectic that was the vision of PIE, the purpose of the latter activity was to enable the former. Other organizations, as a practical matter, had emphasized one dimension more than the other, not both equally. As it happened, much of the white particularity that PIE sought to engage was no more able to grasp the concepts of particularity and pluralism than had been the case when those were the focus of the National Conference of Black Christians and the Black Theology Project. Consequently, neither could most members of the white particularity grasp the essence of the second level of activity — that it involved the equality of partnership and not the subordination of integration.

But it is no more clear that black churches fully grasped the dialectic that PIE so earnestly sought to set in motion. Or perhaps they did — and historical memory prevailed.

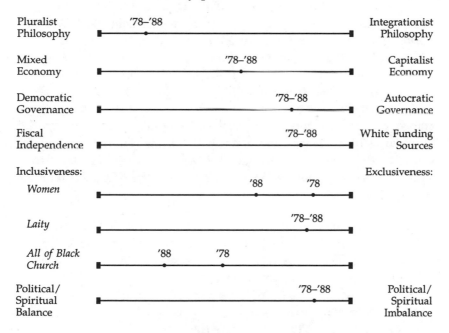

Chapter Seven

INSTITUTION BUILDING
The Congress of National Black Churches

Context

If SCLC's ecumenism engaged the southern grassroots churches, NCBC's the radical northern clergy, and NBEA's the border regions of the Black Church, the ecumenism of the Congress of National Black Churches, Inc. (CNBC), engages the Church establishment itself. In its conciliar arrangement, which seeks to bind the major black denominations in a federation for common action, CNBC is most nearly the "successor" to the Fraternal Council of Negro Churches.

The Congress and the Council are joined in other ways as well. Just as the Fraternal Council initially organized apart from the Federal Council of Churches, so the Congress has embraced a separatist stance, content to contain its conversation and program within the boundaries of the black church family. Even the rationale offered for CNBC by the organization's founder, AME Bishop John Hurst Adams, sounds an echo of his AME predecessor, Fraternal Council founder Bishop Reverdy C. Ransom.

> The one compelling thing which has over-arched [our differences in polity and doctrine] is the pain of black folk. The summons of the Congress has always been to address the needs of black people....Our purposes are really quite clear. We want to do together what we can't do separately, and what we want to do together that we can't do separately is empower black people so that they can be fully human in this world....

152

The true ecumenical development will have to take place at the level of the churches working together and doing together things to relieve the pain and misery of people, and to empower weak people, to heal sick people. The mission of the Church being done together will take place long before there is any true ecumenical understanding in the theological arena. And I think the missional ecumenism is much more important than the theological ecumenism.[1]

But for all the similarities, the Congress is not merely a replica of the Fraternal Council. For one thing, the Congress emerged on *this* side of the rhetoric of the civil rights and black power movements. Given neither to "state of the nation" pronouncements nor to theological flourishes, CNBC instead has set as its agenda nothing less than the mobilizing of resources and building of structures that will render African Americans finally free.

Origins

The first meeting of what was to presage the Congress of National Black Churches was held in Indianapolis in July 1978. Appropriately enough, the meeting began with a worship service. Dr. James Forbes, at that time professor of homiletics at Union Theological Seminary in New York City, was invited to preach the sermon. He chose as his theme "When God Says, 'Never Mind.'" The thrust of his message was that of the two biblical references for God's saying, "Never mind" — in the one instance meaning "forget it," and in the other, "never mind what others are doing" — those persons present should heed the second reference and act without regard for what the ecclesiastical hierarchy might say. "Never mind the history, never mind the divisions, never mind the obstacles. Those of us here at this meeting have a mission: to be a black ecumenical transforming force. And we should act on that mission, 'never minding' what others do or say."[2]

Dr. Forbes was undoubtedly mindful of the long tradition of denominationalism, of the repeated but futile attempts to achieve church union, and of the stumbling blocks encountered in previous cooperative efforts. Thus, his caution to those present that the task they were contemplating would not be easily accomplished. His words serve as a window through which to view that first exploratory meeting, providing a reminder that the Congress of National Black Churches began not as an endeavor to which the Black Church establishment was wholeheartedly committed, but as an improbable venture of a few convention-defying individuals. Bishop Cecil Bishop, Dr. Charles Butler, Rev. Wilbur N. Daniels, Rev. F. Benjamin Davis, Bishop Chester A. Kirkendoll, Bishop German Ross, Rev. Manual Scott, Rev. M. Lorenzo Shepard, Bishop Roy Winbush — these were among the early participants who, in bringing along their churches and their denominations, gave concreteness to an idea that would otherwise surely have been stillborn.

Not only did the Congress survive, but its base of support steadily expanded. Within the first six years of its existence, six of the seven largest historic black denominations had officially voted endorsement of the undertaking. Further, during this period, the Congress designed a bold plan of action that it presented with a persuasiveness that belied its modest beginnings.

Like other black ecumenical movements, the agenda of the Congress was neither structural merger nor doctrinal consensus, but cooperative mission. In contrast to most movements, it was not merely an alliance of individuals motivated by personal ideals, but a body of denominational representatives acting with ecclesiastical authority. CNBC's strategy, in the constant ecumenical quest for justice, was the long-range project of institution building, utilizing the resources — both human and fiscal — of the federated denominations. More than any of the other movements, the Congress represented a "settling in" of black consciousness to the pragmatic task of actualizing the rhetoric of empowerment. Its emphases have been economics more than politics, action more than reflection, social change more than scholarship, structural transformation more than moral persuasion, black communalism more than coalition building, the particularity of the black experience more than the unity of the universal Church. From the beginning its goal was the achievement of independence and self-sufficiency through collective endeavors initiated by the Black Church, but involving the whole of the African American community.

The process by which CNBC arrived at this definition of purpose involved three essential phases: (1) dialogue among black churchpersons and black religious scholars; (2) analysis based on interaction with national experts on social, political, and economic issues impinging on black Americans; and (3) program design and implementation.

The meeting that provided the occasion for Dr. Forbes's sermon — the First Consultation on Interdenominational Dialogue among Black Churches — marked the beginning of the first stage of the organization's life.

Stage One: Dialogue

The Interdenominational Dialogue came about initially through the convergence of fortuitous circumstances. In 1974 the Lilly Endowment, Inc., gained a new Vice President for Religion, Dr. Robert Lynn. Dr. Lynn had for several years had a professional relationship with scholars of the Black Church at Union Theological Seminary, where Dr. C. Eric Lincoln and Dr. Lawrence N. Jones were faculty colleagues.[3] As a result of that experience, Lynn was concerned to include black churches in the religious programs of the Endowment and called upon Lincoln and Jones to serve as consultants.[4] The interests of the Endowment were thereby aligned with the ongoing concern of black churchpersons for the devising of strategies to accomplish the mission of the church. Several such individuals were brought into the discussions as advisers and in December 1976 were invited to a meeting to explore ways in which the Endowment could be supportive of black church efforts. The meeting was convened by Ms. Jacqueline Burton, the Endowment's program officer for Black Church programs. In addition to Dr. Lincoln, it was attended by Bishop John Hurst Adams, the Rev. Charles Adams, Dr. Carl Fields, and Dr. Marshall Grigsby, who was representing Dr. Jones.[5] Wrote Lincoln of the meeting:

> Ms. Burton, because of her own roots in one of the major denominations, had long believed that the time was propitious to explore the possibility of dialogue among various Black denominations. She found an enthusiastic and articulate ally in this cause in the person of one of those with whom she was consulting, the Right Reverend John Hurst Adams.... Though some of the other Lilly consultants were hesitant to see the foundation take on this task, Bishop Adams was convinced that, though the hazards were many, the promise was greater. Ultimately, Bishop Adams was persuasive and subsequently accepted the task of directing the coordination of a consultation of prominent Black

Church officers and consultants, convened by the Endowment in Indianapolis in July of 1978. The consultation provided a forum for a fraternal dialogue about the critical interests of the Black Church in order to determine the most efficient means by which these interests could be implemented.[6]

Invited to attend the First Consultation on Interdenominational Dialogue among Black Churches were the senior bishop and president of the Council of Bishops of each of the three largest Methodist denominations, the president and first vice president of each of the three largest Baptist conventions, and the presiding bishop and associate presiding bishop of the Church of God in Christ. Also invited were the ranking officials of these seven communions within the State of Indiana.[7] Twenty-two representatives of the denominations actually attended, along with six consultants. In addition to Forbes, Jones, and Lincoln, the consultants included the Rev. Mance Jackson, faculty member of the Interdenominational Theological Center; the Rev. H. Carl McCall, New York State Senator and director of the Ministerial Interfaith Association of Harlem; and Dr. Elliott Mason, pastor of Trinity Baptist Church in Los Angeles.[8] Other consultants brought into the process in subsequent meetings included Charles Adams, pastor of Hartford Avenue Baptist Church in Detroit; Calvin Pressley, executive director of the New York City Mission Society; Gayraud Wilmore, then Martin Luther King Professor and Director of the Black Church Studies Program, Colgate Rochester Divinity School; and C. Richard Read, president of the National Media Center Foundation, Parksville, New York. In addition Bishop Adams and the Rev. Thomas Kilgore, Jr., pastor of Second Baptist Church in Los Angeles, served officially in a consultative capacity.

The agenda of the First Consultation included presentations by Robert Lynn on the Endowment's program and objectives; C. Eric Lincoln on "The Black Church and American Society"; Lawrence Jones on "The Black Church and Theological Education"; and H. Carl McCall on "Black Youth and Unemployment." Much of the meeting, however, was given over to discussion of "forces which have hindered cooperative efforts" among the black churches, as well as to "continuing concerns shared by all Black bodies."[9] Out of these deliberations, three issues were identified by the churchpersons and consultants as priorities for further attention. The first was "theological education for black clergy." Second was "the discovery of the power reality in

Black religious organization, a careful assessment of its potential, and strategy by means of which it can be actualized." Third was "the need for continuing the dialogue and perhaps the expansion of groups that are to be included."[10] Upon reaching a consensus with regard to the desirability of convening a second dialogue, a planning committee was appointed consisting of one representative and an alternate from each of the seven participating denominations. The members included John Adams (AME; S. S. Morris, alternate); Herbert B. Shaw (AMEZ; Clinton Hoggard, alternate); John Exum (CME; James L. Cummings, alternate); German Ross (COGIC; Norman A. Quick, alternate); F. Benjamin Davis (NBCA; M. L. Price, alternate); George Lucas (NBC, USA, Inc.; Manual Scott, alternate); and Thomas Kilgore (PNBC; Andrew Brown, alternate).[11] Bishop Adams was designated chairman of the planning committee.

The Second Consultation on Interdenominational Dialogue was held in Atlanta in December 1978, at which time the Dialogue participants determined to develop a formal organizational structure and took the name "Congress of National Black Churches." Proposed by Dr. Lincoln,[12] the name was intended "to signify a continuing forum among the leaders who are representatives of those black denominations having at least national (rather than merely local or regional) constituencies."[13] What had been the planning committee became the executive committee of the new organization. A constitution and by-laws were adopted in May 1979, and in July 1980 the Congress was incorporated in the State of Indiana.

Consultations were held twice a year, in May and December, during 1979, 1980, and 1981. These early meetings were essentially a continuation of the initial dialogue process, in the course of which "Black church leaders began to collectively address a common agenda, the potential of the churches working together became clearer," and the need for such an effort gained a new sense of urgency.[14] To a large extent, the results of these meetings were intangible. Hours upon hours of discussion were invested in the acquisition of factual knowledge about the different denominations, the cultivation of trust relationships, and, above all, the fostering of a spirit of collective endeavor while minimizing any tendencies toward individualism and competitiveness. The Consultations also served as a means for expanding participation in the Congress. A strategy was employed of holding each meeting in a different region of the country, each time inviting district and state officials (e.g., bishops and convention presidents) of

the seven communions located in the host region to attend the proceedings. Thus, from the original twenty-two church officials at the
First Consultation, attendance grew to nearly a hundred participants
at the Consultation held in December 1982.[15]

Beginning with the May 1979 Consultation, a practice was instituted of inviting outside speakers to address a wide range of issues
that emerged out of the ongoing dialogue as priority concerns. In this
fashion, the Consultations increasingly became a forum for educating
the top echelon of church leadership on a broad spectrum of problems
and concerns and for exploring potential remedies. Coinciding with
this activity was the clarification and refinement of areas to which the
Congress wished to give attention. In addition to theological education, these were identified as communications, unemployment, and
evangelism. At the May 1979 Consultation, committees — later called
task forces — were formally designated to address these areas, and
in each succeeding Consultation increasing attention was devoted to
their work. A "Publishers' Roundtable," organized to explore the feasibility of establishing a "Congress Press," was formed in 1980. As the
focus on the work of the task forces intensified, reliance on outside
speakers as the central feature of the Consultation programs diminished. By December 1981, the Congress was making the transition
from dialogue and information gathering into the program implementation phase of its development. Accordingly, the following year
it moved to a format of a single consultation a year in order to give
more attention to the individual task forces and their various projects.

Stage Two: From Dialogue to Design

The year 1982 marked a turning point for CNBC in several additional respects. Since 1978, the organization had been funded by the
Lilly Endowment, which also provided some staff support through
Ms. Burton and her assistant, Rochelle McCann. Accordingly, the
movement identified itself as "a black ecumenical effort enabled by
the Lilly Endowment, Inc."[16] The projection made in 1979, when the
Congress received a three-year operation grant of $112,500, was that
it would become self-sustaining in 1982. Based on the progress made
toward that goal and on the promise the organization had demonstrated for making a significant impact, the Lilly Endowment made a
second three-year grant to the Congress for development purposes.

That grant, in the amount of $119,050, which was contingent on matching funds of $53,500 from the Congress itself, extended to May 1985.[17]

Up until 1982, Bishop Adams's office had served as the national headquarters for CNBC, and Adams himself had assumed much of the responsibility not only for guiding the new organization through its early, vulnerable stages, but for fund raising, proposal writing, and other administrative tasks. With the new grant, the Congress was able to establish separate offices in Washington, D.C., and to employ a full-time executive development officer to assume program development and fund raising responsibilities. Mr. Joseph P. Eaglin, Jr., was appointed to that position in October 1982. In November 1982, CNBC was certified as a nonprofit, tax-exempt organization.[18] And in December of the same year, the organization made its formal debut.

Seeking to avoid the syndrome of individual charismatic leadership that often characterizes social change movements, the Congress elected to maintain a low profile in its early years while cultivating the commitment of the denominations and laying a foundation for the new institution in a quiet and systematic fashion. In June 1981, CBS aired an episode of their Sunday program, *For Our Times*, based on the Consultation held in Nashville in May of that year, and a feature story appeared in the August 1981 issue of the *National Black Monitor*. But with those exceptions, no public announcements were made of CNBC's activities. The precautions were set aside in 1982, however, when the press was notified of the December Consultation held in New York City. The result was a front-page news story in the December 12 issue of the *New York Times*, which was picked up by a number of other newspapers around the nation.

Headlined "Black Churches Forging Coalition to Battle Economic and Social Ills," the article accurately depicted the vision of CNBC participants. While education and training of ministers remained a top priority, emphasis on economic development had emerged as the feature of the Congress most notably distinguishing it, insofar as program emphases were concerned, from other ecumenical endeavors. Among the possibilities discussed at the Consultation were such ambitious undertakings as credit unions, insurance programs, and central purchasing plans among the churches. The Consultation was also the occasion for the announcement of a special summit conference to begin developing an economic plan.[19] An economic

development seminar was subsequently held on April 26, 1983, in
Washington, D.C. Present were seven members of CNBC, eight prominent businessmen, and three officers of the Opportunity Funding
Corporation retained by the Congress to serve as economic advisers.[20]
This seminar, in turn, served as the pilot for the 1983 Consultation, which was devoted almost entirely to economic development.
The 1984 Consultation, then, added a third major focus — the black
family — thus joining BTP and NBEA in acknowledging the area as
central to the agenda of liberation.

As the Congress moved into a more active and visible phase, the
need for structural reorganization became apparent. Accordingly, revised bylaws were adopted at the December 1984 Consultation held
in Memphis. The new bylaws provided for two classes of members:
charter and representational. Charter members, who were designated
members for life, included those individuals who were involved in the
formation of the Congress and who were active as of 1982. They thus
included not only denominational officials, but those persons identified as consultants, as well as the heads of participating seminaries
and the staff members of Lilly Endowment involved in the project.[21]
The second category, that of representational members, included all
the bishops and general officers of the black Methodist denominations and the Church of God in Christ, and members of the executive
boards and the presidents of state and regional conventions of the
National Baptist denominations. Representational membership was
available only to officers of "participating denominations," however,
defined as those denominations that paid annual dues. In 1986 the six
participating denominations were the African Methodist Episcopal
Church, African Methodist Episcopal Zion Church, Christian Methodist Episcopal Church, Church of God in Christ, National Baptist
Convention of America, and Progressive National Baptist Convention. The presence of the Church of God in Christ was particularly
significant, considering that that denomination historically had been
somewhat reticent in its participation in ecumenical efforts. The National Baptist Convention, U.S.A., Inc., on the other hand, while
represented in the Congress through individual charter members, declined for over a decade to participate as a denomination. A persistent
invitation for it to join the Congress was finally accepted in the early
1990s. At the same time, the AME Zion Church, which dropped out
of the Congress in the late 1980s, resumed membership. In addition the newly formed National Missionary Baptist Convention of

America became a member, bringing to eight the total number of denominations participating in the Congress.[22]

From the beginning CNBC expressed a willingness and desire to expand its membership so long as the criterion of a national constituency was met. When the question of participation by blacks in predominantly white denominations was raised in the early dialogues, however, the decision was made to restrict the Congress to the historic black denominations. The determining consideration was control, the prevailing sentiment being that if the Congress was to be independent and self-determining, then it would be contradictory and detrimental to include black churches ultimately controlled by the hierarchies of white denominations. Some of the Congress participants — including the first chair — had been active in the National Conference of Black Christians and undoubtedly found that experience instructive insofar as the issue of autonomy was concerned. Exceptions to the policy were made, however, for those individuals involved in the Congress as consultants who belonged to predominantly white denominations.

The issue of increased representation of laity and women also surfaced from time to time. The membership selection process as provided in the bylaws was such as to include men and ministers almost exclusively. In short, the Congress mirrored the characteristics of the individual denominations insofar as the holders of power and decision makers were concerned. Nevertheless, the Congress considered that it represented all the constituents of all the black denominations — or some 19 million African Americans[23] (Table 7.1).

Task Forces for Action

The years from 1982 to 1987 were a fertile, creative period of brainstorming and idea generation as the Congress explored innovative ways of addressing the needs of those constituents. Ultimately, seven focus areas emerged, each being the responsibility of a task force headed by a consultant or member of the board of directors. Of the seven task forces — Theological Education, Stewardship of Black Resources (Economic Development), Human Development and Social Concerns (Black Family and Youth), Communications, Evangelism in the Black Perspective, Public and Higher Education, and International

162

Table 7.1. Congress of National Black Churches Officials, 1985

Committees and Subsidiaries

Executive:
Chair	John Hurst Adams
V. Ch. at large	F. Benjamin Davis
V. Chair	M. Lorenzo Shepard
V. Chair	Roy L. H. Winbush
V. Chair	J. Clinton Hoggard
V. Chair	C. D. Coleman
Secretary	William H. Graves
Ass't Sec.	Cecil Bishop
Treasurer	Charles W. Butler
Fiscal Officer	Joseph C. McKinney
Parliamentarian	John D. Husband
Historian	W. N. Daniel
Board Consultant	C. Eric Lincoln

Finance:
Charles W. Butler, Chair

Personnel:
F. Benjamin Davis, Chair

Program:
C. D. Coleman, Chair

Church Mngt. Services Corp.:
Roy L. H. Winbush, Chair

Church Missions Trust:
Charles W. Butler, Chair

Board of Directors

AME - Bishop John Hurst Adams
Bishop Vinton Anderson
Bishop Frank C. Cummings

AMEZ - Bishop Cecil Bishop
Bishop Herman L. Anderson
Bishop J. Clinton Hoggard

CME - Bishop William H. Graves
Bishop Marshall Gilmore
Bishop C. D. Coleman

COGIC - Bishop Roy L. H. Winbush
Bishop German Ross
Bishop John D. Husband

NBC - Rev. F. Benjamin Davis
Rev. E. E. Jones
Rev. W. N. Daniel

PNBC - Rev. Charles W. Butler
Rev. M. Lorenzo Shepard, Jr.
Rev. J. Alfred Smith

Task Force Chairs/Consultants (C)

Theological Education
Rev. F. Benjamin Davis
Dr. Lawrence N. Jones (C)

Evangelism
Rev. Manual Scott
Bishop Vinton Anderson
Rev. J. A. Forbes, Jr. (C)

Stewardship of Black Resources
(Economic Development)
Rev. W. N. Daniel
Rev. Thomas Kilgore (C)

Communications
Bishop William Graves
Mr. C. Richard Read (C)

Human Development and Social Concerns
(Black Family and Youth)
Bishop Cecil Bishop
Rev. C. O. Pressley (C)

Public & Higher Education
Bishop German Ross

International Affairs
Bishop J. Clinton Hoggard

Affairs — the first three were the most fruitful in developing and implementing concrete programs and projects.

Following up on an earlier promotional program to recruit seminarians to five major black seminaries, the Theological Education Task Force, shepherded by Dr. Lawrence Jones, developed a Black Church Management Executive Training Program, holding the first training seminars for denominational leaders in 1985. In 1987 the Congress received a $600,000 grant from the Ford Foundation to implement a National Fellowship Program for black pastors, providing for a placement experience with secular organizations that enabled clergy to strengthen their knowledge and skills for working in local communities.

The most significant effort to emerge in the area of the black family was Project SPIRIT, a program first conceptualized at the 1984 Consultation and launched in 1986 with grants of nearly $800,000 from the Carnegie Corporation and nearly $200,000 from the Lilly Endowment. Project SPIRIT — an acronym for Strength, Perseverance, Imagination, Responsibility, Integrity, and Talent — was initiated on a pilot basis in five churches in each of three cities: Indianapolis, Oakland, and Atlanta. Aimed at preventing teenage pregnancy and strengthening the black family, the project consisted of three components: (1) an after-school tutorial program for elementary students designed not only to strengthen basic educational skills but to foster an awareness of ethnic identity and heritage and to develop practical living skills; (2) a parent education program to cultivate more effective parenting; and (3) a pastoral counseling training program to develop pastoral skills in addressing family problems. Significantly, in developing this program area, the Congress took pains to embrace a definition of the family consonant with Christian and African American traditions, rejecting the conventional European tradition of the stereotypical nuclear family.

The most ambitious projections of the Congress — and more particularly of the Congress's chair — were in the area of economic development. Bishop Adams was the chief architect of a complicated plan that began with four basic components: collective purchasing, collective insurance, collective banking, and community development. The plan further included the creation of subsidiary agencies — in insurance, banking, publishing, and telecommunications — which would be owned by a Congress-created but separate for-profit entity, the Church Management Services Corporation (CMSC). Assets from the subsidiaries in turn would flow through CSMC to a not-for-profit body called the Church Missions Trust. Funds from the Trust, then, were to be dispersed on a formula basis, with 50 percent of the monies returning to the member denominations for human service and community development projects, 25 percent going to support the work of the Congress, and 25 percent being invested as an endowment for the Trust.[24] Both CMSC and the Trust were created and incorporated in 1984, but development of the collective programs and the subsidiary agencies — and correspondingly, the envisioned generation of assets — proved to be very long-term endeavors.

The collective banking program was initiated in ten cities in pilot form in 1985, but the loyalty of local churches to their own banking institutions proved too strong to overcome. The banking program consequently was abandoned, although the idea continued to be discussed in later years. The insurance component met with greater success. In 1984 the Church Insurance Partnership Agency, or CIPA, was officially inaugurated as a partnership effort of the Congress and Aetna Life and Casualty, with CNBC holding 70 percent of the interest. Initially CIPA provided property and liability coverage, although it was also licensed to provide health, life, and retirement coverage. The agency began returning a modest profit in 1986. The collective purchasing component and the community development component, oriented toward development of minority businesses, remained on the drawing boards as potential projects of the future.

The activities of other Task Forces were more modest. Of the proposals from the Communications Task Force — for a newsletter, an annual yearbook, production of radio programs, a cable television network, and urban media centers — only the newsletter materialized. A plan for a Congress Press, originally proposed by Dr. Lincoln, was developed by the Publishers' Roundtable, a spin-off of the Communications Task Force consisting of the heads of the respective denominational publishing houses. That project, too, remained on the drawing boards for future consideration.

Under the auspices of the International Task Force, CNBC made some forays into political action, supporting the Free South Africa Movement and participating in fund raising efforts for famine relief in East Africa. The Congress also participated in national voter registration drives and maintained ongoing working relations with the Congressional Black Caucus. But protest politics and electoral politics remained secondary to the emphasis on program development and institution building.

The Task Force on Evangelism sought to establish communications and collaborative efforts among the respective evangelism departments of the participating denominations, but a proposed national conference on evangelism never materialized. The theme of the Task Force, however, was reminiscent of the National Black Evangelical Association, expressed by the Rev. Thomas Kilgore, Jr., as the need to "wed traditional evangelistic goals of soul-winning with social and political action in whatever materials and resources we may develop."[25]

In fact, evangelism, along with stewardship, were the key concepts that together provided a conceptual framework for CNBC's program throughout the 1980s. While the systematic development of black theology was not an activity in which the Congress engaged, its work was emphatically grounded by these two theological ideas — not as conventionally understood, but as interpreted in the context of the black experience. In Bishop Adams's hermeneutics:

There's a certain theological pragmatism about the black church which does not buy into the separation of the secular and the sacred. The grocery store is God's place, as well as the church. The bank belongs to the Lord, as well as the church. So that when we theologize, we are talking about the whole world — both in reference to stewardship of resources, and black evangelism. You can't talk about your spiritual conditions apart from the physical circumstances in which you exist. . . . Evangelism in the black perspective encompasses the social mission of the Black Church. It is the whole church responding as a caring community to the redemptive needs of the whole person and the whole society.[26]

Thus, "the theology of redemption applies to both individuals and institutions. Just as we respond to the needs and hopes of individuals, we must redeem the structures and systems that oppress and limit the opportunity for individuals to be fully and truly human."[27] The other side of redeeming oppressive systems and structures, as envisioned by the Congress, was proper stewardship of potential liberating resources.

We don't handle as well as we could the resources that we have. One of the initial reasons for the black churches coming together was the issue of institutional power; black churches exercise little institutional power in this society. . . . The powers that [influence] our lives, the gifts and talents and money that we have — all of these need to be handled with greater skill. We practice poor stewardship while our people are in oppression, and this has got to be changed so that our stewardship empowers our people.... The ultimate issue about liberation and justice, dignity and freedom, is power; you will be free as long as you have enough power to demand and keep it....

The vision of the Congress is simply organizing the institutional power of the black church to address specific pragmatic needs of the black community. It is to use power to relieve pain; to use power to enhance possibilities....

The Black Church represents Black folks' major investment. Because they have made the Black Church...the biggest and most influential organization in the black community, the Black Church has an obligation to mobilize itself to empower the folk who empowered them.[28]

Save for the Southern Christian Leadership Conference, the vision of the Congress far exceeded that of any other black ecumenical movement. By 1987 the vision was proving to be far beyond CNBC's organizational capabilities. Recognizing a need to bring vision and management into balance, the Congress paused for the better part of two years to take stock and to consider the infrastructure that would be required to support existing and emerging programs. In the course of this self-evaluation, several key transitions occurred. The task force structure was abandoned in favor of board advisory committees corresponding to major program areas; the staff was doubled — from six to twelve members — and assigned primary responsibility for program administration and implementation. Of the twelve, eight were women, including three secretaries, thereby significantly increasing the presence and involvement of women in the work of the Congress. A key new staff position was that of comptroller, signifying a recognition on the part of CNBC that as it grew in visibility and influence, its vulnerability to undue scrutiny increased correspondingly, making sound fiscal management imperative. The office of executive director also underwent change with the departure of Eaglin in December 1987 and the arrival of the Rev. H. Michael Lemmons as interim director in May 1988. Rev. Lemmons became the permanent director in 1989.

Stage Three: Institutionalization

By the end of the transition period, the Congress was well along the road of institutionalization. The program had settled for the most part into the three areas of ministerial development, economic development, and family development. New ground was broken in 1987 with the co-sponsorship of a National Conference on Drug Abuse in Atlanta in conjunction with the CME Church and the Interdenominational Theological Center. Out of this effort, the Congress launched its National Anti-Drug Campaign, which was supported by grants of nearly $600,000 from the U.S. Department of Justice. The Campaign was designed to enable local religious organizations to work in partnership with social agencies and community networks to develop prevention, treatment, and intervention programs. Also in 1987, the Congress, in conjunction with the National Institute on Drug Abuse, held a day-long consultation on strategies for mobilizing churches to address the AIDS crisis in the black community.

Beginning in 1989 the format of the annual consultations shifted. Relying less on invited speakers and more on the developing expertise of the staff, presentations on CNBC's programs were made to attendees, with staff then acting as consultants on strategies for local replication and implementation. Increasingly, the Congress saw its role less as a direct provider of services and more as an experimental station, developing and testing models and passing on to local churches and organizations what proved workable. Formalization of this function was achieved through the establishment of a research and training component called the National Technical Resource and Training Center.[29]

As the 1980s came to a close, the Congress faced what was potentially its most formidable challenge to date: the transition from the organization's founder and leader of twelve years to a successor administration. That precarious ground was ably traversed by the Rev. Dr. Charles Butler, who served as CNBC's second chair from 1989 through 1991. With the succession of the third chair, CME Bishop William H. Graves, in 1992, the institutional soundness of the Congress was confirmed and its future well assured (Table 7.2). (For further information on the organizational structure of CNBC, see Appendix II.)

In recognition of Bishop Adams's many years of devoted visioning and laboring, a Leadership Award Dinner was inaugurated at

Table 7.2. CNBC Chairs and Directors

1978–82	Bishop John H. Adams	—
1982–87	"	Mr. Joseph P. Eaglin, Jr.
1988	"	Rev. H. Michael Lemmons (Interim)
1989	Dr. Charles Butler	Rev. H. Michael Lemmons
1990	"	"
1991	"	"
1992	Bishop William H. Graves	"
1993	"	"
1994	"	"

the 1989 Consultation. Subsequently, that event became a regular feature of the annual gathering, serving both as a means of recognizing leadership contributions and as a major avenue of fund raising to support CNBC's programs.

In the 1990s the annual consultations have continued to be the primary source of new program initiatives, providing forums for information exchange and dialogue on major issues confronting the Black Church and the black community (Table 7.3). Out of these deliberations come ideas to be tested first as pilot projects, then modified for adoption at the local level. Health care was the particular focus of the 1990 and 1991 Consultations, both having the theme of "Health, Wholeness and Healing," and both supported by the U.S. Department of Health and Human Services. These were followed in 1992 by a groundbreaking meeting, insofar as black ecumenical circles are concerned, on "Theological Perspectives on Sexuality in the African American Community." Among the topics explored — with both temerity and courage — were AIDS, homosexuality, sexually transmitted diseases, birth control, and male-female relationships. The same year the Congress was a co-sponsor of a conference on "The Crisis of Substance Abuse among African American People," held at the Hazelden Foundation in Minnesota in June 1991.

The result of these events was the adoption of a health initiative as a program focus comparable to Economic Development, Family Development, and Leadership Development and Theological Education. The new focus began with two primary emphases: (1) preservation of existing black health care institutions, and (2) partnership with health care agencies and professional associations to promote health care in areas ranging from nutrition to screening and testing to stress control techniques. In 1993 the Congress was the recipient of a $300,000 grant from the U.S. Department of Health and Human Services to

Table 7.3. Chronology, Congress of National Black Churches

Date & Location	Primary Issues	Date & Location	Primary Issues
7/78 Indianapolis	Interdenominational Dialogue Church and Society Theological Education Youth Unemployment	12/82 New York	Politics Economics Health Care Education Media Economic Development
12/78 Atlanta	Background of Dialogue Theological Education Evangelism and the Black Perspective Communications Liberation in Africa Black Unemployment	12/83 Chicago	Economic Development Black Politics
		12/84 Memphis	Black Family
		12/85	—
5/79 Chicago	Theological Education Communications Unemployment	12/86 Washington	CNBC Program Development
12/79 San Francisco	National Black United Fund U. S. Census Voter Registration Communications Black Theology Public Affairs	12/87 Atlanta	Drug Abuse
		12/88	—
		12/89 Atlanta	Economic Development
5/80 Washington	International Affairs Publishing Urban Policy Higher Education Ethnic Pluralism Economics	12/90 Detroit	Health, Wholeness and Healing, Part I
		12/91 Detroit	Health, Wholeness and Healing, Part II
12/80 Houston	Post-election Climate Theological Education Evangelism Publishing Black Youth	12/92 Richmond, Va.	Biblical and Theological Perspectives on Sexuality in the African American Community
5/81 Nashville	Public Affairs Jobs and Economy International Affairs	12/93 New Orleans	Violence in America
		12/94 Memphis	
12/81 Washington	Africa Black Youth Black Aged Economics/Employment Black Survival		

implement an immunization program in local churches. As health programs were being developed, other programs evolved in new directions in a never-ending dialectic of assessment and innovation.

In the Leadership Development unit, the National Fellowship Program for Black Pastors continued to be operative, while two new components, both supported by the Ford Foundation, were added: the Ministerial Institutes Program to train ministers in administration and fund raising, and the Leadership Development Alumni Network Project to follow up on clergy completing the Fellowship component. A new program appropriately titled "Love in Action" was instituted to assist churches in addressing the issue of AIDS. Other groundbreaking initiatives were being explored in the mid-1990s, including leadership training of nonclergy men and women, leadership training on the African continent, and a women's leadership development project "to empower women in various aspects of the church."

Under Family Development, Project SPIRIT was operative in fifty-five churches in ten cities, with regional expansion underway in ten states. Continuing support was provided by the Carnegie Corporation and Lilly Endowment. Other involvements of the unit included research on reduction of breast cancer, anti-smoking campaigns, adolescent health status and care, and latchkey children. Meanwhile, the National Anti-Drug Campaign, which was functioning in some thirty-five urban communities, still with the support of the Justice Department, had expanded the scope of its concerns to encompass violence, abuse, AIDS, and advocacy of prison ministries. The 1993 consultation focus was on urban youth, with a theme of "Violence in America: The Black Church Responds."

The insurance agency, CIPA, went through a major transition as a result of Aetna's internal restructuring which rendered Aetna's program no longer competitive. In 1993 CNBC assumed 100 percent ownership, which allowed CIPA to work with a range of carriers, Aetna being only one of them. As the program moved to add health, life, disability, and retirement coverage and to provide coverage for storefront churches, the potential for generating sufficient revenues to support the Economic Development staff as well as some other Congress programs was greatly enhanced. In addition the Economic Development unit continued to explore economic initiatives in publishing, collective banking, and convention planning. Most promising was a collective purchasing venture in the area of telecommunications in partnership with Sprint and MCI.

To strengthen its outreach, CNBC embarked on the creation of an affiliate structure. Fourteen sites were initially proposed in cities, states, or portions of states, with the development of each site being the responsibility of a board member resident in that geographic area. In another dimension of expansion, the affiliate agreements provided for membership by all local denominations rather than just the eight member denominations of CNBC. By 1993 affiliates had been organized in Detroit and Georgia, with preliminary planning underway in New England, Memphis, Miami, and Dallas.

As projects continued to emerge, the organization created a new Development Program to handle the tasks of fund raising, public relations, and program evaluation. While the goal of economic self-sufficiency was far from accomplished, by the mid-1990s significant progress had been made in that direction (Table 7.4).

Overall, CNBC's annual budget grew from $60,000 in its first three years, to $500,000 in the mid-1980s, to $1.5 million in the 1990s. Core operating costs continued to be supported by an annual Lilly Endowment allocation of some $125,000. But support for operating costs was forthcoming from a variety of other sources as well. Member denominations paid annual dues of $10,000 each. A registration fee of $100 had been instituted for attendees of the annual consultation, which averaged 200 to 250 participants. The Annual Leadership Awards Dinner, noted earlier, also generated significant revenue. An annual direct appeal campaign involving local churches that had been involved with Congress activities in one form or another generated some $50,000 annually. As of 1993 CNBC's participation in the National Black United Federation of Charities, which allows federal employees to contribute a portion of earnings through automatic payroll deductions, was generating some $100,000 in pledges. The affiliate structure, once in place, held promise of becoming an additional source of income, as did the Congress Endowment Fund, to which each member of the board of directors annually contributed $500.

In contrast to operating costs, however, CNBC's programs continued to be underwritten entirely by foundations and federal agencies, which included Lilly, Ford, Carnegie, Hoffman-LaRoche, William Randolph Hearst, Pew Charitable Trust, Kellogg, the U.S. Department of Justice, and the U.S. Department of Health and Human Services. Exceptions to the rule of program funding were the local Project SPIRIT efforts, which were supported in whole or in part by sponsoring congregations or local ecumenical groups. Annual consultations

Table 7.4. CNBC Programs, 1994

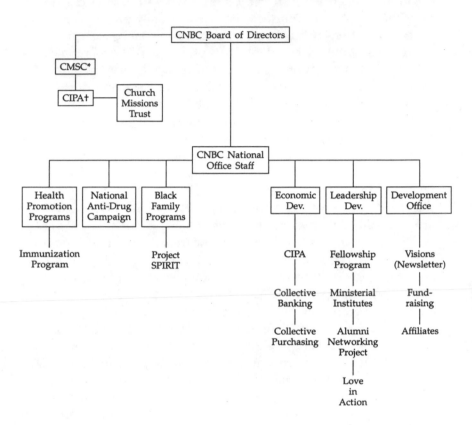

*Church Management Services Corporation Board of Directors
†Insurance Board of Directors

were also underwritten by foundations or agencies that found in CNBC an important avenue for reaching African American populations through black churches. This funding enabled the Congress to absorb expenses of board members to attend the spring board meeting as well as the December consultation. In addition air travel was provided for up to fifteen attendees from each member denomination, as well as for participating consultants, a practice that at least partially alleviated the cost problem encountered by most other ecumenical efforts in convening annual meetings.

Summary

In its organizational structure CNBC in the 1990s has become without question the most elaborate and complex of all the black ecumenical efforts. But its focus remains singular and straightforward: to empower black churches to meet the needs of their constituents. In the words of former chair Charles Butler, "We act out of a common understanding of the church in the black community as a liberating instrument, in the sense that it frees us to be ourselves, to conform to the significance that we consider important, rather than necessarily conforming to the demands of the Europeanized culture." That the operative model for the Congress is one of pluralism is evident in this further comment: "We are not talking about something that's necessarily radical or revolutionary, but about something that liberates us as a group in our society to do the same thing that other groups have done: A Pole to be a Pole in the American context, an Irish to be an Irish in the American context, a black African to be a black African in the American context."[30]

Yet philosophically and practically the Congress has operated out of a male-dominated, hierarchical model and within the framework of the capitalist economic system. At the same time, as Dr. Butler put it, "The hope is that better understanding, as a result of our deliberations, of how capitalism works, will lead to an understanding of how it might be adapted and used to our own ends." Better distribution and a broader participation in the economic system were certainly desirable, but as Butler noted, "The basic question is whether participation and acquisition of a bigger piece of the pie also entails the ability to manage that to our own ends and goals, because acquisition means nothing if we are still controlled by the larger system."[31]

Because of its conciliar structure, women and lay men were nearly totally excluded from organizational deliberations through the first fifteen years of its tenure. In the mid-1990s the move to create local affiliates held great promise of opening up the opportunities for participation not only by women and lay men, but by local clergy as well. Within the parameters of board membership, however, the Congress evidenced an unusual degree of democratic governance through a collective process of policy formulation.

The growth in CNBC's programs over the years is its own testimony to the organization's increasing skill in tapping outside sources

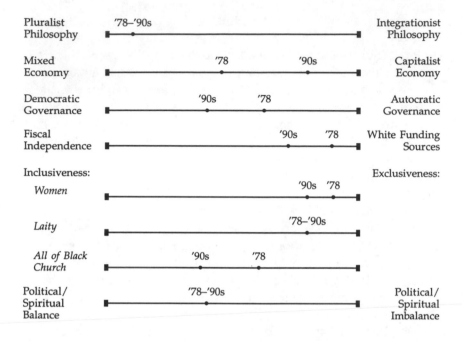

of revenue. But paralleling that achievement has been the quiet, persistent movement toward building structures for self-generation of revenues to address the sorrowful conditions of America's inner cities. If the theory and the theology were the legacy of predecessor movements, the creativity and tenacity to begin actualizing the vision of self-determination are the unique contributions of CNBC's leadership and staff. The ultimate outcome of the organization's effort will not be known for years to come, but its potential is of nearly unimaginable proportions.

It bears repeating that, for all the emphasis on finances, money has never been the sole, or even primary, focus of the Congress. Revenue generation took center stage only as the means to feed the bodies and souls of member denominations' constituents. Feeding the soul of the Congress itself has been no less a priority, which accounts for the participants' practice of "holding church" at board meetings and consultations. Over the years prayer, song, and sermon have been essential features in fulfilling CNBC's self-description as a "voluntary, nonprofit organization... [whose purpose is] to promote unity, charity, and fellowship among the member denominations."[32] Indeed, the very bringing together of the historic denominations for a sustained period, given differences in doctrine and polity and given their sometimes adversarial histories with one another, is itself a signal accomplishment. The membership of the Congress is not broad-based, but among the ecclesiastical authorities who participate, the fellowship is rich, the degree of unity extraordinary — and charity comes first.

Chapter Eight

THEMES OF BLACK ECUMENISM

The contemporary expression of black ecumenism is bracketed on the one side by the Fraternal Council of Negro Churches and on the other by the Congress of National Black Churches. Intervening were the years of civil rights and black power, when normal discourse was suspended while the nation took time out to inspect its sins and debate the addressing of them. Momentarily. The Reagan and Bush years were then devoted precisely to the avoidance of such soul-searching. The Black Church has been far more steadfast in its attention to these matters than has been the nation as a whole. Within the Black Church, that steadfastness is most apparent in its ecumenical expressions. In spite of their substantial diversity and often brief tenures, there is a continuity in the ecumenical movements that is manifested as a singularity of purpose. As far removed as the ecclesiastically oriented Congress of National Black Churches of the 1990s is from the free-wheeling activism of the Southern Christian Leadership Conference of the 1960s, an unmistakable and poignant echo of the latter is sounded as participants at Congress meetings join in singing the civil rights anthem, "We Shall Overcome."

With but one or two exceptions, the movements have been tied together by a body of "ecumenical personalities," that is, individuals who have been or are active participants in three or four different movements and who provide an ongoing exchange of ideas, of lessons learned, and goals aspired to. If not an "interlocking directorate," they constitute some degree of interlocking membership. Similarly, the emphases have varied among the different movements — ranging from civil rights to political action to education to economic development.

176

Yet each in its own way is committed to the empowerment of African Americans.

The fact of this continuity, the differences among the movements notwithstanding, points to a fundamental and essential feature of the Black Church that transcends its structural and doctrinal fragmentation. It is this transcendent feature, the devotion to the cause of freedom, which is embodied in the transdenominational — i.e., ecumenical — movements. These movements, in turn, in enlarging the consciousness of church representatives of that common purpose and passion, serve to make the Church more whole.

The commitment to the achievement of freedom — the one overriding theme of black ecumenism — is rather like the baton passed from runner to runner in a relay race; the characteristics and longevity of the runners vary, but the baton endures, undaunted. To push the analogy, however, if the objective is to win the race — that is, to secure freedom and not merely perpetuate the quest for it — then the attributes of the runners invite scrutiny. Several sets of characteristics were suggested in the Introduction as key factors in the performance of ecumenical movements: cultural ideology, economic philosophy, form of governance, sources of funding, degree of inclusiveness, and political/spiritual balance.

Characteristics of Black Ecumenical Movements

Inclusiveness. A recurring theme in the stories of these movements is that their leaders and participants constitute a "remnant" of the Black Church. The question of inclusiveness of all of the Black Church thus goes to representativeness: Are African Americans in predominantly white denominations represented? Or are only the traditional black denominations represented? What of smaller sects and denominations? Are the movements clergy-dominated? Do they represent the mainstream or a political or ecclesiastical minority? In answer, most of the organizations have had representatives from the largest historic black denominations, as well as from the black constituencies of the predominantly white denominations — a circumstance that is often both a strength and a source of tension. Except for the National Black Evangelical Association, they do not include smaller denominations and sects. That matter aside, none of the movements has been inclusive of all segments of the Black Church. One appeals to grassroots church folk, one to the theologically conservative, another to the politically radical, still another to the church hierarchy. Some — NCBC and CNBC — involve clergy almost exclusively, with scarcely any lay presence whatsoever. A critical perspective and representation is thus omitted from the deliberations of these entities. For both clergy and laity, "who participates" is very often a function of economics. Particularly where national meetings are concerned, who has access to personal or church or denominational resources is often the determinative factor.

The exclusion of laity also acts to exclude women, since clergy in the Black Church remain overwhelmingly male. In those organizations that do include laypersons, the participation rate of women is still vastly disproportionate to their numbers in black churches — about one-third in NBEA and 20 percent in PIE. As the numbers of women clergy and scholars increased in the 1980s, they assumed prominent roles in the administrative and governance structures of BTP and PIE. Women were an important voice in the final years of NCBC; in the early 1990s women came to be well represented on the staff of CNBC; and SCLC/Women was a vital complement to SCLC itself. Clearly the trend was toward a larger presence of women in black ecumenism, and that trend will accelerate as more women are ordained. Nevertheless, the fact remains that women have occupied the top leadership positions in none of the organizations save the Black Theology Project. To the extent that women continue to be underrepresented, to that extent will the analysis and problem solving being brought to the very complex circumstances that characterize African American family and community life remain incomplete. Significant, too, is the fact that none of the movements have formed youth components, although several have sought to include seminarians. At least one local movement provides for a youth membership category, while SCLC has a student category.

Cultural ideology. The ideological theme of integration versus nationalism winds through black ecumenical history, as it does through Black Church history generally. What is distinctive about black ecumenism is the resolution it found in embracing the model of particularity and pluralism — an approach that allows for the preservation of ethnic identity and heritage, while at the same time providing avenues for participating as full partners in the larger society and in the universal Church. Thus, under the leadership of Martin Luther

King, Jr., SCLC moved from a goal of integration into the system as it existed to a strategy of group solidarity and coalition for the sake of transforming the social and economic systems that oppress and exploit. NCBC, rejecting both integration and radical nationalism, helped formulate in more systematic terms the alternative model of pluralism.

Speaking at an early Consultation of CNBC, Gayraud Wilmore, former chair of NCBC's Theological Commission, commented on the "powerful new way of thinking about the Christian faith ... which we can credit to black theology: the pluralism of God's revelation — or another way of saying it, our magnificent diversity within the unity of the one holy, catholic, apostolic church." And he said, "If I were to choose a text to express this rediscovery of black theology, this rediscovery of pluralism, I'd pick Psalm 104:25":

> Oh Lord, how manifest are thy works
> In wisdom, thou has made them all.[1]

PIE, BTP, CNBC — all then operated on the model of pluralism, with some overtly articulating its value and others tacitly living it out.

The movements varied, however, in the extent to which they chose to relate to other particularities. NCBC and BTP both had a strong international focus, reaching out to Africa, the Caribbean, and Latin America. BTP also sought initially to relate to other ethnic caucuses within Theology in the Americas. With the exception of SCLC and the Black Clergy of Philadelphia and Vicinity, no other movements ventured to build coalitions with Latinos, American Indians, other ethnic minorities, or poor whites within the United States. A proposal by PIE to reach out to Hispanics was soundly rejected by much of its membership. Thus, the primary interaction remained that of black and white particularities.

A distinction may be made between those movements having a relationship with the larger ecumenical movement and those spurning ties with the white church establishment. To recap: The black denominations joined the Federal Council of Churches and then, disillusioned with that experience, formed the Fraternal Council of Negro Churches. Captivated by the promise of integration of the National Council of Churches, the Fraternal Council was enticed into inertness. But in its stead came the National Conference of Black Christians, formed in part to mediate black power demands as they related to the white churches, and later, Partners in Ecumenism, which represented an effort to establish church-based coalitions to address urban problems. SCLC, NBEA, the Black Theology Project, and the Congress of National Black Churches, on the other hand, represent more independent initiatives, with no significant impetus coming from ties to white ecumenical bodies. In other words, the causes for the founding of the former were more reactive, while the latter groups were more proactive. That characteristic alone, however, does not determine any given movement's effectiveness.

Fiscal independence. Other characteristics do have a bearing on the longevity of the movements, as well as the expansiveness of their respective programs. Foremost among these factors is funding — not only the level of funding, but also the source. Only SCLC and CNBC have secured sufficient revenues to maintain an active program and staff over an extended period — and SCLC faltered badly after the death of Martin Luther King due to its reliance on white funding sources. NBEA's program has been seriously hampered by dependency on white funding sources, while NCBC and PIE's dependency proved fatal. CNBC has been the most deliberate in working toward becoming self-sustaining. If it succeeds, it will be the first of the movements to do so since the Fraternal Council of Negro Churches.

Beyond sheer survival, of course, is the matter of autonomy to candidly assess the needs and critique the strategies of black communities, and to establish priorities without regard to the availability of foundation grants or the preferences of white churches. While white funding agencies have undeniably played invaluable roles in facilitating various movements, the limitations of some movements must also be attributed at least in part precisely to such arrangements. Significantly, it is on this point of fiscal independence that the ecumenical movements depart most markedly from the characteristics of the Black Church itself.

The issue involved is not simply one of "who owns the money." In fact, much of the money administered by foundations, government agencies, and predominantly white ecumenical bodies comes from the exploitation of black labor, from African American taxpayers, and from black congregations and denominations. From this perspective, much of the money arguably belongs to the African American nation. The issue is control. An increased African American presence on foundation staffs and boards in recent decades certainly has facilitated greater attention being paid to problems and needs in black communities, but by and large real power remains vested elsewhere. Grantees are always vulnerable to the shifting priorities and political inclinations of their benefactors, making their future precarious to the extent that they are dependent on those sources.

At the same time, implicit in the very idea of coalition is the pooling of resources to address common concerns. The central issue then becomes whether the role of predominantly white agencies in fact is that of benefactor or partner. Once again, partnership requires equal power relations. Equal power relations would seem to mandate that black ecumenical organizations be self-sufficient at least with regard to basic operating costs. The securing of funds from other sources for particular programs and projects then becomes less of a threat to the survival of the group.

A fair critique of black ecumenism's funding history and future must acknowledge that black denominations have nowhere near the elaborate bureaucratic structures of the large, mainline denominations. Neither, in consequence, do they have the means of accumulating revenues to fund major projects and programs. The support for individuals to participate in ecumenical activities often comes from the local congregation — but the church that is large enough to sustain such support is the exception. Most black congregations are relatively small in size, and most are hard pressed to pay utilities, insurance, and the pastor's salary, for the economic status of the black religious community mirrors the economic profile of the community at large. Both the modesty of local resources and the lack of national structures severely impede the aggregating of funds for underwriting ecumenical efforts. While the Church itself is a partial resource, ecumenical movements that would be fiscally independent are compelled either to turn to other sources within the African American community or to generate their own revenues.

Governance. A second key issue in the fate of ecumenical movements is leadership and governance style. To a considerable degree, the movements have replicated the patriarchal, charismatic model characteristic of black churches. Most movements exhibit either an autocratic (dominance by one individual) or oligarchic (dominance by a small group) form of leadership. SCLC in its early years offers the most conspicuous example of charismatic leadership — both of what it can accomplish and the hazards it poses. The Fraternal Council persevered for as long as it did through the sheer force of one personality; William Jernagin's death proved to be the final blow to an already faltering endeavor. NBEA has persisted through the tenacity of its executive director, Aaron Hamlin, and a small group of devoted individuals — Eddie Lane and Ruth Bentley, among others — who provide leadership year after year. NBEA does, however, also involve the membership in policy formulations at its annual meetings. NCBC ceased to meet altogether following the death of its president, Kelly Miller Smith, but was on the wane long before. PIE, which to a substantial degree functioned by virtue of the commitment of its director, failed the test of succession, although other critical factors were involved as well — financing, for one, as previously noted. CNBC is the one group that has most deliberately sought to institute a model of collective leadership. Not even SCLC — which is institutionalized to a greater degree than other movements — appears to have evolved the bureaucratic structures that would assure effective transition, for SCLC remains heavily dependent on the personality and authority of its president.

Decision making in most of the movements — informally or otherwise — has been vested in one or two persons, or at most a small executive committee. Consequently, the organizations move forward or remain static depending on the accessibility and inclinations of those particular individuals. As the history of these movements makes clear, in situations of dramatic social change when maximum flexibility is imperative, the charismatic style of leadership, with authority vested in one or a few personalities, is most effective. Even then, however, participatory mechanisms are both possible and imperative — if for no other reason than to provide critiques and checks on the potential excesses of autocratic leadership. Once the agenda shifts from direct action protest to long-term change, then a more managerial and bureaucratic model becomes essential in order to systematize and institutionalize programs. The stability of management procedures and bureaucratic structures also becomes an insurance policy on rational planning, accountability, and fiscal integrity. Bureaucratic structures, of course, also mean that decisions are more deliberate and change more cumbersome. It is always a trade-off, and the diminished opportunity for spiritual renewal is a particularly costly price. A challenge for ecumenical movements lies in how to preserve the best of both approaches, without succumbing to the hazards of either.

The more democratic such arrangements — the higher the rate

of participation in the decision making process — the more tedious the pursuit of goals may become. Yet it is the accommodation of such broad-based participation that allows for the infusion of creative ideas and assures the interests of all constituents being taken into account. For the most part, national ecumenical movements have not developed the structures that would allow for this type of participation — namely, local and regional affiliates. Among the consequences are the lack of adequate systems of communication and accountability from the local to the national levels, and vice versa. Local units — to the extent they exist — often act autonomously, if they act at all. Where local chapters do exist and are connected with the national body, those movements are strengthened and evidence greater endurance — SCLC being the compelling case in point. The importance of a grassroots foundation is recognized in theory by most of the movements and fully acted on by few. NBEA is very "chapter conscious," as was PIE, and continues to try to build local units. NCBC, on the other hand, never got beyond proposing a regional structure, although it did have important connections to local independent ecumenical movements. CNBC's affiliates, as of the mid-1990s, had much potential for radically altering the magnitude and character of participation in the organization's programs; how they might participate in decision making and policy formation was yet unclear. Greater attention by national movements to the development of such structures may well be the next critical stage in black ecumenism.

Political/spiritual balance. Mention of spiritual renewal raises the larger issue of the balance of the spiritual and the political in ecumenical life. Certainly there often is a correlation between charismatically led organizations and the keeping of spirituality in the forefront of the movement, although autocratic or oligarchic leadership itself does not assure the correlation. Nor is it assured by theological leadership — that is, by leaders who define their ecumenical mission as being in part systematic theological formulations. This, of course, was very much a part of the self-definition of the National Conference of Black Christians and, to a lesser extent, the Black Theology Project and the National Black Evangelical Association. Successor organizations to NCBC saw their mission less as the formulating of black liberation theology and more the actualizing of its mandates. In either case, the focus became heavily political — the core of black liberation theology being the gospel mandate of social, political, and economic empowerment.

An early critique of black liberation theology was its overemphasis on the political to the near exclusion of the spiritual. Again, NCBC was the organization most vulnerable to this criticism; NBEA perhaps the least so. Other organizations landed at different points on the continuum, with PIE's director, for example, pushing for a spiritual emphasis but meeting strong resistance from most of the leadership. In the 1980s and 1990s the insistence on the inclusion of the spiritual dimension became more emphatic not only where black liberation theology was concerned, but for the liberation theologies of other oppressed peoples as well. Something of the same quest for balance is being evidenced in Catholic base communities, in mainline Protestant denominations, in many black congregations — everywhere, it would seem, but on the religious right. It may be that this larger struggle holds lessons for black ecumenical organizations; or it may be that answers for participants of the other endeavors will be forthcoming from these very organizations, anchored as they are in both liberation theology and the spiritual tradition of the Black Church. One organization pointing the way may be the Black Clergy of Philadelphia and Vicinity.

A separate but related issue facing religio-political movements concerns the relationship of praxis to reflection — of action to evaluation and critique. All of the movements engage in reflection insofar as a critique of the external sociopolitical situation is concerned, but few extend the reflection to a critique of their response to the external situation. Under Dr. King's leadership, opportunity for the latter was created through meetings and retreats with SCLC staff and advisers. CNBC has been deliberate in setting aside time for self-scrutiny and self-assessment. The Black Theology Project envisioned the creation of theological clusters throughout the country that would function as reflection groups, but they were not necessarily action oriented and so bifurcated the two components of the praxis/reflection model instead of enabling them to function in tandem. A mechanism for sustaining the essential dialectic of action and reflection is rare in most social change efforts, black ecumenical movements — indeed, black political movements of any type — being no exception.

In part the failure to institute and sustain this dynamic may be attributable to the aversion of many black religious leaders to ideological dogmatism. To the extent that the process of critique is engaged, it most often is framed as a biblical ethic of justice or, in recent decades, an ethic of empowerment — approaches that are eminently appropriate, given that *all* ideologies — capitalist, socialist, or otherwise — must be submitted to a transcendent critique. But secular frames of reference also have their usefulness, for in their absence, capitalism is generally tacitly embraced, receiving no critical attention whatsoever.

The major exception to this pattern in recent years has been the effort by James Cone and a handful of other liberation theologians to incorporate a Marxist orientation in their work — not as political dogmatism but as an approach to sociological analysis. By and large this emphasis has been poorly received by the Black Church as a whole — although individual congregations often greet it with enthusiasm. At an intuitive level, many African Americans, like other oppressed peoples, recognize in a socialist analysis truth statements that speak to their condition. But the public heralding and actualizing of a socialist model is fraught with anxiety. As a practical matter, however, the range of options available for pursuing the objectives of liberation and justice are substantially limited to those corresponding to one of two ideological orientations: liberal reform or radical transformation.

Economic philosophy. The Southern Christian Leadership Conference, the National Conference of Black Christians, the Black Theology Project, the National Black Pastors Conference — all of these groups, at one time or another, under the influence of one leader or another, teetered on the edge of a radical critique of America's economic order. While SCLC never used the language of socialism, NCBC, BTP, and NBPC did. Two of the latter three no longer exist, and BTP is scarcely any longer radical. The correlation of language and announced intentions with the tenure of the groups may well be coincidental. Or it may reflect two realities: one is that the ecumenical movements were more radical than the mainstream of the Black Church, and accordingly were denied essential support; the other is that the language of socialism is anathema in "anti-communist" America. In fact, the ecumenical groups that engaged in a critique of capitalism were never revolutionary in their prescriptions, instead pointing toward some form of mixed economy that would be more consistent with economic democracy. But an organization need not *be* radical to know opposition; it need only *threaten* to be radical. Black ecumenical organizations did just that, at a period in the country's history when African Americans were joined by students, anti-war activists, and women in challenging the assumptions of America's liberal ideology — i.e., that economic growth, individual effort, and upward mobility could resolve all social problems, with no alteration in the fundamental structures of society.[2]

Since the 1970s the liberal consensus has reasserted itself and radicalism has diminished correspondingly. But the social problems — certainly the problems of African Americans — have by no means been resolved. To their credit, black ecumenists were among the few voices in the reactionary era of the 1980s who continued to proclaim and to protest the discrepancy between the American creed and American practice. But in contrast to earlier movements, the movements functioning in the 1990s have generally lacked a radical dimension — radical in the etymological sense of going to the roots of the matter. They decry the problems but in their program designs do not penetrate to the source of the problems. That is not to say that the projects and proposals of groups such as NBEA and BEAM have no empowering dimensions. But they empower only insofar as the limits of reform permit. If fully implemented, their programs might well improve the life conditions of black Americans relative to white Americans in such areas as income, education, health, and housing, and that would be an accomplishment emphatically undeserving of disparagement. They are not likely, however, to modify America's core value system of individualism, materialism, consumerism, militarism, and imperialism — in the absence of which black empowerment and liberation will surely remain compromised, for these are the very values that create and sustain the black underclass.

Progressive personalities of the Black Church — who have also often been ecumenical leaders — have always excelled in the mediums of moral protest and liberal reform. There is no denying that these strategies have substantially benefitted the black middle class — indeed, helped *create* a black middle class. They have, as a group, been less inclined toward radical analyses and prescriptions that would touch the lives of the masses of the people. It was, of course, at the point of departing from this norm that Martin Luther King, Jr., was silenced. That is surely no coincidence, and it is a matter of speculation whether the failure of recent black ecumenical movements to build on King's platform reflects a lack of discernment with regard to his thinking in the last years and months of his life, or whether it is simply the better — and safer — part of discretion. But if the consequence of King's stance is still too intimidating to allow the hearing of his analysis, then there is the equally incisive analysis of his elder. Writing in 1953, W. E. B. Du Bois shared this retrospect on his earlier assessment of the central problem of the century:

> I still think today as yesterday that the color line is a great problem of this century. But today I see more clearly than yesterday that back of the problem of race and color, lies a greater problem which both obscures and implements it: and that is the fact that so many civilized persons are willing to live in comfort even if the price of this is poverty, ignorance and disease of the majority of their fellowmen; that to maintain this privilege men have waged war until today war tends to become universal and continuous, and the excuse for this war continues largely to be color and race.[3]

There are exceptions, of course — or more accurately, a continuum of positions — among the movements with regard to economic radicalism. SCLC endures and has conjoined the issues of racial discrimination, poverty, and militarism in a forthright manner that attests to a consciousness of the international and interlocking nature of the various forces of oppression. CNBC departs from the reform modality not only in its collective endeavors and its attention to value clarification, but in its designs for constructing a black economy — an aspiration which, if realized, could potentially alter the political and social status of black Americans in absolute terms. What is also notable about CNBC is that it does not make rhetorical pronouncements in the language of radical ideology, but seeks instead to make operational programs that have potential for far-reaching change.[4] On balance, however, if black ecumenical organizations stand as the more progressive representation of the Black Church, radicalism remains relative.

The Measure of Ecumenism

Among the more compelling messages bequeathed by Dr. King is that, while authentic empowerment and liberation necessitate transformation of basic societal structures and values, such transformations, in turn, require solidarity. At issue, therefore, is not only the

ideological underpinnings of specific programs, but the extent to
which ecumenical movements are, literally, "ecumenical." The task
of black ecumenism may be seen as twofold: first, to bring together
the separate components of the institutional church, but, second, to
reduce the distance between the ecclesiastical expression of black religion and the unstructured, grassroots expression of black religion
in which is preserved the orientation and cohesiveness of a people
sharing a common historical experience. The extent to which the
ecumenical movements have achieved either objective is scarcely a
quantifiable matter, but certainly contributions toward those ends
have been made.

The black consciousness movement of the 1960s gave new impetus to the primacy of unity, and as the awareness of ethnic identity
and the self-perception of "nationhood" were heightened, a revitalization of black religion was initiated at both levels of the religious
system. The sense of commonality of predicament and perspective
that was renewed and reinforced was expressed both in a celebratory
stance toward the black heritage, as well as in a new analysis of the
systemic nature of the oppression to which blacks as a people were
subjected and of the need for collective action to achieve liberation.
These informal "ecumenical" dynamics, set in motion to a substantial
degree by the Southern Christian Leadership Conference, gave impetus to deliberate ecumenical activity within the institutional church.
The resulting cooperative, social change movements in turn served to
further the informal ecumenical process.

At the level of the institutional Church, ecumenical movements
have by no means eliminated denominational demarcations. They
have, however, provided means of transcending those divisions. Almost without exception, the movements have avoided a preoccupation with the minutiae of doctrine and polity, instead addressing
themselves to the ultimate life concerns of black Americans: survival, freedom, self-determination, equity, dignity. In the process, they
have fostered a reawakening of the liberation-oriented heritage and
tradition of the Black Church, so that individual churches, whether
formally attached to ecumenical organizations or not, are encouraged
to engage in "ecumenical" — that is, unifying — types of activity. Pragmatically, the ecumenical movements have enabled greater
familiarity with denominations other than one's own; cultivated relationships of trust across denominational lines; brought Baptists,
Methodists, and Pentecostals into proximity with one another in a

way that merger discussions do not; and moved conservative and fundamentalist blacks, as well as blacks in the white denominations, into closer relation with the historic black denominations. The movements have encouraged the pooling of resources to address common problems; etched out a theological formulation indigenous to the black experience; defined black religion as a separate phenomenon from white Christianity; and established the position of the Black Church and black ecumenism in relationship to the white church and the white ecumenical movement.

In short, the parameters of the black cosmos, insofar as the institutional church is concerned, have not only been made clearer but assigned a more positive valuation. Indeed, the most important contribution of the movements may consist in having made the very idea of a "black cosmos" more acceptable. In so doing, they have at least partially resolved certain conflicts that have long afflicted the Black Church concerning whether or not self-development as a race-conscious people and separation in a race-defined church were compatible with the Christian tenets of the unity of humankind and the universality of the church.[5] On the other hand, to the extent the Black Church remains ambivalent on these questions, and therefore assumes a moderate or even conservative stance, the ecumenical movements provide critically important forums for dissenting church men and women to join with like-minded individuals free of those constraints. In the process, a certain mind-set and orientation is reinforced in which church members and pastors are enabled to think and act in terms of the mission and purpose of "the" Church, rather than "my" church, or "our" denomination.

In addition to their influences within the Church, ecumenical movements have given support and encouragement to unifying and liberating activities being carried out by segments of the community unattached in any formal way to the institutional church. In this capacity, they have served as a bridge connecting the two levels of the religious system and, in so doing, have contributed to making the concept of "Black Church" — in its ethnic, inclusive, noninstitutional sense — a more valid concept than it would have been a few decades ago. Just as there remains fragmentation within the institutional church, however, so are there yet separations in the community at large.

The Persistence of Division: Gender and Class

The ecumenical dynamics set in motion by the black consciousness movement largely eradicated several long-standing sources of division among African Americans, including color, regionalism, and urbanization. Concomitantly, the tendency toward individualism, a value orientation underlying the perceived desirability of integration, was substantially diminished and replaced by a more collective orientation conducive to a strategy of pluralism. In spite of those developments, however, other critical sources of division within the black community have scarcely been modified — namely, those divisions that are a function of gender, sexual orientation, and class.

As the 1980s progressed, the stresses of the black family — e.g., single heads of households, teenage parenthood, poverty rates — increasingly commanded the attention of the ecumenical movements, as well as of the community at large. So, too, the plight of black men surfaced as a compelling item on the agendas of secular and ecclesiastical organizations. But the oppressive realities of sexism and homophobia continued to challenge the moral conservatism of the Black Church and continued to wound countless men and women who found their personhood assaulted and their God-given dignity denied.

Among ecumenical organizations, the Black Theology Project was the most forthright in identifying such issues as concerns commanding attention, holding workshops at its first convocation, in 1977, on "Black Feminism, Black Women, and the Church," and on "Changing Ideas of Family Life and Sexuality." The matter of gender inequity reappeared on BTP's agenda in the latter 1980s, no doubt in part because of the higher level of participation by women than in other organizations. Like the Black Church as a whole, however, most ecumenical movements studiously avoided the topic of sexuality and most particularly the subject of homosexuality. As late as 1990 the recalcitrance of the Church was attested in this offhand comment by one of its most respected pastors: "Homosexuality is tougher than the woman issue . . . and we're not doing so well with that." A test of black ecumenism of the future will be its willingness to take on the tough issues. Certainly no one should have to fear exclusion or distancing, as was the case with one of SCLC's most creative thinkers and loyal supporters, Bayard Rustin.

Not until the early 1990s did some organizations — notably the

Southern Christian Leadership Conference and the Congress of National Black Churches — begin to address courageously the issues of drug abuse, violence, and AIDS, which had become such a threat to the welfare of the entire community. While the reluctance of many local churches and church leaders to address these issues is a function of their theological conservatism, that conservatism often obscures a class bias, which in turn speaks to the breach in the African American community between the black middle class and the black working class and underclass. Again, the Black Theology Project stood out in naming classism as an issue within the black community as well as in society at large.

Brought to this land in the first place for economic motives and sustained as long as they were economically profitable, African Americans have become — for purposes of America's capitalistic agenda — substantially expendable. In a highly technological economy that is no longer labor intensive and in a sociopolitical era in which high unemployment rates are regarded as acceptable, certainly little incentive exists in the society at large to render African Americans competitive in the job market through the provision of education, job training, or affirmative action. Nor is the motivation strong for middle class blacks to jeopardize what security they may have by aggressively aligning themselves with that segment of the black population that has no security whatsoever.

With the transition to the Clinton administration in the early 1990s, hope was renewed that support for addressing urban conditions might again be forthcoming from the federal government and other secular entities. Certainly changes in values and priorities at the national level would render more feasible efforts within the religious community to address the sources of division. But regardless of the larger context, it is these divisions — along with the iniquitous protraction of racism — that provide the most compelling challenge for contemporary ecumenical endeavors, a challenge that seems scarcely less in magnitude or urgency than those faced by blacks of the antebellum North and the post-Reconstruction South. Black ecumenism will empower and liberate only insofar as it includes within its purview the vast numbers of the black underclass and the marginal working class. Conversely, for black ecumenical movements to disregard these realities is to risk becoming the antithesis of ecumenism.

Internal Dynamics: Unity and Autonomy

Division emerges as an issue within the ecumenical fold as much
as in the black cosmos as a whole — not only with regard to inclusiveness of women and laity as earlier mentioned — but in terms of
the multiplicity of movements. Like black denominations, ecumenical movements are subject both to schism and to efforts at unification.
The split in the Black Theology Project that occurred shortly after its
first major conference is the most clear-cut example of "schism." Less
well-known is the fact that the movement of the late 1970s referred
to as the National Black Pastors Conference (NBPC) was initially
proposed as a project of CNBC for the purpose of connecting the
Congress with local black clergy across the nation. A Special Committee on the Pastors' Conference was created at CNBC's December 1978
Consultation to plan a convocation of black pastors. The First Annual
Black Pastors Conference subsequently held in Detroit in November
1979 was funded primarily by the Progressive National Baptist Convention, whose president at the time was the Rev. William A. Jones.
By virtue of that office, Rev. Jones was also a member of CNBC's executive committee. At that initial conference, planning and steering
committees were appointed, each having two representatives from
each of the participating denominations, thereby retaining an ecumenical format. The Congress per se, however, was excluded from
subsequent activity of the Pastors Conference, which was represented
as an independent entity.[6] In 1980 NBPC elected its own board of directors, with William Jones as president, and was incorporated in the
State of New York. Two additional annual conferences were convened,
one in Chicago in October 1980 and one in Houston in October 1981,
before the organization ceased to function. While it existed, NBPC
generated widespread enthusiasm among local clergy of all denominations and persuasions who embraced the organization's agenda
of political activism. Its meetings were attended by as many as eight
hundred pastors from around the country. By the second year, however, the disparity between the radical posture of the leadership and
the more conservative orientation of rank-and-file members had become apparent. Equally critical in the movement's demise, if not more
so, was the lack of financial support.[7]

A more direct, but even less successful, challenge to CNBC was
posed by the National Assembly of Black Churches, whose announced purpose and program bore a striking resemblance to the

Congress. The National Assembly was put together by a Mr. James Hurt, with Rev. T. J. Jemison, president of NBC, USA, Inc., and AME Bishop Frank Cummings serving as co-chairs. The Assembly, organized in September 1983, less than a year after the public announcement of the Congress, held one national meeting in New Orleans in April 1984 before fading from the scene.

If the spirit of ecumenism is denied by such episodes as these, it is affirmed by contrary events. In 1980 CNBC initiated a "Black Ecumenical Group Conversation" with four other bodies — the National Conference of Black Christians, the Black Theology Project, Partners in Ecumenism, and the National Black Pastors Conference. A meeting of the top officials of the groups was held in Washington, April 17, 1980, for the purpose of seeking "cooperation, support, and reinforcement" among the groups and, conversely, avoiding conflict and duplication of effort.[8] A proposal was actually made at this meeting for the different groups to become divisions of the Congress, each functioning in the area of its expertise — e.g., theological development, urban policy, or political activism — but nothing came of the idea. A year later, a Special Summit Meeting was called jointly by the heads of NBPC, NCBC, and CNBC to address the "current religio-political climate" — i.e., the Reagan administration and the religious right. Although it was resolved at that meeting "that a Joint Commission of Black Ecumenism be established as the umbrella for the joint ministry of NBPC, CNBC, and NCBC,"[9] the plan was never implemented.[10] Later the same month — April 1981 — a "National Gathering of Black Clergy" was convened in Atlanta by the Metropolitan Atlanta Black Clergy and co-sponsored by CNBC, ITC, NCBC, and SCLC.[11] In 1982 PIE hosted a meeting attended by Philip Potter, president of the World Council of Churches, and the heads of CNBC, NCBC, and NBPC, as well as representatives from SCLC and the National Urban League.[12] While none of these initiatives achieved any degree of permanency, they at least fostered a level of communication beyond the informal exchange of overlapping memberships. Even after several of the groups became defunct, at least one ecumenical leader — John Adams — continued to countenance an organization with components performing the functions that each of the individual groups at one time performed. Such an arrangement, he ventured, is the "hope for black ecumenical development."[13]

The alternating impulses of competition and consolidation in black ecumenism mirror the dynamics of denominationalism and merger displayed historically by black churches. These dynamics, in turn, point to what would appear to be two intrinsic characteristics of the black religious experience. The first characteristic is a "will to unity," a desire to come together that was early manifested by blacks, beginning with the "invisible institution" of the slaves and the African Societies of free men and women. This inclination is countered, however, by a second characteristic — namely, a "will to autonomy," a desire to be independent and self-determining, which was announced in the black independent church movement inaugurated by Peter Spencer, Richard Allen, and James Varick. While the two "impulses" plausibly have roots respectively in the cosmos of Africa and in the chaos of racism, they likely found reinforcement in the particular polities of the churches through which most African Americans were initially introduced to Christianity. That is, the connectional arrangement of Methodism reinforced the "will to unity," while the determined independence of the Baptists fostered the "will to autonomy."

The tension of these two characteristics is manifested in the inability of black denominations either to achieve union or to cease pursuing union. Similarly, the proliferation of cooperative interdenominational movements is at once an expression of the impulse to unite and of the impulse to be autonomous. The competing motivations are hinted as well in the contrasting orientations of the movements, as was demonstrated by two groups that came into being at the same time in the late 1970s, namely, CNBC and PIE. From the beginning CNBC was the project of members of the church hierarchy, visualized as a national endeavor whose policies and programs would "filter down" to the local level. The objectives were to "connect" the denominations in a formal, structured fashion and to create a consciousness of interrelatedness. It may not be incidental that the founder and first chair of CNBC was a Methodist bishop. Nor is it insignificant that the largest of the Baptist denominations — NBC, USA, Inc. — for so long declined to participate. The situation, in short, represented a stalemate of unity and autonomy. Partners in Ecumenism, on the other hand, was initiated by ministers and staff of ecumenical agencies functioning at the local level, and the struggle of PIE was always to develop programs planned and administered as close to the lives of people in local communities as possible. Emphasis was placed on addressing the particular needs of individuals in their own locale according to their own definitions. It may well be significant that Baptist ministers were a strong presence at PIE meetings, and that two of PIE's first three presidents were Baptist. Indeed, the first president was a member of NBC, USA, Inc.

The existence of the two "impulses" and two corresponding orientations — to the extent that is indeed the case — is not inherently a negative circumstance. The issue, to adapt a phrase of Martin Luther King's, is whether the "tension" of the two orientations is "creative" or whether it is debilitating and immobilizing. In the case of CNBC and PIE, both drew on the black power motif that SCLC helped spawn and NCBC refined. From this common legacy came two different approaches for pursuing the common goal of liberation. In many respects, the approaches were complementary. CNBC brought together the hierarchies of the denominations, while PIE provided a forum for individual clergy and laity to come together, much as NBPC was designed to do and as NCBC initially did. CNBC worked exclusively with black denominations, while PIE included black representatives from the predominantly white denominations. CNBC assigned priority to economic development, while PIE gave precedence to political activism. CNBC's thrust has been empowerment through institution building, while PIE's was empowerment through networking and coalition building. Each approach has its merits. Brought together in a coordinated plan of action, both would possibly be strengthened and the benefits to the community multiplied.

Complementarity of the movements — a condition that certainly extends beyond PIE and CNBC to include other organizations as well — argues the merits of a cooperative, or even federated, arrangement. It does not necessarily thereby make a case for merger. On at least two counts, efforts to compress or restrict black ecumenical movements to a single monolithic entity may be inadvisable. First, the religious domain is still an important arena for the honing and exercising of leadership. To restrict the quantity and range of opportunities in ecumenical endeavors, it might be argued, would be as limiting as to create a single Black Church superstructure. Perhaps an even more important consideration is vulnerability. Simply, a single organization is easier to undermine, and any consolidating that enhances power in fact or appearance is highly likely to draw fire from without and obstruction from within. Empowerment does require solid infrastructures. But it does not impel monopoly so much as functional networks and alliances. There is room for a multiplicity of approaches to a given problem; there is justification for a variety of ecumenically oriented groups employing different strategies in pursuit of common goals.

The Future of Ecumenism

That is not to say that some approaches will not be more effective than others. It is not to say that some are not more appropriate than others, given the peculiar social, economic, and political realities of the day. Martin Luther King's question, "Where do we go from here?," is surely as timely as when first he voiced it. Where does black ecumenism go? Where do black and white ecumenical relations go?

The answer to the latter question is in large part the responsibility of white ecumenists, for it is the degree of their openness and commitment that determines the propriety of black ecumenists investing time and effort in building partnership. On the other hand, if black denominations and churches then decline to take ownership of cooperative efforts, white ecumenists are effectively disempowered to act. A mutually agreeable reciprocity has yet to be established, and that task presents itself as the essential prelude to any future joint action. But it is terrain unlikely to be successfully negotiated unless all parties bring an understanding of and respect for pluralism and for the interrelationship of love and power.

Many of the same issues obtain as black ecumenical organizations enter into relationships beyond the Christian family — whether those relations involve interfaith efforts with Muslims and Jews or networking with secular organizations that share common concerns. At the same time, withholding from such relations until such time as other entities approach a state of perfection in their understanding effectively precludes participation in the transformation of oppressive systems and mind-sets. Certainly a critical consideration is the extent to which black ecumenists come to the interaction from a position of strength and clarity of purpose.

In the meantime, the status and future of black ecumenism itself invites review. Clearly the decade of the 1980s had a dampening effect on ecumenical movements, as it did on nearly all social change efforts of the liberal or radically left persuasions. The time may be propitious for a resurgence of social justice movements, though they undoubtedly will have a character different from the movements of the 1960s and 1970s. The mood and the need in urban America is vastly different, vastly more complex than in decades past. But the residents of these areas may themselves be pointing the way in the self-help projects and programs that are emerging in communities across the nation. It may be that ecumenists are called to support and enhance these efforts.

The development of models and the provision of technical assistance to implement those models at the local level, as is being done by the Congress of National Black Churches, also seems critical, as does the long-range project of economic institution building. But equally important is the development of a mechanism to network black clergy and local black churches across the country and to bring the influence of that network to bear on national policy formulation and resource allocation. This may well by the contribution of Black Ecumenical Advocacy Ministries (BEAM). Not to be overlooked is the ongoing project of consciousness raising, pastoral training, and theological education that is central to CNBC's program, as well as to NBEA's.

The organizing of additional local ecumenical efforts — either as independent bodies or as affiliates of national organizations — looms large as a key factor in moving beyond rhetoric to the implementation of programs that genuinely make a difference in people's lives. It is at the local level, too, that multicultural coalitions can be actualized and lines of gender, class, and sexual orientation transcended. The breaking open of such possibilities at the grassroots level then may point the way to effective action at the national level with regard to those concerns that transcend race — homelessness, poverty, health needs, unemployment and underemployment, deficient education, and inadequate child care — indeed, all forms of violation of human rights and human dignity.

In all these endeavors — and certainly they do not exhaust the possibilities — consideration of the factors contributing to the successes and failures of past efforts seems prudent. So, too, does the instituting of processes for ongoing, constructive self-criticism and of mechanisms by which organizations can be held accountable to their constituents. Above all, responsible stewardship emerges as an absolute mandate, for the challenge facing black ecumenical efforts is formidable, and the available resources none too abundant.

But they are sufficient.

Throughout its history, the Black Church has known challenge upon challenge, and in the face of seemingly insurmountable odds not only endured but substantively advanced the cause of freedom. In the presence of such a witness, one hesitates to slight the power of faith or to render suspect the adequacy of grace.

Appendix I

SOURCES OF BLACK DENOMINATIONALISM

Unlike their brethren of European ancestry, African Americans brought to the shores of the New World no sectarian preferences. They came, rather, as a mosaic and fettered representation of the religious diversity of West Africa, which, while including an unknown number of devotees of Islam, in all probability was devoid of practitioners of the Christian faith.[1] Through the sparse ventures of the Society for the Propagation of the Gospel and the more fruitful evangelism of the early nineteenth-century revivals, Africans denied opportunity to practice the rituals of their homelands were introduced to the fundamentals of Christianity.[2] The result was a "congregation" of enslaved believers furtively clustered across the South in what came to be known as the "invisible institution."[3]

In the free North, the first formal congregating of African believers separate and apart from white churches occurred in the self-help and benevolent associations called African Societies, the most famous of which was the Free African Society of Philadelphia organized by Richard Allen and Absalom Jones in 1787. As quasi-religious bodies, the Societies frequently gave rise to one or more churches, the well-known products of the Philadelphia Society being St. Thomas Episcopal Church and Bethel Church, the Mother Church of the African Methodist Episcopal denomination. Either through the medium of the Societies or the process of schism — or both — the number of congregations grew until in 1810, AME minister Daniel Coker

This appendix appeared previously in *Phylon: The Clark Atlanta University Review of Race and Culture* 49, nos. 3–4 (Fall and Winter 1993–94), and is reprinted with permission.

reported the existence of fifteen African churches representing four denominations in ten cities from South Carolina to Massachusetts.[4] Those early separate churches, Will Gravely has suggested, point to "the emergence of an Afro-American community in the new United States." Implicit in this early movement of independent churches was the possibility of a "community or union church," in contradistinction to the phenomenon of denominationalism then taking hold in the larger society.[5] It was a possibility never realized.

The process of denominationalism among blacks occurred over a period of a century in three major stages: the Methodist stage at the turn of the nineteenth century, the Baptist stage in the second half of that century, and the Holiness-Pentecostal stage at the turn of the twentieth century.

The initial steps to denominationalism were taken when the constituency of the Philadelphia Free African Society, upon deciding to organize a church, determined also to model the church on an existing polity. Unable to agree on whether to emulate the Anglicans or the Methodists, the Society was divided into two churches, one of which affiliated with the white Episcopal denomination, while the other became the nucleus of a new, if still Methodist, denomination.

The first black denomination to be formed, however, was the Union Church of Africans organized by Peter Spencer in Dover, Delaware, in 1813, eight years after he and other members had withdrawn from Asbury Methodist Episcopal Church in Wilmington.[6] The Union Church was later renamed Union American Methodist Episcopal Church. Spencer, though among the delegates attending the 1816 meeting in Philadelphia convened by Richard Allen to organize the African Methodist Episcopal (AME) Church, declined to become a part of Allen's new denomination. Similarly, the New York AME Zions, following discussions with Allen in 1820, opted to organize a separate denomination, which they did the following year. This decision — predicated largely on resentment of Allen's use of a former Zion member to do mission work in New York for Allen's own denomination — suggests that the implications of proliferating black denominations was not a matter that weighed heavily on the minds of church leaders. That is not to imply that the formation of additional denominations was undertaken in a frivolous or cavalier fashion; rather, it argues a certain "taken for grantedness" about the phenomenon of denominationalism that blacks never challenged.

If the separation of black churches from white had a theological impetus — namely, the belief that the demeaning treatment accorded blacks was an affront to God and to all those created in the image of God — the explanations for the creation of multiple black denominations are more decidedly sociological. Gravely identifies three circumstances that undoubtedly contributed to the pattern of church organization established by the antebellum black Methodists. To begin with, freedom of religion had officially been guaranteed only as recently as 1791 with the adoption of the Bill of Rights. The first black denominations thus emerged in an era when the legal structures pertaining to religious independence were just beginning to be defined; it was the opportunity to participate in this early litigation that even made possible the separation of black churches from white denominations. Bethel Church, for example, became free of the control of the Methodist Episcopal Church only after appealing to the state Supreme Court.[7]

The corollary of this process of developing a body of legal precedents was the formalizing of denominational boundaries within American society.

> In the post-Revolutionary generation, there was a fluidity in the process of forming denominations because of the new context of religious freedom. All of the denominational polities and structures within which African churches were formed were being shaped, revised, challenged, defended, and implemented. In the 1780s Episcopalians and Methodists were moving from a colonial to an American organization of church government. Presbyterians did not hold their first general assembly until 1789. Baptists were only regionally organized until 1813, when they established the first national network for the purpose of missionary cooperation.[8]

By and large, as black congregations within these new bodies split off, they retained the name and polity and doctrines of the denomination from which they separated. Those black churches organized as free-standing congregations took on the identity of the particular representatives most significant in introducing their members to the gospel. In this evangelical era of the Second Great Awakening, they were primarily Methodists and Baptists.

Many black congregations, of course, chose to remain within the white denominations, and in those denominations where blacks were relatively few or the mission outreach to blacks tepid, no separate

black bodies materialized. This pattern, in turn, was related to a third
factor, which Gravely suggests influenced the course of black denominationalism. In those white denominations in which the numbers
of black members were small, slavery was a far less divisive issue
than in the denominations having substantial black memberships. In
this the Presbyterians were an exception, joining the Methodists and
Baptists in splitting into northern and southern segments over the
issue of slavery, while the Episcopalians and Congregationalists and
Lutherans remained intact. But even before these formal divisions occurred, the diminution in opposition to slavery within these churches
may well have encouraged black separatism. Gravely points out that

> in the case of the Methodists, . . . all three African separations oc-
> curred *after* the failure of the general conferences between 1800
> and 1808 to remove slaveholders from membership and from
> clerical orders. Indeed, the conferences of 1804 and 1808 printed
> expurgated copies of the Church's *Discipline* for the southern
> states without the legislation on slavery. Even Asbury, who had
> despised slavery from the first, gave in to proslavery pressures,
> conceding in his journal that it was more important to save the
> African's soul than to free his body.[9]

These three factors, then — access to legal authority condoning a
multiplicity of religious expressions, the "fashionableness" of denominationalism, and diminishing anti-slavery sentiment — all conjoined
to foster the establishment of black denominations. At that, the over-
whelming majority of black Methodists initially remained within the
white denomination. Of the 42,300 blacks in the Methodist Episcopal Church in 1816, only 1066 withdrew to follow Allen into the new
AME Church. The AME Zion Church was organized in 1820 with but
1406 Methodists. In short, "at no time was there a wholesale rush out
of the Methodist Church."[10] This situation changed dramatically after
the Civil War, however, when former slaves, for the first time, had a
choice of religious affiliation.

In 1860, shortly before Emancipation, the total black population
of the United States was 4.4 million. Of these, 4.2 million were in
the South, while a mere 200,000 were in the North.[11] With the abo-
lition of slavery, the factors already operative in black separatism
and denominationalism became even more pronounced. In addition
to those cited, C. Eric Lincoln identifies the "longing to be rid of the
unremitting stress of living in a white-dominated world," the "dearth

of leadership opportunities elsewhere in the society," and the heterogeneity among blacks that generated both a capacity and a need for
diverse religious expressions.[12]

The importance of this heterogeneity for black denominationalism
was greatly magnified following Emancipation. Indeed, internal differences within the black population became as compelling, if not
more so, than the external factors involved in denominationalism.
Among these categories of differentiation — each of them products
of the slave system — were legal status, role assignment, and skin
color.[13] Class divisions within the white-defined black caste stemmed
from prior status of free or slave and, within the former slave population itself, from relationships and skills that had been developed
in their capacity either as house servants or field hands. Often a
correlation obtained between these assignments and skin complexion. Thus, light-skinned blacks were more likely to have had contact
with whites, to have cultivated social and artisan skills, to have been
exposed — if tangentially — to white churches and to educational systems. These differences became the source of considerable elitism and
conflict in the years and decades following Emancipation, a divisive
circumstance not substantially modified until the black consciousness
movement of the 1960s.

Nor did these divisions among blacks bypass the church, which
too often became a mirror of the distorted values bequeathed to blacks
by the larger society. George Simpson maintains that "the blacks who
were attracted to the Presbyterian and Episcopal Churches tended
to be closer in class affiliation and complexion with the whites than
was the case among the black Baptists and Methodists,"[14] and Lincoln adds that "while black churches attached to white denominations
tended to be more color-conscious than others, the problem was not
unknown in the authentic Black Church of independent tradition,
although it was considerably less pronounced."[15]

The class divisions took on sectional dimensions as tensions developed between better-educated northern blacks who were a generation
or more removed from slavery — or who had never been slaves — and
southern blacks newly liberated. Many of the northern black leaders
had been engaged in the abolitionist movement and were accustomed
to political activism. Southern blacks had a different experience and
agenda, preoccupied, as they were, with learning how to live free in
a virulently hostile climate. Furthermore, the intense resentment of
southern whites toward northern missionaries, as well as northern

politicians and military personnel, made identification with radical northern elements — black or white — a dangerous proposition for southern blacks.

In spite of these realities, thousands of freed slaves did respond to the overtures of AME, AME Zion, and Methodist Episcopal emissaries from northern churches. But the social and political circumstances also played a major part in the formation of yet another black Methodist denomination, the Colored (now Christian) Methodist Episcopal Church, organized in Jackson, Tennessee, in 1870. The members of this new body represented the residual black membership of the Methodist Episcopal Church, South, which declined to come under the jurisdiction of any of the other Methodist bodies, partially out of resentment of the northerners' aggressive tactics of taking over established congregations, along with their church property.[16]

Some of the same sectional hostilities and tensions served to prolong the process of achieving a united black Baptist denomination. Independent black Baptist churches began separating from white Baptist bodies in the North as early as 1805. These churches, of course, were preceded by black Baptist congregations in the South dating from the early 1770s; indeed, by far the majority of black Baptists were in the South, most of them gathered within the "invisible institution" of slave religion. Upon gaining their independence, they clung fiercely to it, declining to come under the episcopacy of the Methodist churches.

The first black Baptist associations were formed in Ohio in 1834 and 1836, and in Illinois in 1839. These were followed in 1840 by the first regional convention. A second regional convention organized in 1864 joined with the first in 1866 to form the first national black convention, called the "Consolidated American Baptist Missionary Convention." But financial difficulties and regional differences over such issues as the political role of church leaders and emotionalism in worship services caused this effort to be short-lived.[17] Disbanded in 1879, it was succeeded in 1880 by the Baptist Foreign Mission Convention and in 1886 by the American National Baptist Convention. Not until 1895 did these two groups join with yet a third, the National Baptist Educational Convention, to become the first enduring national black Baptist denomination: the National Baptist Convention, U.S.A. Class and sectional divisions again entered into the formula of black denominationalism, however, when two years later the Lott Carey Foreign Missionary Convention was organized by some of the more highly educated members of the National Convention from North Carolina, Virginia, and the District of Columbia.

The year 1897 also marked the founding of what has become the largest of the black Holiness-Pentecostal denominations, the Church of God in Christ. COGIC, along with numerous other black denominations, was initially a product of the Holiness Movement dating from the 1860s. As the Methodists had become more middle class, they also had become disparaging of the old "folk" ways of worship, in reaction to which a reform movement was initiated within the churches. The movement gradually became schismatic, however, as the "come-outers" among Methodists, Baptists, and other denominations — black and white alike — formed their own independent congregations and associations, some of which then became new denominations.[18]

While social class conflicts were a distinctive feature of the movement, this stage of denominationalism — in this instance more aptly termed "sectarianism" — did have a theological dimension as well. The complaint was that Methodists had abandoned the Wesleyan doctrine of sanctification, or spiritual perfection, an experience deemed as necessary to salvation as conversion, or spiritual rebirth. It was from this emphasis that the appellation "holiness" derived as a description of those who participated in the protest.

The Pentecostal Movement, then, stemming from the Azusa Street Revival held in Los Angeles from 1906 to 1908 under the leadership of a black minister, W. J. Seymour, was distinctly theological in origin.[19] The Pentecostals posited a "third work of grace" designated as "baptism in the Holy Ghost" and evidenced by the phenomenon of "speaking in tongues," or glossolalia. Yet the movement also had class overtones and held particular appeal for the masses of blacks migrating to the North and West during the War and Depression decades in search of a brighter future.

In its nearly ninety-year history, the Pentecostal Movement has produced as many as seventy separate black groups, most of them with memberships of less than a thousand. Many of these groups are both Holiness and Pentecostal, COGIC being a case in point. The Pentecostals, in turn, have divided — again on doctrinal grounds — into Trinitarian churches and Apostolic, or "oneness," churches.[20]

There are, of course, other Methodist and Baptist communions as well. The National Baptist Convention, U.S.A., experienced schism a second time in 1915, which produced the National Baptist Convention

Table A.1. Major Black Denominations' Membership

	Est. U.S. Members
African Methodist Episcopal	1,700,000
African Methodist Episcopal Zion	1,100,000
Christian Methodist Episcopal	850,000
Church of God in Christ	3,500,000
National Baptist Convention of America, Inc.	*
National Missionary Baptist Convention of America	*
National Baptist Convention, U.S.A., Inc.	7,100,000
Progressive National Baptist Convention, Inc.	1,000,000
TOTAL	17,450,000

Source: Executives and published reports of the respective denominations and conventions. Figures are estimates for 1984.

*The membership of the National Baptist Convention of America before dividing into these two groups was estimated to be 2.2 million. The distribution of the membership in the two groups was unclear as of the early 1990s, but it appeared the majority had affiliated with the newly incorporated body.

of America, and again in 1961, which resulted in the Progressive National Baptist Convention, Inc. In both instances the conflicts revolved around matters of personality and organizational control, although in the case of PNBC a theological difference over the appropriateness of political activism was also at issue.[21] In 1988 yet another division occurred when the National Baptist Convention of America split into the National Baptist Convention of America, Inc. and the National Missionary Baptist Convention of America. These four Baptist Conventions, together with the three largest Methodist Churches and the Church of God in Christ, accounted for nearly 17.5 million church members in the late 1980s (see Table A.1).

To these could be added approximately 1.2 million church members in smaller black communions. Among them are the National Primitive Baptist Convention of the U.S.A.; the United Free Will Baptist Church; the National Baptist Evangelical Life and Soul Saving Assembly of the U.S.A.; the Union American Methodist Episcopal Church; the Church of the Living God (or Christian Workers for Fellowship, known locally as C.W.F.W.); the National Convention of the Churches of God, Holiness; the Apostolic Overcoming Holy Church of God; Triumph the Church and Kingdom of God in Christ; Pentecostal Assemblies of the World; Bible Way Churches of Our Lord Jesus Christ, World Wide; the United Holy Church of America; and

Table A.2. Blacks in White Denominations/Sects, U.S.

Orientation	Estimated Members
Protestant	
United Methodist	400,000
American Baptist	580,000*
Southern Baptist	147,000
Presbyterian	62,000
Episcopal	49,000
United Church of Christ	70,000
Evangelical Lutheran Church of America	48,000
Seventh-day Adventist	122,000
Jehovah's Witnesses	170,000
Assemblies of God	63,000
Church of the Nazarene	8,000
Various Pentecostal and Spiritual	50,000
	1,769,000
Catholic	1,200,000
	2,969,000

Source: Denomination officials and reports. Figures are variously for 1988 and 1989.

*This figure includes some double counting, since many black Baptists dual affiliate with a black Convention and American Baptist Churches.

the Church of the Lord Jesus Christ of the Apostolic Faith, Inc. — all of which had memberships ranging from 25,000 to 100,000.[22]

An additional 1.8 million blacks were estimated to be members of predominantly white denominations, ranging from 48,000 black Lutherans to 400,000 black United Methodists. The highest rate of growth in recent decades may be in the Roman Catholic Church, which as of 1990 counted some 1.2 million black members in the United States. The American Baptist Churches and Southern Baptist Convention also reported substantial increases in black membership, although in many instances these undoubtedly entail dual affiliation with one of the National Baptist conventions (see Table A.2).

Significantly, over 80 percent of all black church members are gathered in the eight largest black denominations. These, in turn, represent but three different orientations — namely, those orientations corresponding to the three major stages of denominationalism among black Christians. Thus, if a single united church has eluded African Americans, the dynamic of denominationalism has never fragmented this population as extensively as has been the case for

Euro-Americans. One may see in this circumstance an extraordinary holding in tension of inheritances from vastly differing cultural sources. Black denominationalism, in its moderation, is at once an acknowledgement of diversity within the black nation and an emphatic statement of ethnic solidarity.

Appendix II

ORGANIZATIONAL STRUCTURES

Fraternal Council of Negro Churches

In the 1934 constitution, representation for purposes of voting was based on one representative for the first ten thousand members of a given denomination and five representatives for each additional ten thousand members. Dues were assessed at the flat rate of one dollar per year for each representative. By 1950 a much more elaborate structure had been devised wherein national denominational dues ranged from $25 to over $200, depending on the size of the denomination. In addition units of the various denominations — annual conferences, district conferences, state conventions, synods, presbyteries, associations, local ministers' conferences, and local churches — were entitled to one or two representatives upon payment of from $5 to $35. Dues for individuals with voting privileges were $2; without voting privileges, $1. Life membership could be obtained for $50.

Officers of the Council, who were nominated by committee and approved by voting members at the annual meeting, included the president, vice president at large, vice president for each participating denomination, recording secretary, treasurer, and statistician. Except for the latter, these officers, along with the executive secretary, the founder (Bishop Ransom), and designated representatives of the participating denominations (the number of representatives being determined by the size of the denomination) constituted the executive committee, which elected its own officers. Expenses of the executive committee were to be paid by the Council — "provided the condition of the Treasury permits."

The executive committee appointed the executive secretary, who served as the administrative head of the Council and directed the work of the various committees and commissions. Except for the secretary and treasurer, officers were initially elected for two-year terms and, after 1950, for one-year terms with a limit of two terms. The presidency was supposed to rotate from denomination to denomination until each had been represented, though in actuality that office was always held by a member of one of the five largest denominations — AME; AMEZ; CME; NBC, USA, Inc.; NBCA — or of the Methodist Central Jurisdiction.

Southern Christian Leadership Conference

Throughout its history, SCLC's board members were elected, with renewable terms. In reality, many of the members on the board in the mid-1990s had been on the board since the 1960s. Officers included the chair, vice chair, secretary, treasurer, financial secretary, and chaplain. There were also seven regional vice presidents, although the regional designations had no real structural or program functions. The board met twice a year, in the spring and fall. In practice, the board functioned in a largely *pro forma* manner, endorsing the proposals of SCLC's president.

Although the language of "affiliates and chapters" was still used, in actuality "affiliates" were no longer a functioning element of SCLC's structure. Chapters, which ranged in size from fifty to two or three thousand members, paid a chapter membership fee of $300. The individual members of chapters were also subject to being assessed a fee, one-half to two-thirds of which was then remitted to the national office. Constitutions and bylaws of chapters were required to be approved by the national office.[1] Among the largest and most active chapters were Baltimore; Dayton, Ohio; Los Angeles; Chicago; Kansas City, Mo.; Virginia State Chapter; and several chapters in Alabama.

Other categories of membership in SCLC aside from chapters included student ($5), general ($10), sustaining ($25), silver ($50), gold ($100), and MLK:Life ($500). Corporate and institutional (churches and nonprofit organizations) memberships were each $1000.

SCLC memberships were a relatively minor source of income, while *SCLC, The Southern Christian Leadership Conference National Magazine* had become a major source of revenue. SCLC continued to receive some foundation grants; its Wings of Hope Program was sup-

ported by the U.S. Department of Justice. SCLC/Women held fund
raisers to support their own programs as well as SCLC nationally
and had itself been the recipient of substantial grants, including $1.3
million from the Center for Disease Control in support of its AIDS
Awareness Program. Some funds continued to be raised through direct mail solicitations conducted by the SCLC Foundation based in
Chicago.

National Conference of Black Christians

Membership dues in NCBC were $25 for regular members and $10
for students. In 1974 a category of congregational membership was
added, with dues of $100.

New constitutions were adopted in 1970, 1974, and 1977, but the
official organizational structure was never altered substantially. In
1970 officers included the president, vice president at large, six regional vice presidents, treasurer, secretary, and chair and vice chair of
the board. Not until 1978 were women elected officers, with Thelma
Barnes serving as secretary and Carole Hoover as consultant for development. The envisioned regional structure never materialized, and
those offices were ultimately dropped. Nor did NCBC ever have local
chapters. Over the years the size of the board of directors fluctuated from twenty-two to forty-six, and gradually shifted from an even
distribution between black denominations and predominantly white
denominations to proportionately more representation from black denominations. Officers and members of the board were elected by the
general membership, variously for two- or three-year terms.

In 1979 NCBC was placed under the governance of a smaller body
referred to as the "trustees." Also that year it was reincorporated as a
nonprofit organization in the State of Ohio.[2]

National Black Evangelical Association

Although membership in NBEA as of 1993 was primarily on an individual basis, local churches and other church-related organizations
could also join; denominational membership, however, was not an option. Individual membership fees were $30 annually; organizational,
$100. Officers, elected by the general membership, included president,

first and second vice presidents, board chair and co-chair, recording secretary, and treasurer. Over the years women had held the offices of vice president, co-chair, and recording secretary. Officers were elected for two-year terms and could serve a maximum of three terms.

Black Theology Project

BTP never enjoyed financial affluence. In the earlier years some denominational contributions were received, as well as modest foundation grants. But the primary sources of income were membership fees and church contributions, sustaining an annual budget in the area of $10,000.

In the late 1980s, BTP membership fees were $15 for students and senior citizens, $35 for individual subscribers, $100 for sustaining memberships, $250 for congregational memberships, and $1500 for denominational memberships.

Partners in Ecumenism

PIE's office of president had a two-year, renewable tenure. All officers were elected by the general membership at the national conference. Six regional representatives were appointed by the regional vice presidents, while other at-large members were selected by the steering committee itself. Officers were stipulated in the "Standing Rules of Partners in Ecumenism." The "Rules" were adopted in 1984, but were not strictly adhered to. In the 1984–86 term, seven of the forty committee members were women, and ten were laypersons. Twenty-two were members of the historic black denominations (twelve Methodist; nine Baptist; one COGIC). Thirteen come from mainstream white denominations, and five from other traditions including Roman Catholic, Unitarian-Universalist, and Friends.

Membership fees in PIE were $15, although individuals were not required to join officially in order to participate in PIE. A congregational membership structure established in 1983 called for dues of from $25 to $1000, depending on the size of the congregation. A proposal was made the same year for a "National PIE Sunday" to be observed the first Sunday of each May, when collections would be taken in participating congregations as a means for PIE to become self-sustaining, but the structure for such an undertaking never developed.

Congress of National Black Churches

According to the bylaws in effect in 1993, the board of CNBC was to consist of no fewer than three and no more than forty-five members. In the early 1990s the core number usually was thirty-two, with four board members being put forth by each participating denomination and then elected at the annual meeting for one-year terms. The members of the original executive committee were lifetime members of the board. All current officers of the Congress were also members of the board. The board itself was authorized to elect additional members if it so desired. In addition the six original consultants continued to meet with and engage in board deliberations.

Officers of the Congress included the chair, vice chair at large, four denominational vice chairs, secretary, assistant secretary, treasurer, parliamentarian, and historian. The chair was elected for a three-year term; officers were elected annually by the board of directors for one-year terms and could serve no more than three consecutive terms. The office of the chair was to rotate until all participating denominations had been represented. The executive committee, responsible for the "day-to-day affairs of the Congress," consisted of the officers, the executive director, and one at-large member. The chair, however, had "active executive management of the operations of the Congress, subject...to the control of the Board of Directors."[3]

For many years the board met quarterly, but as the organization became more stable, and with the addition of professional staff, the meetings were reduced to twice a year, one of them being held in conjunction with the annual consultation. Through the latter part of the 1980s, board administrative committees were Audit and Finance, Personnel, Programs, and Church Management Services Corporation. To these were added in the 1990s Networking (affiliate development) and Development (fund raising).

As of 1994 the Congress had a staff of twenty, including six support staff. Of the other fourteen, eight were women; five were ministers, including one of the women.

NOTES

Introduction

1. See Appendix I, "Sources of Black Denominationalism."

2. For a more detailed discussion of the black presence in the larger ecumenical movement, see Mary R. Sawyer, "Blacks in White Ecumenism," *Mid-Stream: The Ecumenical Movement Today* 31, no. 3 (July 1992): 222–36.

3. Howard Thurman, *The Luminous Darkness* (New York: Harper and Row, 1965), x.

4. Of particular import were the Edinburgh Conference of 1910; the International Missionary Council, a federation of seventeen national missionary organizations, founded in 1921; the Universal Christian Conference on Life and Work, convened in 1925; and the World Conference on Faith and Order, meeting in 1927 and again in 1937.

5. For a discussion of this theme, see C. Eric Lincoln, *Race, Religion and the Continuing American Dilemma* (New York: Hill and Wang, 1984), and Gayraud S. Wilmore, "Black Christians, Church Unity and One Common Expression of Apostolic Faith," *Mid-Stream: An Ecumenical Journal* 24, no. 4 (October 1985).

6. Linda-Marie Delloff, "COCU Is Dead; Long Live COCU!" *Christian Century*, December 12, 1984, 1164.

7. "Toward a Common Expression of Faith: A Black North American Perspective," *Mid-Stream* 24, no. 4 (October 1985): 413. This report was the product of a Black Church consultation held in Richmond, Virginia, in December 1984 under the auspices of the Faith and Order Commission of the National Council of Churches to prepare a response to the WCC's Apostolic Faith study. An account of the Richmond Consultation is provided in Cornish Rogers, "The Gift of Blackness," *Christian Century*, June 5–12, 1985, 572–73. The October 1985 issue of *Mid-Stream* is devoted entirely to the black response to the WCC study. The Consultation's report was presented to WCC by Gayraud Wilmore. Also present were Jacquelyn Grant and Thomas Hoyt.

8. Gayraud Wilmore, "Politics and the Black Church," address at the Fifth Partners in Ecumenism Conference, Washington, D.C., September 1985.

Nearly a decade later, the WCC had evidenced no more responsiveness than when the Consultation's report was first presented.

9. For a history of merger efforts, see Mary R. Sawyer, "Efforts at Black Church Merger," *Journal of the Interdenominational Theological Center* 13, no. 2 (Spring 1986): 305–15 (published Fall 1987).

10. Practically speaking, ecumenical organizations encompass the eight largest black denominations and the black constituencies and clergy in the mainline white denominations. Sects and cults generally do not engage in ecumenical activities since, by definition, they are engaged in the reverse process of withdrawal and isolation. Even if, as some have suggested, black sects constitute more a reformation than a separatist movement, calling the mainstream denominations back to the expression of authentic black religion, they are nevertheless disinclined to participate in ecumenical activities. An exception, as will be seen, was the Fraternal Council of Negro Churches.

11. John Hurst Adams, interview, Washington, D.C., March 19, 1985.

12. C. Eric Lincoln, ed., *The Black Experience in Religion* (New York: Anchor Books, 1974), 3. Also see C. Eric Lincoln, *The Black Church since Frazier* (New York: Schocken Books, 1974), 115, and C. Eric Lincoln, "Contemporary Black Religion: In Search of a Sociology," *Journal of the Interdenominational Theological Center* 5 (Spring 1978): 91–104.

13. Wilmore, "Black Christians, Church Unity and One Common Expression of Apostolic Faith," 357.

14. Peter Paris, "Response to Bishop Adams," *Journal of the Interdenominational Theological Center* 8, no. 2 (Spring 1981): 129, and Peter Paris, *The Social Teaching of the Black Churches* (Philadelphia: Fortress Press, 1985), 129–30. None of the functional definitions, it may be noted, necessarily precludes from membership those marginal individuals whose identification with the spiritual experience of black life is strictly ontological.

15. See Gayraud S. Wilmore, *Black Religion and Black Radicalism: An Interpretation of the Religious History of Afro-American People*, 2nd ed, rev. and enl. (Maryknoll, N.Y.: Orbis Books, 1983).

16. Lawrence N. Jones, "The Black Church: A New Agenda," in Martin E. Marty, ed., *Where the Spirit Leads* (Atlanta: John Knox Press, 1980), 49.

17. James H. Cone, *For My People: Black Theology and the Black Church* (Maryknoll, N.Y.: Orbis Books, 1984), 11–24.

18. A pivotal figure in recent years in the discussion of the relationship of race and class in determining life-chances of African Americans is William J. Wilson, author of *The Declining Significance of Race* and *The Truly Disadvantaged*. Wilson's work set off a torrent of debate in the 1980s, a sampling of which is collected in the December 1989 special issue of the *Journal of Sociology and Social Welfare*.

19. Kenneth Aman, ed., *Border Regions of Faith* (Maryknoll, N.Y.: Orbis Books, 1987), 421.

20. King's analysis is presented, for instance, in his speech, "Beyond Vietnam," delivered at Riverside Church, New York City, April 4, 1967. Both his Chicago campaign and the Poor People's campaign in Washington, D.C., point to this analysis as well.

21. C. Eric Lincoln and Lawrence H. Mamiya, *The Black Church in the African American Experience* (Durham, N.C.: Duke University Press, 1990), chapter 1.

22. Each chapter concludes with a discussion of this model relative to the respective organizations. A comparative discussion will be found in the final chapter of the book.

23. Martin Kilson, Meeting of the Working Group on Afro-American Religion and Politics, W. E. B. Du Bois Institute for Afro-American Research, Harvard University, October 29, 1988.

Chapter One: To Uplift the Race

1. Richard R. Wright, Jr., "Where is the Federal Council of Negro Methodists," *Christian Recorder*, 1917 (?), cited in Milton C. Sernett, "If Not Moses, Then Joshua," unpublished paper, September 1988, 8.

2. Monroe N. Work, ed., *Negro Year Book, 1931–32* (Tuskegee, Ala.: Tuskegee Institute, Negro Year Book Co., 1931–32), 254.

3. For a discussion of Bishop Ransom's experiences with the FCC and his advocacy of merger, see Calvin S. Morris, "Reverdy C. Ransom," Ph.D. dissertation, Boston University, 1982, 80–81. In his autobiography Ransom writes: "Some of us saw clearly that [the Federal Council of Churches] could not bring its full influence to bear upon many questions that were vital to Negroes and other minority groups. We therefore organized the Fraternal Council of Negro Churches to promote the interests and objectives we had in mind" (Reverdy C. Ransom, *The Pilgrimage of Harriet Ransom's Son* [Nashville: Sunday School Union, n.d.], 296). Ransom's despairing of the success of merger efforts notwithstanding, the two ideas of merger and cooperation continued to receive concurrent attention from the black church community. For a discussion of the history of black merger efforts, see Mary R. Sawyer, "Efforts at Black Church Merger," *Journal of the Interdenominational Theological Center* 13, no. 2 (Spring 1986): 305–15.

4. Randall K. Burkett, *Garveyism as a Religious Movement* (Metuchen, N.J.: Scarecrow Press and the American Theological Library Association, 1978), 113.

5. Ibid., 146–48.

6. See Maloney's "Plea for Unity of the Negro Church," reprinted in Randall K. Burkett, *Black Redemption: Churchmen Speak for the Garvey Movement* (Philadelphia: Temple University Press, 1978), 94–97.

7. Gunnar Myrdal, *An American Dilemma* (New York: Harper and Brothers, 1944), 2:817.

8. *1972 Heritage Brochure: Facts about the National Fraternal Council of Churches, U.S.A., Inc.*, Assembled and Issued by the Washington Bureau, National Fraternal Council of Churches, July 1972, 10.

9. Samuel Kelton Roberts, "Crucible for a Vision: The Work of George Edmund Haynes and the Commission on Race Relations, 1922–1947," Ph.D.

dissertation, Columbia University, 1974, 237, cited in Spurgeon E. Crayton, "The History and Theology of the National Fraternal Council of Negro Churches," master's thesis, Union Theological Seminary, 1979, 11–12, and David W. Wills, "An Enduring Distance: Black Americans and the Protestant Establishment" in Wm. R. Hutchison, ed., *Between the Times: The Travail of the Protestant Establishment* (New York: Cambridge University Press, 1989).

10. See Wills, "An Enduring Distance."

11. Reverdy C. Ransom, ed., "The Fraternal Council of Negro Churches in America," *Year Book of Negro Churches, 1935–36,* Wilberforce University, Wilberforce, Ohio, 24.

12. "Forward," *1972 Heritage Brochure.*

13. Ransom, *Year Book of Negro Churches,* 24–25.

14. See, for example, Sid Thompson, "Some Highlights in the Fraternal Council," *Negro Journal of Religion* 4, no. 5 (June 1938): 13.

15. Membership in the Council fluctuated over the years, but at one time or another, in addition to the four Methodist denominations and two National Baptist conventions, it included the following: the African Orthodox Church; the Church of Our Lord Jesus Christ of the Apostolic Faith; Church of God in Christ; the Pentecostal Church; Freewill Baptists; Primitive Baptists; Church of God, Holiness; Church of God and Saints of Christ (Black Jews); the Bible Way Church of Washington, D.C.; the Metropolitan Community Church of Chicago; and the Central Jurisdiction of the Methodist Church. Also represented were "Negro Churches of Interracial Denominations" — Episcopal, Presbyterian, Congregational, Disciples of Christ (Christian), and the Conference of Community Churches. The constituency of the Council was always considered to be the total membership of the participating denominations — some eight to nine million blacks as of 1947.

16. Crayton, "History and Theology," 4.

17. Morris, "Reverdy C. Ransom," 73–75.

18. *1972 Heritage Brochure,* 9.

19. Ibid., 3–4.

20. "A Message to the Churches and to the Public from the Fraternal Council of Negro Churches," reprinted in Ransom, *Pilgrimage,* 297–300. In all probability, the "Message" was written by Bishop Ransom.

21. *1972 Heritage Brochure,* 8–10.

22. Monroe N. Work, ed., *Negro Year Book, 1937–1938* (Tuskegee, Ala.: Tuskegee Institute, Negro Year Book Company, 1937–38), 215.

23. Signs of Progress," *Negro Journal of Religion* 4, no. 5 (June 1938): 4.

24. Andrew Fowler, interview, Washington, D.C., August 2, 1985.

25. "The Fraternal Council of Negro Churches," *Negro Journal of Religion* 6, no. 3 (April 1940): 4. The monthly journal began publishing in February 1935 and continued at least until May 1940. It was edited by Lendell Charles Ridley and published at Wilberforce University, with contributing editors from seven different denominations.

26. *1972 Heritage Brochure,* 27.

27. Fowler interview, August 2, 1985.

28. *Washington Afro-American,* February 22, 1958, n.p.

29. Ibid.

30. *Washington Afro-American*, October 23, 1954, n.p.

31. The FBI files were obtained under FOIPA requests 295,620 and 295,621 in 1989. Among the "front" organizations cited are the Committee on Jobs for Negroes in Public Utilities, United Negro and Allied Veterans of America, American League for Peace and Democracy, National Committee for Peaceful Alternatives to the Atlantic Pact, and the African Council. With regard to the Fraternal Council, one memo states: "This council appears to be a very militant group, which advocates full Negro rights, but at the present time is not known to be guided by any political philosophies foreign to this country. However, the council is working very close with such groups as the Fellowship of Reconciliation, March on Washington Movement, and Brotherhood of Sleeping Car Porters, all of which are known to be generally guided by individuals following a Socialist philosophy of government." Approximately half of the papers released under the FOIPA request were excised, allegedly for reasons of "national security" or to protect the identity of a "confidential source." Many pages were not released at all, for the same alleged reasons, as well as to avoid "unwarranted invasion of personal privacy."

32. It is clear from the FBI files that the alleged informant staff member was Pauline Myers, formerly the National Organizer of the March on Washington.

33. See Ralph Lord Roy, *Communism and the Churches* (New York: Harcourt, Brace Co., 1960), 199–205.

34. Randall K. Burkett, "The Black Church in the Years of Crisis: J. C. Austin and Pilgrim Baptist Church, 1926–1950," unpublished paper, presented at the W. E. B. Du Bois Institute's Working Group on Afro-American Religion and Politics, Harvard University, March 9, 1989, 12–13.

35. *1972 Heritage Brochure*, 23.

36. Fowler interview, August 2, 1985.

37. News release of the Associated Negro Press, August (?) 1944 and October 16, 1944. Claude A. Barnett Papers, Box 387–7, Chicago Historical Society. Bishop Wright's "offense" was that he had accepted a position as vice chairman of the National Citizens Political Action committee without resigning his position with the Council, thus appearing to have committed the support of the nonpartisan Fraternal Council to a partisan political organization.

38. Press release and transcript of phone call, February 27, 1947, to the Associated Negro Press, Claude Barnett Papers.

39. Letter from Bishop Greene to C. A. Barnett, Associated Negro Press, May 24, 1957, Claude Barnett Papers.

40. *1972 Heritage Brochure*, 35.

41. Cited in Crayton, "History and Theology," 42.

42. *1972 Heritage Brochure*, 21.

43. Crayton, "History and Theology," 28.

44. "Fraternal Council's Bureau Growing in Social Action," *Pittsburgh Courier*, May 26, 1945.

45. Calvin K. Stalnaker, "The ABC's of the National Fraternal Council of Negro Churches, U.S.A.," 1947; *1972 Heritage Brochure*, 19–20, 43; *Brochure*

of Examples of Work Done by the Fraternal Council of Churches, issued by the Washington Bureau, September 1964, passim.

46. J. T. McMillan, phone interview, February 18, 1985.

47. *1972 Heritage Brochure,* passim.

48. Burroughs served on the National Coordinating Committee of the Fraternal Council in Civilian Defense. Jernagin to Burroughs, April 15, 1942, Nannie H. Burroughs Papers, Library of Congress, Washington, D.C.

49. Press release to the Associated Negro Press, June 8, 1949, Claude A. Barnett Papers, Chicago Historical Society.

50. *1972 Heritage Brochure,* 9.

51. "Program," Lincoln Thanksgiving Pilgrimage, September 22, 1954, Claude A. Barnett Papers, Chicago Historical Society.

52. Morris, "Reverdy C. Ransom," 86.

53. Crayton, "History and Theology," 52. This is based on an interview with Rev. George W. Lucas, who was executive secretary of the Fraternal Council at the time the invitation was extended to King.

54. Ibid.

55. Irma Lucas, interview at the Conference of Partners in Ecumenism, Washington, D.C., September 25, 1985.

56. Joan Campbell, interview at the Conference of Partners in Ecumenism, Washington, D.C., September 24, 1985.

57. John Satterwhite, interview, Washington, D.C., January 1985.

58. Cited in Crayton, "History and Theology," 53.

59. Bishop John Adams, founding chair of the Congress of National Black Churches; Rev. Joan Campbell, general secretary of NCC; and Irma Lucas, widow of George Lucas, all attest to the veracity of this statement.

60. Cited in Crayton, "History and Theology," 54. Lucas's letter was written in 1969.

61. See chapter 8 for a more extended and comparative discussion of these continuums.

Chapter Two: To Save the Soul of America

1. Aldon Morris, *The Origins of the Civil Rights Movement* (New York: Free Press, 1984). Morris maintains that rather than speaking of church support for the NAACP, "It is much more accurate to say that in many cases the church ran the local Southern units, but within the constraints of the National office of the NAACP" (37).

2. Ibid., 25

3. Adam Fairclough, *To Redeem the Soul of America: The Southern Christian Leadership Conference and Martin Luther King, Jr.* (Athens: University of Georgia Press, 1987), 17.

4. See Morris, *Origins,* chapter 3.

5. Morris cites Jacquelyn Grant's study of the MIA and ACMHR for this percentage (ibid., 74).

6. Fairclough, *To Redeem the Soul*, 29–30.

7. Eugene P. Walker, "A History of the Southern Christian Leadership Conference, 1955–1965," Ph.D. dissertation, Duke University, 1978, 30–32; L. D. Reddick, *Crusader without Violence* (New York: Harper & Row, 1959), 184.

8. Morris, *Origins*, 85.

9. Fairclough, *To Redeem the Soul*, 86.

10. Accounts vary as to the name. Walker, "A History," 46, indicates it was "Southern Negro Leadership Conference," while David Garrow reports it was "Southern Leadership Conference." See David J. Garrow, *Bearing the Cross: Martin Luther King, Jr., and the Southern Christian Leadership Conference* (New York: William Morrow, 1986), 90.

11. Reported dates of this meeting are inconsistent. Walker, "A History," 46, says August 7 and 8, while Garrow, *Bearing the Cross*, 97, says August 8 and 9.

12. Garrow, *Bearing the Cross*, 97.

13. Walker, "A History," 46.

14. Fairclough, *To Redeem the Soul*, 32–33. The motto was changed in later years to "To Redeem the Soul of America."

15. Morris, *Origins*, 90.

16. Fairclough, *To Redeem the Soul*, 34.

17. "This Is SCLC," reprinted in August Meier et al., eds., *Black Protest Thought in the Twentieth Century* (Indianapolis: Bobbs-Merrill, 1971), 302–6; emphasis in original.

18. Ibid.

19. Ibid.

20. Ibid.; emphasis in original.

21. Subsequently provisions were made for at-large members where no local affiliate existed.

22. Morris, *Origins*, 90–91.

23. Ibid.

24. Doug McAdam, *Political Process and the Development of Black Insurgency, 1930–1970* (Chicago: University of Chicago Press, 1982), 134, Table 6.4. These figures are based on actions from 1955 to 1960, but one may speculate that the pre-SCLC actions were not significantly different in kind from actions following SCLC's establishment.

25. Walker, "A History," 108; Daniel W. Wynn, *The Black Protest Movement* (New York: Philosophical Library, 1974), 178.

26. Fairclough, *To Redeem the Soul*, 5.

27. Morris, *Origins*, 91.

28. Adam Fairclough, "The Southern Christian Leadership Conference and the Second Reconstruction, 1957–1973" in David Garrow, ed., *We Shall Overcome: The Civil Rights Movement in the United States in the 1950s and 1960s* (Brooklyn, N.Y.: Carlson Publishing, 1989), 1:234.

29. For accounts of these campaigns, see Fairclough, *To Redeem the Soul*, Garrow, *Bearing the Cross*, and Taylor Branch, *Parting the Waters: America in the King Years, 1954–63* (New York: Simon and Schuster, 1988).

30. Gayraud Wilmore, *Black Religion and Black Radicalism: An Interpretation of the Religious History of Afro-American People*, 2nd ed, rev. and enl. (Maryknoll, N.Y.: Orbis Books, 1983), 177.

31. Fairclough, *To Redeem the Soul*, 52; Fairclough, "Second Reconstruction," 187. Fairclough is inclined to give somewhat less weight to King's early reliance on moral persuasion than other scholars.

32. Fairclough, "Second Reconstruction," 187.

33. Fairclough, *To Redeem the Soul*, 168.

34. Ibid., 169, 171; Fairclough, "Second Reconstruction," 235; Morris, *Origins*, 93.

35. Walker, "A History," 86, 106, 127, 162; *The SCLC Story* (Atlanta: Southern Christian Leadership Conference, 1964), 15; Fairclough, "Second Reconstruction," 234; Morris, *Origins*, 113.

36. Paul Good, " 'No Man Can Fill Dr. King's Shoes' — but Abernathy Tries," in August Meier and Elliott Rudwick, eds., *Black Protest in the Sixties* (Chicago: Quadrangle Books, 1970), 287.

37. Morris, *Origins*, 113.

38. Ibid., 102–5, 112–15.

39. Fairclough, *To Redeem the Soul*, 49–50.

40. Garrow, *Bearing the Cross*, 584.

41. Morris, *Origins*, 114; Fairclough, *To Redeem the Soul*, 369. The five women board members in 1967 were Marian Logan, Victoria Gray Adams, Johnnie Carr, Annie Divine, and Margaret Shannon (correspondence from Dana Swann, SCLC staff member, November 1992).

42. Fairclough, *To Redeem the Soul*, 4.

43. Ibid., 96.

44. Ibid., 256.

45. Herbert H. Haines, *Black Radicals and the Civil Rights Mainstream, 1954–1970* (Knoxville: University of Tennessee Press, 1988), 101–4.

46. Ibid.; Fairclough, *To Redeem the Soul*, 256; Morris, *Origins*, 116–19.

47. Fairclough, *To Redeem the Soul*, 256.

48. Exhaustive research on the resources of major civil rights organizations has been conducted by Doug McAdam, as well as by Herbert Haines, whose work draws in part on McAdam's. Because SCLC's records are incomplete, so are their data. That matter aside, their figures differ. McAdam gives this range of SCLC income: 1957 — $35,000; 1960 — $180,000; 1963 — $875,000; 1965 — $1.5 million. Morris, on the other hand, claims that SCLC raised $50,000 annually from 1957 to 1960, with 65 percent of the income going to salaries, rent, and travel and 35 percent to programs. See Morris, *Origins*, 117; Haines, *Black Radicals*, 84, T-8; Doug McAdam, *Political Process and the Development of Black Insurgency, 1930–1970* (Chicago: University of Chicago Press, 1982), 253. "External income" as Haines uses the term constitutes the overwhelming preponderance of SCLC's total income, the major exception being affiliate fees.

49. Fairclough, *To Redeem the Soul*, 345.

50. Fairclough, *To Redeem the Soul*, 170–71.

51. Garrow, *Bearing the Cross*, 468, 584, 597, 611.

52. Fairclough, *To Redeem the Soul*, 172–73. The most complete account of the FBI's treatment of King and SCLC is to be found in David J. Garrow, *The FBI and Martin Luther King, Jr.* (New York: W. W. Norton, 1987).

53. In *Where Do We Go from Here: Chaos or Community?* (Boston: Beacon Press, 1967), King wrote, "Let us . . . not think of our movement as one that seeks to integrate the Negro into all the existing values of American society." Rather, "Let us be those creative dissenters who will call our beloved nation to a higher destiny, to a new plateau of compassion, to a more noble expression of humaneness" (133).

54. Martin Luther King, Jr., *Stride toward Freedom* (New York: Harper & Row, 1958), 72, 76.

55. Martin Luther King, Jr., *Why We Can't Wait* (New York: Signet Books, 1964), 23.

56. Ibid, 137–41.

57. Martin Luther King, Jr., *The Trumpet of Conscience* (New York: Harper & Row, 1967), 16–17.

58. For a fuller discussion of this shift in King's position, see Mary R. Sawyer, "Legacy of a Dream," in C. Eric Lincoln, ed., *Martin Luther King, Jr.: A Profile*, rev. ed. (New York: Hill and Wang, 1984), 260–70. Also, see Fairclough's article in the Lincoln book, "Was Martin Luther King a Marxist?," 228–42, and Fairclough's further discussion in *To Redeem the Soul*, 324–25, 351–54.

59. This speech, variously titled "Beyond Vietnam" and "Why I Oppose the War in Vietnam," is reprinted under the title "A Time to Break Silence" in James M. Washington, ed., *A Testament of Hope: The Essential Writings of Martin Luther King, Jr.* (San Francisco: Harper & Row, 1986), 231–44. The same ideas are expressed in King's book, *Where Do We Go from Here: Chaos or Community?* 133. Writes King, "There is a need for a radical restructuring of the architecture of American society. For its very survival's sake, America must re-examine old presuppositions and release itself from many things that for centuries have been held sacred. For the evils of racism, poverty and militarism to die, a new set of values must be born. Our economy must become more person-centered than property- and profit-centered. Our government must depend more on its moral power than on its military power."

60. This address also appears in Washington, ed., *A Testament of Hope*, under the title, "Where Do We Go from Here," 245–52.

61. Ibid. King initially offered this critique of capitalism and communism in his book, *Stride toward Freedom* (New York: Harper & Row, 1958), 92–95.

62. Garrow, *Bearing the Cross*, 436, 455–56, 585.

63. Ibid., 132.

64. Fairclough, *To Redeem the Soul*, 348–49.

65. Cited in ibid., 360.

66. King, *Stride toward Freedom*, 20–21.

67. Fairclough, *To Redeem the Soul*, 34–35; Fairclough, "Second Reconstruction," 237.

68. Cited in Branch, *Parting the Waters*, 695–96.

69. Wilmore, *Black Religion and Black Radicalism*, 179.

70. Branch, *Parting the Waters*, 228, 501.

71. Interview with Mance Jackson, Atlanta, July 6, 1989.

72. Morris, *Origins*. See chapter 4 in particular.

73. Cited in ibid., 88.

74. Interview with Mance Jackson, July 6, 1989.

75. Fairclough, *To Redeem the Soul*, 393–94.

76. James Tinney, "A Theoretical and Historical Comparison of Black Polit-ical and Religious Movements," Ph.D. dissertation, Howard University, 1978, 119–20, 155, 161; Fairclough, *To Redeem the Soul*, chapter 15, "The Abernathy Years."

77. Phone interview with Randel Osburn, SCLC administrator, Atlanta, July 1992; *SCLC Magazine*, August/September/October 1992.

78. "SCLC Convention calls for Unity of Civil Rights Labor Forces," *Southern Fight-Back*, Fall 1989, 2.

79. Jefferson P. Roger, "Black Ecumenicity Defined," n.d. (mimeographed).

Chapter Three: To Empower the People

1. For an excellent treatment of nineteenth-century religious nationalism, see Gayraud S. Wilmore, *Black Religion and Black Radicalism: An Interpreta-tion of the Religious History of Afro-American People*, 2nd ed, rev. and enl. (Maryknoll, N.Y.: Orbis Books, 1983).

2. James H. Cone, *For My People: Black Theology and the Black Church* (Maryknoll, N.Y.: Orbis Books, 1984), 11 and 24.

3. Ibid., 18.

4. Ibid., 17 and 85.

5. Gayraud Wilmore, remarks at the Congress of National Black Churches Convocation, December 1979, San Francisco. Speaking at the 1986 Convoca-tion of the Black Theology Project in Washington, Wilmore had this to say: "As far as the modern history of black theology is concerned, I'm sure it could not have come into existence without Martin Luther King, Jr. I would trace its modern history from at least 1955, because we all stand on the shoul-ders of Martin Luther King, Jr., as black theologians. I doubt very much whether the events which came after 1955 and propelled us toward the artic-ulation of a black theology could have occurred without Montgomery, 1955, and without the coming together of the affiliate groups to SCLC in the pe-riod between '55 and the end of the decade." See also, for example, Paul R. Garber, "Black Theology: The Latter Day Legacy of Martin Luther King, Jr.," *Journal of the Interdenominational Theological Center* 2 (Spring 1975).

6. Wilmore, *Black Religion and Black Radicalism*, 200. At least one attempt was made to coordinate the activities of NCBC and SCLC. Wilmore writes: "At the Third Annual [NCBC] Convocation in Oakland, November 11–14, 1969, a national committee was organized representing the National Confer-ence of Black Churchmen (NCBC), SCLC, IFCO, and the Black Economic Development Conference (BEDC). The stated purpose was to "coordinate

policies and programs, to do long-range planning for the politicization and empowerment of the Black community, and to confirm our mutual responsibility for and accountability to one another" (from the minutes of the Third Annual Convocation, cited in Gayraud S. Wilmore and James H. Cone, eds., *Black Theology: A Documentary History, 1966–1979* [Maryknoll, N.Y.: Orbis Books, 1979], 11, n. 1). The Committee never became functional.

7. James Tinney, "A Theoretical and Historical Comparison of Black Political and Religious Movements," Ph.D. dissertation, Howard University, 1978, 128, n. 42. The vocabulary of black theologians coincided with, if it was not influenced by, the Latin American liberation theology movement.

8. Cited in Charles V. Hamilton, *The Black Preacher in America* (New York: William Morrow, 1972), 133.

9. Linda Ocker, "The National Committee of Negro Churchmen," master's thesis, Columbia University (1968?), 63.

10. This brief account of NCC's relation to the black liberation movement obscures the personal and professional struggles in which many white NCC representatives became engaged — some of whom persisted as allies of the movement long after their colleagues had withdrawn. For a comprehensive treatment of NCC's involvement with the civil rights movement — with race relations generally and with NCBC in particular — see James F. Findlay, Jr., *Church People in the Struggle: The National Council of Churches and the Black Freedom Struggle* (New York: Oxford University Press, 1993). Certainly NCC has paid a price in diminished financial support for the stands it took on issues that polarized America's society as a whole.

11. Nathan H. VanderWerf, *The Times Were Very Full*, report of the National Council of the Churches of Christ, 1975, 59.

12. Donald Jacobs, phone interview, Cleveland, April 3, 1985. The Commission on Religion and Race was replaced with the Racial Justice Working Group under NCC's Board of Church and Society.

13. Wilmore, *Black Religion and Black Radicalism*, 196.

14. "Black Power," Wilmore and Cone, eds., *Black Theology: A Documentary History*, 25–27; emphasis in original.

15. Wilmore, *Black Religion and Black Radicalism*, 196; Ocker, "The National Committee of Negro Churchmen," 13–14.

16. Leon Watts II, "The National Committee of Black Churchmen," *Christianity and Crisis*, November 2 and 16, 1970, 239.

17. "Racism and the Elections: The American Dilemma, 1966," Wilmore and Cone, eds., *Black Theology: A Documentary History*, 33–34.

18. See Ocker, "The National Committee of Negro Churchmen," 18 and 63.

19. Ibid., 24, 26.

20. Although he never served as president or chair, no one played a more important role in the most active years of NCBC than Gayraud Wilmore. Wilmore initiated the first meeting, held in Payton's office, was the author of many of NCBC's most cogent and important statements, and was responsible for "connecting" James Cone and other black theologians with NCBC. His skills as peacemaker and mediator kept the movement together when

it might otherwise have floundered. James Cone describes him as the "ac-knowledged leader of the revolt of black clergy radicals" and credits him with "providing the theological knowledge and vision upon which black theology was based" (James H. Cone, *For My People* [Maryknoll, N.Y.: Orbis Books, 1984], 18 and 217, n. 71).

21. According to Mance Jackson, executive director of NCBC, the National Committee of Black Churchmen was actually dissolved in 1973 and a new organization with the name National *Conference* of Black Churchmen formed later that year by some of the participants in the original organization (personal correspondence, April 2, 1986).

22. J. Metz Rollins, phone interview, New York City, February 19, 1986; Gayraud S. Wilmore, interview at the Black Theology Project Convocation, Washington, D.C., February 5, 1986. Also see Wilmore, *Black Religion and Black Radicalism*, 266, n.9.

23. Timothy Mitchell, phone interview, Flushing, New York, January 23, 1986.

24. Other women active in NCBC, several of whom were board members or steering committee members, included Sr. Mary DePorres Grey, Sarah Nel-son, Mary Jane Patterson, Mary Kinnard, Yvonne Delk, Rhoda Rhodes, Mary Ann Bellinger, Sr. Alice McNair, Olivia Pearl Stokes, Erna Ballentine Bryant, Thelma Barnes, and Carole Hoover. Also see Appendix II, NCBC.

25. Rollins interview, February 19, 1986.

26. Ibid. There were a few larger grants. NCBC received $50,000, for example, from the United Methodist Board of Missions in 1969.

27. Cornish Rogers, "NCBC: Retooling for Economic Liberation," *Christian Century*, December 1, 1971, 1407.

28. J. Metz Rollins, "Black Churchmen Meet in Atlanta," *Presbyterian Life*, January 15, 1971, 30, 31.

29. Watts, "The National Committee of Black Churchmen," 35.

30. 1970 Constitution of NCBC.

31. Gayraud Wilmore, remarks at the Black Theology Convocation, Wash-ington, D.C., February 6, 1986.

32. "Black Theology," statement by the National Committee of Black Churchmen, June 13, 1969, in Wilmore and Cone, eds., *Black Theology: A Doc-umentary History*, 101. Also, see the discussion of this statement in Wilmore, *Black Religion and Black Radicalism*, 214–15.

33. The Society for the Study of Black Religion, which as of the early 1990s convened annually, reportedly had a membership of around seventy scholars.

34. The three stages of the development of black theology are outlined in the General Introduction of Wilmore and Cone, eds., *Black Theology: A Documentary History*. The third stage, involving the Black Theology Project, is discussed later in this chapter. For an elaboration of the development of black theology within NCBC, see Cone, *For My People*, 11–19.

35. "Black Theology in 1976," statement by the Theological Commission of the National Conference of Black Churchmen, in Wilmore and Cone, eds., *Black Theology: A Documentary History*, 341–42.

36. Wilmore and Cone, eds., *Black Theology: A Documentary History*, 447. Wilmore also chaired the Commission on African Relations at one point. He was succeeded by Maynard Catchings (Gayraud Wilmore, interview at the Black Theology Project Convocation, Washington, D.C., February 5, 1986).

37. Rollins interview, February 19, 1986.

38. For a discussion of these proposed entities, see Ocker, "The National Committee of Negro Churchmen," 24–27, 111.

39. Wilmore, *Black Religion and Black Radicalism*, 200–201.

40. Rollins interview, February 19, 1986. Also, see Rollins, "Black Churchmen Meet," 31.

41. Wilmore interview, February 5, 1986; Ocker, "The National Committee of Negro Churchmen," 57–60.

42. The story of the black caucuses — some of which actually existed in some form for over a century — is one that invites further research and documentation. For a brief overview, see Ocker, "The National Committee of Negro Churchmen," 47–56. The caucuses included Black Churchmen of the American Baptist Convention, Coordinating Committee of Black Lutheran Clergymen, Black Caucus of the Unitarian-Universalist Association, Black Methodists for Church Renewal, Black Presbyterians United, Union of Black Clergymen and Laymen of the Episcopal Church, United Church of Christ Ministers for Racial and Social Justice, National Black Sisters, and Black Catholic Clergy Caucus.

43. "The Church and the Urban Crisis," Wilmore and Cone, eds. *Black Theology: A Documentary History*, 45–47. This statement also had words for NCNC itself, calling upon the group to establish national headquarters, establish regional offices, and "to divest itself of internal partisan politics and ecclesiastical gamesmanship."

44. Wilmore, *Black Religion and Black Radicalism*, 266, n. 8.

45. SCLC became a member of IFCO in 1970. See "Another Jim Forman?" *Christianity Today*, October 9, 1970, 42. NCBC and several caucuses also became members of IFCO. See "Black Churchmen Plan NCC Takeover," *Christianity Today*, December 5, 1969, 33.

46. Wilmore and Cone, eds., *Black Theology: A Documentary History*, 21.

47. Gayraud Wilmore, "A Black Churchman's Response to the Black Manifesto," in Wilmore and Cone, eds., *Black Theology: A Documentary History*, 94–95.

48. Wilmore, *Black Religion and Black Radicalism*, 208; Wilmore interview, February 5, 1986.

49. Wilmore, *Black Religion and Black Radicalism*, 208–9, n. 23; Rollins interview, February 19, 1986.

50. Wilmore interview, February 5, 1986.

51. Wilmore, *Black Religion and Black Radicalism*, 201, 209.

52. Wilmore interview, September 25, 1985; "Black Churchmen Plan NCC Takeover," 33.

53. Cornish Rogers, "NCBC: Streamlining for New Directions," *Christian Century*, October 25, 1972, 1060.

54. Rollins interview, February 19, 1986.

55. A thorough critique of NCBC's statements and actions was provided by Vincent Harding at the 1970 Annual Convocation in Atlanta. Harding determined the organization to be far less radical than its rhetoric implied. The critique was published in the October–November 1970 issue of *Renewal*.

56. Gayraud S. Wilmore, "Our Heritage and Our Hope," [1977] (typewritten).

57. The National Black Pastors Conference is discussed briefly in chapter 8.

Chapter Four: Grassroots Prophecy

1. "Black Religion: Past, Present and Future," position paper submitted by the Philadelphia Council of Black Clergy, 1968, Appendix F in Warner R. Traynham, *Christian Faith in Black and White: A Primer in Theology from the Black Perspective* (Wakefield, Mass.: Parameter Press, 1973), 103, 105.

2. Minutes from the Local Black Churchmen's Steering Committee Meeting, Boston, September 26, 1968.

3. Marshall Lorenzo Shepard, interview at the CNBC Consultation, Atlanta, December 1989.

4. Cited in Joe Adcock, "Black Ministers Agree to Operate Seminary," *Philadelphia Bulletin*, April 4, 1971, n.p.

5. William W. Lawrence, "7000 Mourn King at Service in Civic Center," *Philadelphia Bulletin*, April 8, 1968, n.p.

6. C. Eric Lincoln, *The Black Church since Frazier* (New York: Schocken Books, 1974), 119–22.

7. Muhammed Isaiah Kenyatta, phone interview, November 3, 1989.

8. Letter from Ann Petett to Rev. Michael Haynes, August 1, 1968.

9. "The Establishment of the Massachusetts Black Ecumenical Commission," Boston, August 1969, 2–3 (typewritten).

10. Ibid., 7–8.

11. Ibid.

12. Ibid., 10.

13. Ibid., 11.

14. Cited in Darrell Holland, "Post Backs Action on Black Grant," *Pilgrim State News*, newsletter of the Massachusetts Conference of UCC, January 1970, 1–2.

15. "The Massachusetts Council of Churches, Its Constituent Denominations, and the Black Ecumenical Commission," February 12, 1970 (typewritten).

16. Rev. John Wesley Mosley, Jr., phone interview, November 4, 1993.

17. Program, Ninth Annual Salute to Black Fathers Awards Banquet, Concerned Black Clergy of Metro Atlanta, June 18, 1993.

18. Project SPIRIT is discussed in chapter 7.

19. C. Eric Lincoln and Lawrence H. Mamiya, *The Black Church in the African American Experience* (Durham, N.C.: Duke University Press, 1990), 155–56.

Chapter Five: Praxis and Reflection

1. Certainly not all black evangelicals were drawn into NBEA, nor even a majority. Once again, one must speak of a "remnant."

2. See Gayraud S. Wilmore and James H. Cone, eds., *Black Theology: A Documentary History, 1966–1979* (Maryknoll, N.Y.: Orbis Books, 1979), 253. By the time the Black Theology Project was organizing, theological development in NCBC had waned. Many of the same individuals were active in both organizations, so that there was considerable continuity. Also see Gayraud Wilmore, "Origin and Future of the Black Theology Project: Some Reflections," paper presented at the Tenth Anniversary Convocation of the Black Theology Project, Atlanta, 1987.

3. Leon N. Watts, "Black Ecumenicity," *Renewal*, n.d., 32.

4. Linda Ocker, "The National Committee of Negro Churchmen," master's thesis, Columbia University (1968?), 66.

5. William H. Bentley, *National Black Evangelical Association: Evolution of a Concept of Ministry*, rev. ed. (Chicago: Wm. H. Bentley, 1979), 12, 14–15, n. 6, 17; emphasis in original.

6. Wilmore and Cone, eds., *Black Theology: A Documentary History*, 249.

7. Bentley, *National Black Evangelical Association: Evolution of a Concept of Ministry*, 22, 25, n. 8.

8. Interview with Gayraud Wilmore, September 25, 1985.

9. See William H. Bentley, "Toward a Biblical Black Theology," *The Other Side*, July–August 1975, 20–23. For a recounting of NBEA's process in engaging and developing black theology, see Bentley, *National Black Evangelical Association: Evolution of a Concept of Ministry*, chap. 7. Evangelicals involved in writing about black theology, other than Bentley, included Howard Jones, William Pannell, Bobby Harrison, Ron Behm, Tom Skinner, and Ron Potter. It is noteworthy that NBEA is the only ecumenical organization whose constitution and literature contain a "Statement of Faith." The first of the eight points of the statement reads: "We believe the Bible to be the inspired, only infallible, authoritative word of God." Equally significant is that structured time at the annual convention is divided almost equally between workshops and worship services variously called "Prayer Time," "Prayer and Praise Time," or "Inspirational Hour."

10. See Bentley, *National Black Evangelical Association: Evolution of a Concept of Ministry*, 27. Bentley, a Pentecostal who located himself in the radical camp as a "Black Nationalist," remarked: "Radical politics and conservative theology hardly seem to go together, except largely, in this country, among Black Christians" (40–41, n. 6).

11. Ibid., 10, 12, 17; Aaron Hamlin, phone interview, Portland, Oregon, May 23, 1986.

12. See Bentley, *National Black Evangelical Association: Evolution of a Concept of Ministry*, chapters 4–6. Phone interview with Aaron Hamlin, July 20, 1993.

13. Of the founders, Dr. Bentley, Bishop Holman, Rev. Banks, and Rev. Rowe are deceased.

14. Hamlin interview, May 23, 1986.

15. Virgie W. Murray, "The NNEA: 'Important Crossroads,'" *Christianity Today*, May 7, 1971, 37.

16. Hamlin interview, May 23, 1986.

17. On the subject of ethnicity, see Bentley, *National Black Evangelical Association: Evolution of a Concept of Ministry*, 11, 30, 35–37. One key member, former board chair Charles Williams, did not return. Instead, Rev. Williams started a new group in Portland, Oregon, which incorporated independently and continued to function into the 1990s with the original name, National Negro Evangelical Association of the Northwest.

18. For an account of the internal dissension in the earlier years, see Bentley, ibid., 20–22. The lingering effects of these differences are addressed in Randy Frame, "For Black Evangelicals, A Silver Anniversary," *Christianity Today*, May 13, 1988, 43–44.

19. Bentley, *National Black Evangelical Association: Evolution of a Concept of Ministry*, 27.

20. William H. Bentley, "Understanding The History of NBEA," NBEA Twenty-fifth Anniversary Conference Program, 15–16.

21. Bentley, *National Black Evangelical Association: Evolution of a Concept of Ministry*, chapter 10, especially 99 and 101. See also 20.

22. Hamlin interview, May 23, 1986.

23. See Bentley, *National Black Evangelical Association: Evolution of a Concept of Ministry*, chapter 9, for discussion of these two organizations.

24. The issue of women in ministry is thoroughly explored in a book by black evangelical Dr. Arthur D. Griffin entitled *By Your Traditions: A Theological Perspective on Women in the Gospel Ministry* (Chicago: Black Light Fellowship, 1989). Neither NEA nor NBEA had addressed racism in the 1960s or 1970s. This action was thus a major breakthrough for both groups (interview with William Bentley, Chicago, April 29, 1990).

25. Hamlin interview, July 20, 1993. In a 1987 survey by the Princeton Religion Research Center, 44 percent of black respondents identified themselves as born again or evangelical Christians (cited in C. Eric Lincoln and Lawrence H. Mamiya, *The Black Church in the African American Experience* [Durham, N.C.: Duke University Press, 1990], 228).

26. Hamlin interview, May 23, 1986.

27. *Rationale, Goals, Objectives, Program and Structure*, BTP pamphlet, 1985.

28. Gayraud Wilmore, interview at the Black Theology Project Convocation, Washington, D.C., February 5, 1986.

29. Remarks by John H. Satterwhite, Black Theology Project Convocation, Washington, D.C., February 6, 1986.

30. For an elaboration of the history of TIA and African Americans' relation to it, see James H. Cone, *For My People: Black Theology and the Black Church* (Maryknoll, N.Y.: Orbis Books, 1984), 161–72. Also see Wilmore and Cone, eds., *Black Theology: A Documentary History*, 446–47 and 602–3.

31. Charles Spivey, interview at the Black Theology Project Convocation, Washington, D.C., February 6, 1986.

32. "Focus on Black Theology," *TIA Newsletter* 2, no. 3 (September 1977). Some of the individuals involved in the early days of the Black Theology

Project, in addition to Rev. Spivey, Dr. Cone, Sr. Copeland, and Rev. Kenyatta, included Rev. Gayraud Wilmore, Dr. Henry Mitchell, Bishop Donald Lester, Bishop Will Hertzfield, Father William Reese, Sr. Jamie Phelps, and Rev. Frederick Douglass Kirkpatrick.

33. Wilmore and Cone, eds., *Black Theology: A Documentary History*, 9.

34. Ibid., 253.

35. Ibid., 346.

36. Ibid., 11.

37. Ibid., 348–49.

38. For a critique of black theology, see Cornel West, *Prophesy Deliverance: An Afro-American Revolutionary Christianity* (Philadelphia: Westminster Press, 1982), 111–21.

39. "Focus on Black Theology."

40. Wilmore, "Origin and Future." Wilmore writes, "At a sad juncture the Board split into two Black Theology Projects. One led by Kenyatta, [Frederick Douglass] Kirkpatrick and a few young women out of Harlem and North Philadelphia activist groups, and the other led by Charles Spivey, James Cone and others who were more closely identified with the churches and with the old NCBC" (7).

41. Howard Dodson, phone interview, New York City, April 1, 1985; Jualynne Dodson, interview at the Black Theology Project Convocation, Washington, D.C., February 6, 1986.

42. Cone, *For My People*, 165.

43. Wilmore, "Origin and Future." This paper contains an excellent comparative analysis of the 1977 and 1980 statements.

44. Jualynne Dodson, remarks at the Black Theology Project Convocation, Washington, D.C., February 6, 1986. Also see Cone, *For My People*, 171; BTP *Bulletin*, no. 5, September 1985.

45. Jualynne Dodson interview. An organizational structure was designed in the early years of the Project and set forth in BTP's pamphlet, *Rationale, Goals, Objectives, Program and Structure*, but generally was not adhered to.

46. Phone interview with Iva Carruthers, Chicago, August 13, 1993.

47. Ibid.

48. "The Black Theology Project" brochure.

49. Ibid.

Chapter Six: The Ecumenical Dialectic

1. Nathan H. VanderWerf, *The Times Were Very Full*, report of the National Council of the Churches of Christ, 1975, 83.

2. Joan Campbell, interview at the Partners in Ecumenism Conference, Washington, D.C., September 24, 1985.

3. Ibid. The president of NCC in 1986, AME Bishop Philip R. Cousin, was the first to be elected from a historic black denomination.

4. In the 1989–90 reorganization of NCC, CORLE became the office of Ecumenical Networks.

5. Maynard Catchings, "Report on Partners in Ecumenism Project," NAES Conference, Granby, Colorado, June 27–July 1, 1976 (typewritten). Catchings's report indicated the proposal was made in 1973.

6. Campbell interview, September 24, 1985.

7. Donald G. Jacobs, "Spotlight On: Partners in Ecumenism," *Ecumenical Trends*, November 1984, 153. Jacobs gives 1974 as the date of the formulation of the plan. Catchings and Jacobs apparently are referring to separate initiatives that converged in 1974.

8. Ibid.

9. Donald Jacobs, phone interviews, Cleveland, Ohio, March 14 and April 3, 1985.

10. Catchings, "Report on Partners in Ecumenism Project."

11. Ibid.

12. Jacobs interviews, March 14 and April 3, 1985.

13. Rev. Campbell left NCC in 1986 to serve as head of the U.S. office of the World Council of Churches. She returned as general secretary of NCC in the early 1990s.

14. Jacobs interviews, March 14 and April 3, 1985.

15. "Job Description Reviewed and Approved by P.I.E. Steering Committee," October 9, 1985 (typewritten). Donald Jacobs, "Report to CORLE," November 4, 1984 (typewritten).

16. Joan Campbell, phone interview, New York, November 26, 1985.

17. "Today's Crisis and Black Survival," PIE publication, vol. 1, no. 1, [1979].

18. "Fact Sheet," Partners in Ecumenism, March 29, 1979; emphasis in original.

19. "Today's Crisis and Black Survival."

20. "Foundation Proposal for Seed Money," Partners in Ecumenism, June 1982 (typewritten).

21. PIE newsletter, vol. 3, no. 1, Spring 1985.

22. Jacobs interviews; Campbell interviews. In a departure from the established pattern, the 1986 PIE conference was scheduled in October in Cleveland, Ohio, in order to meet in conjunction with the World Council of Churches.

23. Campbell interview, September 24, 1985.

24. Jacobs interviews, March 14 and April 3, 1985.

25. Ibid.

26. The Interdenominational Theological Center (ITC) is a consortium of six black seminaries founded in 1957. ITC itself constitutes an important ecumenical endeavor, with the specific goal of education for ministry.

27. "Intern Program Trains Black Students," NCCC *Chronicles*, September 1984, n.p.

28. PIE brochure, "Accomplishments as of October, 1983."

29. "Partners in Ecumenism: Background Information," March 3, 1988 (typewritten).

30. PIE brochure.

31. "Black Church Group Wins $50,000 Ford Grant," NCCC *Chronicles*, Spring 1984, n.p.

32. Jacobs interviews, March 14 and April 3, 1985.

33. PIE Budget, 1984–86.

34. Campbell interview, November 26, 1985.

35. PIE budget, 1984–86. Phone interview with Andrea DeUrquiza, CORLE staff member, January 29, 1990.

36. In 1988 a "Proposal of Empowerment" was developed soliciting the "partnership" of the historic black denominations in PIE's program. The document proposed a three-year commitment of a $3500-per-year contribution to pay the salary of an executive director. Among the elements of empowerment cited in the proposal was acknowledgement that "it will take the joint insistence, and assistance of the historic Black Church to motivate the ecumenical community to live up to their witness of inclusivity; for without the involvement of the historic Black Church, the ecumenical community will continue to reflect ideology and theology from the perspective of middle class white America." It is not clear the document itself was ever presented to the denominational representatives. A meeting was held in which the general content was discussed, but no follow-up occurred and the response of the black representatives was tepid at best — a circumstance that reflected on the failure of the office of general secretary to build relations with the historic black denominations as much as it did on the denominations themselves.

37. Linda-Marie Delloff, "NCC Reshapes Its Future," *Christian Century*, November 21, 1984, 1084. A survey of concerns of black participants in NCC, conducted by Jacobs in 1983 and published in the first PIE newsletter of that year, is also revealing of a variety of tensions and dissatisfactions.

38. Frank Madison Reid, "An Invitation to Partnership," NCCC *Chronicles*, Fall 1983, n.p.

Chapter Seven: Institution Building

1. John Hurst Adams, interviews, Washington, D.C., January 17 and 22, March 19, 1985.

2. Sermon by Dr. James Forbes, Consultation on Interdenominational Dialogue among Black Churches, the Lilly Endowment, Inc., Indianapolis, July 25, 1978. Dr. Forbes subsequently became minister of Riverside Church in New York City.

3. During the developmental years of the Congress, Lincoln was Professor of Religion and Culture at Duke University, while Jones was dean of Howard University Divinity School.

4. Robert W. Lynn, interview at Lilly Endowment, Indianapolis, April 9, 1985. Since its founding by Eli Whitney in 1937, the Endowment has been distinguished by its strong emphasis on religious concerns. Religion, in fact,

is one of three major program divisions, the other two being Education and Community Development. Lynn retired from this position in 1989.

5. Jacqueline L. Burton, "Program in Support of the Black Churches," Policy Papers of the Religion Division, Lilly Endowment, [1977].

6. C. Eric Lincoln, Historical Interpretive Statement, "The Congress of National Black Churches: The Search for Community in an Ongoing Tradition," [1979] (typewritten).

7. Memo from John Hurst Adams to Jacqui Burton, March 6, 1978, John Hurst Adams Files.

8. Consultation Program, July 25–26, 1978.

9. [Lawrence N. Jones and C. Eric Lincoln], "Summary Report," Consultation on Interdenominational Dialogue among Black Churches, July 25–26, 1978.

10. Ibid.

11. Ibid. Rev. Lucas and Bishop Shaw died in 1981 and were succeeded on the committee by their respective alternates.

12. Adams interviews, January 17 and 22, March 19, 1985.

13. C. Eric Lincoln, Historical Interpretive Statement.

14. "Introduction," program of the Second Consultation on Interdenominational Dialogue among Black Churches, December 11–13, 1978, Atlanta.

15. This account is based on programs of the Consultations, as well as discussions with various participants.

16. See, for example, CNBC's letterhead in that period.

17. Grant Agreements, December 12, 1978, November 21, 1979, and November 23, 1982.

18. Joseph Eaglin, interview in Washington, D.C., January 22, 1985.

19. Kenneth A. Briggs, "Black Churches Forging Coalition to Battle Economic and Social Ills," *New York Times*, December 12, 1982, 1.

20. Summary of the Economic Development Seminar of the Congress of National Black Churches, Inc., April 26, 1983, Washington, D.C. (typewritten).

21. Adams interviews. See also Executive Committee Meeting minutes, March 3, 1981, Washington, D.C.

22. Adams interviews. The local churches belonging to NCBC, Inc., could and did participate in Congress programs, however. In fact, more local NBC, USA, Inc., churches may ultimately have been involved than any other, simply because there are greater numbers of them.

23. Ibid. See Appendix II for further information on the governance and structure of CNBC.

24. Interview with Joseph Eaglin, Washington, D.C., January 22, 1985.

25. CNBC minutes, December 16–18, 1980, Houston.

26. Adams interviews.

27. John Hurst Adams, "Two Sleeping Giants: The Black Church and Black Politics," *Focus*, April 1984, 7.

28. Adams interviews.

29. Interview with Rev. H. Michael Lemmons, Washington, D.C., November 10, 1989.

30. Interview with Dr. Charles Butler, CNBC Consultation, Atlanta, December 12, 1989.

31. Ibid.

32. CNBC brochure, 1993.

Chapter Eight: Themes of Black Ecumenism

1. Gayraud Wilmore, Congress of National Black Churches Consultation, San Francisco, December 1979.

2. See Godfrey Hodgson, *America in Our Time* (New York: Vintage Books, 1976), passim.

3. W. E. B. Du Bois, "Fifty Years After," in *The Souls of Black Folk* (Greenwich, Conn., 1961), xiv.

4. Says Bishop Adams: "Basically, we reject the secular ideological terms, by definition, just as we reject the secular, Western sociological definitions of family. I find them completely European, having very little, if anything, to do with either Africa or the Bible. And so we have to come at these things in terms of the categories with which we do. Black churches have been addressing the agenda of a just political, social, and economic order for generations. The definitions which our secular, political society imposes on us are not necessarily the ones with which we function" (John H. Adams, interview, Hillsborough, N.C., November 22, 1985).

5. Peter Paris discusses these conflicts in *The Social Teaching of the Black Churches* (Philadelphia: Fortress Press, 1985). See especially chapters 2 and 4.

6. CNBC minutes, December 11–13, San Francisco; CNBC Spring Consultation Program, May 1–3, 1979, Chicago.

7. William A. Jones, phone interview, New York, November 18, 1985.

8. John Hurst Adams, interview, Washington, D.C., March 19, 1985; John Adams personal files.

9. Special Summit Meeting, minutes, United Nations Inter-Church Center, April 1, 1981.

10. Adams interview, March 19, 1985.

11. Veneita Wesley, "Physical and Economic Violence Addressed at National Gathering of Black Clergy," *SCLC Magazine*, June/July 1981, 50–53.

12. Donald Jacobs, phone interview, Cleveland, Ohio, April 3, 1985.

13. John Hurst Adams, interview, Washington, D.C., January 22, 1985.

Appendix I

1. C. Eric Lincoln, "The American Muslim Mission in the Context of American Social History," in E. H. Waugh et al., eds., *The Muslim Community in North America* (Edmonton, Alberta, Canada: University of Alberta Press, 1983).

2. Milton C. Sernett, *Black Religion and American Evangelicalism* (Metuchen, N.J.: Scarecrow Press and the American Theological Library Association, 1975).

3. Albert J. Raboteau, *Slave Religion: The "Invisible Institution" in the Antebellum South* (New York: Oxford University Press, 1978).

4. Will B. Gravely, "The Rise of African Churches in America (1786–1822): Re-examining the Contexts," *Journal of Religious Thought* 41, no. 1 (Spring–Summer 1984): 58.

5. Ibid., 58, 64–65.

6. Lewis V. Baldwin, "The A.U.M.P. and U.A.M.E. Churches: An Un-explored Area of Black Methodism," *Methodist History* 19 (April 1981): 177–78. Baldwin writes: "In September 1813, Spencer and 26 of his followers organized the Union Church of Africans, which was incorporated at Dover, Delaware. By December of 1813, this church had become a connectional body with the addition of two small congregations in New York and Pennsylvania. By 1816, the year the A.M.E. Church was incorporated as an independent African Methodist connection, the number of congregations comprising the Union Church of Africans had increased to five."

7. Gravely, "The Rise of African Churches," 66–67.

8. Ibid., 68.

9. Ibid., 71.

10. Harry V. Richardson, *Dark Salvation: The Story of Methodism as It Developed among Blacks in America* (Garden City, N.Y.: Anchor Press/Doubleday, 1976), 148.

11. Ira Berlin, *Slaves without Masters* (New York: Oxford University Press, 1974), 46–47, 136–37, Appendix 1.

12. C. Eric Lincoln, *Race, Religion, and the Continuing American Dilemma* (New York: Hill and Wang, 1984), 81.

13. Ibid., 74–77.

14. George E. Simpson, *Black Religion in the New World* (New York: Columbia University Press, 1978), 228.

15. Lincoln, *Race, Religion, and the Continuing American Dilemma*, 77.

16. Richardson, *Dark Salvation*, 195–98, 235–36.

17. James M. Washington, *The Origins and Emergence of Black Baptist Separatism*, 1863–1897 (Ann Arbor, Mich.: University Microfilms, 1983). See chapter 4, "The Dissolution of the Consolidated Convention, 1869–1879."

18. For an overview of the emergence of the Holiness Movement, see chapter 2 in Vinson Synan, *The Holiness-Pentecostal Movement in the United States* (Grand Rapids, Mich.: Wm. B. Eerdmans Publishing Co., 1971).

19. The Azusa Street Revival is treated in chapter 4 of Synan, entitled "The American Jerusalem — Azusa Street."

20. James Tinney, "Selected Directory of Afro-American Religious Organizations, Schools, and Periodicals," in Dionne J. Jones and Wm. H. Matthews, eds., *The Black Church: A Community Resource* (Washington, D.C.: Howard University Institute for Urban Affairs and Research, 1977), 199–200, 214–15.

21. Specifically, the conflict revolved around the opposition of the Convention's president, Joseph Jackson, to the direct action protest tactics of the civil

rights movement. It was Martin Luther King's supporters in the Convention who challenged Jackson and ultimately led the schismatic movement to form the PNBC. See chapter 2 above.

22. Tinney, "Selected Directory of Afro-American Religious Organizations, Schools, and Periodicals," 160–215, passim.

Appendix II

1. See "SCLC: Chapter Development and Policy Manual," Southern Christian Leadership Conference, Atlanta, n.d. (typewritten).

2. "NCBC in 1979" (typewritten).

3. Bylaws of the Congress of National Black Churches, Inc., as revised December 1984.

Index